She hath thighs like pillars of alabaster;
and between them, there vaunts a secret place,
a sachet of musk, that swells, that throbs,
that is moist and avid . . .

O hail! the jewel in the lotus.

THE JEWEL
IN THE
LOTUS

A Historical Survey of the
Sexual Culture of the East

Allen Edwardes

Introduction by Dr. Albert Ellis

BANTAM BOOKS
TORONTO · NEW YORK · LONDON

THE JEWEL IN THE LOTUS

*A Bantam Book / published by arrangement with
Crown Publishers, Inc.*

PRINTING HISTORY

Julian Press, Inc. edition published June 1959

2nd printing	..September 1959	6th printing	....November 1961
3rd printing	....November 1959	7th printing	.............June 1962
4th printing	............April 1960	8th printing	.......January 1963
5th printing	.............June 1961	9th printing	....December 1963

10th printing............November 1964

Bantam edition / November 1976

ISBN 0–553–10289–3

Published simultaneously in the United States and Canada

*Bantam Books are published by Bantam Books, Inc. Its trade-
mark, consisting of the words "Bantam Books" and the portrayal of a bantam, is registered in the United States Patent
Office and in other countries. Marca Registrada, Bantam
Books, Inc., 666 Fifth Avenue, New York, New York 10019.*

PRINTED IN THE UNITED STATES OF AMERICA

Contents

Ome! munnee pudmeh hum

O hail! the Jewel in the Lotus

Introduction

It is amazing how little is known about the customs of the East by the peoples of the West; and this is particularly true of Western ignorance of the sexual attitudes and behavior of Orientals. In searching for authoritative articles on Asiatic sex practices for an *Encyclopedia of Sexual Behavior* which I am now in the process of editing, I found it unusually difficult to track down accessible scholars who could accurately describe Eastern and Middle Eastern beliefs and acts, although I had no trouble whatever locating many authorities on American and European behavior.

It is with some degree of enthusiasm that I welcome the publication of Allen Edwardes' *The Jewel in the Lotus,* since it is virtually the only existing work in English which systematically describes and analyzes the sex customs and ideas which were prevalent in the East and, especially the Middle East, in pre-twentieth century times. Selecting discriminately from the writings of Sir Richard F. Burton, the greatest of all students of Persian-Arabian eroticism, and from classic Oriental sources, Edwardes has patiently classified the most important aspects of Asiatic sex life and has produced a surprisingly large amount of exceptionally relevant information which has hitherto been unknown to most American and European readers. Although none of the material he presents is inaccessible to the painstaking scholar, most of it is not likely to come to the attention of the educated layman who does not read a summary such as is quite adequately presented in *The Jewel in the Lotus*.

In presenting this material on Eastern and Middle Eastern sex mores, the author has wisely, I believe, retained the full literary flavor of much of his source material, thus making his book more authoritative and interesting. Whereas sex, when it is spoken about in public in the West, tends to be expressed in fairly down to earth terms, Oriental speech patterns, at least in former days, appear to be more flowery and euphemistic; and in sticking to Burton's and others' mid-Victorian English translations, the flavor of the original sex expressiveness is probably best retained.

In spite of the euphemistic language of much of the Oriental sex passages included in this book, it is gratifyingly surprising how well the lusty, and in many ways relatively unrepressed, sexuality of the Islamic people comes through. In spite of their over-sufficiency of sex superstitions and, as the author incisively points out, their anti-feminine biases, the Arabs of bygone days (as well as, apparently, of today) were in many respects gloriously prosexual and made a considerable part of our own antisexual behavior inept and pallid by comparison.

It is also most interesting to note, in Edwardes' pages, some of the similarities between the Oriental practices and our own. Thus, it is clearly indicated that Arabian homosexuality, which tends to be considerably more widespread than our own, does not spring from purely biological causes but is closely related to the Islamic custom of segregating young males from young females as well as to other environmental factors. Some of the material which Edwardes presents in this connection is surprisingly close to that which I present in a chapter in my recent book, *Sex Without Guilt,* which is entitled "How American Women Are Driving American Males Into Homosexuality."

Again, *The Jewel in the Lotus* contains a fascinating description of how Arab *ginks,* or extreme sex inverts, had themselves castrated in order to appear like females. Here we have the Oriental counterpart of the

Christine Jorgensen-type castration attempts of some transsexualists of today. Apparently, many sex customs repeat themselves even in widely differing cultures; and when certain restrictions and pressures are placed on human sexuality, such as the discouraging of heterosexual relationships, certain aberrations, such as widespread homosexuality or transsexualism, will tend to occur. As is usual in the entire animal kingdom, overt sexuality is a product of *both* significant biological and social factors.

While the author of *The Jewel in the Lotus* has done a careful and scholarly job of delineating many Middle Eastern sex beliefs and practices, the reader must be warned that, because of the necessarily limited nature of his sources, some of the material in the book must be taken with something of a grain of salt. Thus, many of the customs exposited are taken from stories, myths, and tales which have more literary than scientific substance. Just as our contemporary novels are indicative but not necessarily precisely descriptive of our own sex-love attitudes and acts, so the *Book of a Thousand Nights and a Night* and other fictional sources which are quoted in this book are often suggestive rather than scientifically accurate in their depictions of Arabian sex activities.

It must nonetheless be noted that even the exaggerations and inaccuracies of the Oriental sex tales are themselves indicative of very real aspirations, wish-fulfillments, and fears of the Asiatic peoples in regard to sex. Thus, when the Oriental scribe consistently depicts his female protagonists as being exceptionally ardent and inclined to commit adultery whenever the harem eunuch's eyes are turned, he may by no means be describing the actual propensity of most Islamic women, but he may very well be demonstrating the conscious and unconscious desires of Arabian men to have ardent female lovers and their dire fears of being cuckolded. These desires and fears are themselves an important aspect of Oriental love life, however unrealistic or exaggerated they may be.

In any event, considering that such large populations of the world have resided and still reside in the

Orient, and considering that we know, through many careful anthropological studies, much more about the sex lives of many primitive tribes than we do about those of some of our oldest civilized peoples, it is most desirable that information about Eastern and Middle Eastern sex habits becomes much more widely disseminated in the West than is presently true. It is particularly desirable that definitive articles and books on contemporary Oriental beliefs and practices be published. *The Jewel in the Lotus* does not, as its author frankly makes clear, cover this modern ground. But it does contain a great deal of information, including some of the minutest details, of many unique sex rites, rituals, and cults of the East and Middle East. If read for what it is, rather than for what some of us might like it to be, I think that it will prove rewarding for most Americans and Europeans.

Albert Ellis, Ph.D.

New York City

Preface

Many of the customs described herein are no longer practiced today. There has always been change in the supposedly unchanging East; and never, perhaps, have the changes been as great as under the impact of the conqueror West in recent centuries. And now as the East is shaking off Western power by adopting Western nationalism, the changes are being accelerated.

Certain basic attitudes, however, remain. One of these is the candid and realistic Oriental feeling about sex, and this is to be seen remaining in the changed or moderated sexual practices of the East.

It is in this light and in the illumination it can shed on Western attitudes and ways that this book on the sexual customs of the East (primarily the Middle East) is offered to the reader.

For a better understanding of our sexual culture it is essential that we be familiar with the scope and content of other cultures. These cultures may have been similar to our own or may have represented a form of social behavior so opposed to our own ideas that in defense we have developed, in a form of negative adjustment, strict patterns to resist their influence. For example, the Victorian Westerners were so shocked by the licentiousness of Eastern sexual mores that a rigidity and repression were imposed which recent studies have evaluated as being as destructive as that which was being resisted, if not more so.

However, in this context it is also important to note that regardless of how free and glorified was sexual expression in the Eastern cultures, it never rose to the heights where woman was acknowledged as an equal partner to man. The roles she was forced into in the East were those of chattel and concubine; whereas the nonfree, "rigid and repressive" attitude of Western Christian tradition did, by some inadequately understood process (and this is something for present-day scholars to investigate seriously) lead to an awareness of both the individual and the social value of the free, equal, and responsible woman. This development promises a future when man and woman can look forward to a fuller, more meaningful harmony in their sexual union and in all their other relationships.

This is not meant to suggest the equation Rigidity + Repression = Freedom. The statement is made with the hope that people will perceive that there is more to History-Tradition-Understanding than meets the careless eye. The study of peoples and cultures must not proceed from a point of view biased by either the exclusively negative or the exclusively positive. Both negative and positive factors contribute to what history has properly evaluated as the reality.

The purpose of this book is to study and learn what is the face behind the masks—those which have been called Islam and Hindooism; masks to too great a degree fashioned by Occidental delusion and pedantry. One way to a productive study of culture is to survey its sexual practices. These reveal the basic character of a people better than many other social expressions.

The "self-righteous" Western civilization of yesteryear drew a veil over the truth. An attempt was made to deny or dim the naturalness of basic human sexual relations. But this ghost of Victorianism is vanishing; we are aware, today, that ours is a world peopled by humans molded of bone, flesh, and blood—and sex and other glands.

Occidental conceptions of harems and chivalrous princes are disastrously quaint, engendered and nurtured by the nursery rhyme, Oriental *galland,* and Hollywood fantasy.

Richard Burton and others of his stature presented a truer picture of the East. However, the inebriate stench of nineteenth-century Puritanism and egomania was all but deadly; the diffusion of sexual knowledge had been blocked. Pretension and fantasy refused to accept the truth because the truth was strange, uncouth. Thus the squeamish tin gods of Europe barred off communication of the realities of the East as contaminations from "lucrative sinks of iniquity peopled by degenerate niggers."

In the Orient, virtue and vice were generally regarded in juxtaposition. Sensuality or continence was but a matter of taste; and, declared the witty Brahmin in explaining away the bald iniquities of Hindooism, who can account for taste?

Such philosophy, viewed in the light of Christian morality, appeared utterly depraved and despicable. "Ah! better an acknowledged sinner than a lecherous saint," retorted the Easterner who seemed well acquainted with Occidental disposition.

There is no Good, there is no Bad: these be the whims
    of mortal will;
What works me weal: that, call I *Good;* what harm and
    hurts, I hold as *Ill;*
They change with place, they shift with race; and, in the
    veriest span of Time,
Each Vice has worn a Virtue's crown: all Good was
    banned as Sin or Crime.

This was the strong feeling of one Hadjee Abdoo-el-Yezdee, who had thoroughly scrutinized the world's temperament, and it speaks for itself. Evil, deified in one society, became ungodly in another.

Cease, Man, to mourn, to weep, to wail: enjoy thy shin-
    ing hour of sun;
We dance along Death's icy brink, but is the dance less
    full of fun?

The Eastern ideal in practice was "Live for Today; let Past and Future look to themselves." Yesterday, Today, and Tomorrow meant the same; and Time, a

Western monstrosity, meant nothing. What did not occur today occurred tomorrow, or many tomorrows
hence. What need to worry?

    "Unborn To-morrow and dead Yesterday" . . .
"Why fret about them if To-day be sweet!"

    "Drink of yon Mirage-stream, and chase the tin-
kling of the Camel-bell!" says Hadjee Abdoo-el-Yezdee in true spirit.

> Be thine own Deus, make Self free: liberal as the circling
>   air;
> Thy Thought, to thee, an Empire be: break every prisoning
>   lock and bar.

    This manner of reasoning crops up in almost every
piece of Oriental literature. Even the Old Testament
does not lack its share of fatalism: "Let us eat and
drink; for tomorrow we shall die."

    The entire *Rubaiyat of Omar Khayyam* bears a
keenly necessitarian tone, bordering on self-delusion:

> And Lip to Lip it murmur'd: "While you live,
>   'Drink!'—for, once dead, you never shall return."

    The *Rubaiyat*'s appeal, however, lies not in its
pathetic outbursts of abandonment but in its earnest
search for the unattainable Truth. This quest, sadly
enough, often ends in abandonment of common sense
and clinging to hopeless fanaticism, like the passion of a
Hindoo ascetic: "I, Myself, am Heav'n and Hell!"

    Hadjee Abdoo-el-Yezdee, rational throughout, de-
fies the assumed omniscience of man with:

> What know'st thou, Man, of Life?—and yet, for ever 'twixt
>   the womb, the grave,
> Thou pratest of the Coming Life: of Heav'n and Hell
>   thou fain must rave.

    In his turn, the brilliant but melancholy Persian
intones:

> Of threats of Hell and Hopes of Paradise!
> One thing at least is certain—This Life flies;
>   One thing is certain and the rest is Lies;
> The Flower that once has blown for ever dies.

Beholding life in this aspect, the almost instinctive reaction is self-sorrow and deterministic resignation. Perceiving little difference in life and death, pleasure and pain, Omar Khayyam, arm in arm with the Hindoo agnostic, damns existence and says:

Drink! for you know not whence you came, or why: Drink! for you know not why you go nor where.

Such sensual resignation, arising out of failure to understand that which never can be understood nor delineated, pervaded the Orient. Ego debased Reason. What in the beginning was a philosophical acceptance of life's mysteries ended in selfish indulgence.

If one could not grasp the purpose for living, what sense lay in human existence? From North Africa to Japan rang the saying: "Naked about thy genitories, and perfume under them: eat, drink, copulate—and let the world go to ruin."

Thus the East steeped itself in both thoughtful seclusion and open debauchery. It has required centuries for the West to sense some understanding of Oriental temperament.

When Omar the Tent-Maker divorced "old barren Reason" from his Bed, and "took the Daughter of the Vine to Spouse," antisocial groups, abortions of fatalism and cynicism, avowed defiance of life and invited pleasurable death. Among them were the sadomasochistic Thugs and Assassins.

Life is transient like a flash of lightning, and this world is as unsubstantial as a spark of fire. For what is the world? It is even as the bough of a tree on which a bird rests for a night and, in the morning, flies away.

This theory, coupled with man's guilty need for retribution, merely because life is so short, so cruel, so inscrutable, led to the famous words of the saint Kubeer: "Illusion dies; dies not, the Mind, though dead and gone the flesh." This in essence explains why Sir Richard Burton was led to remark that "the more I study religions, the more I am convinced that man never worshiped anything but himself."

And man, worshiping Self in the image of a god or Self as an ill-fated insubstantial being, made a principle of sensuality.

"Our Arab, at his worst," says Burton, "is a mere barbarian who has not forgotten the savage. He is a model mixture of childishness and astuteness, of simplicity and cunning, concealing levity of mind under solemnity of aspect. His stolid instinctive conservatism grovels before the tyrant rule of routine, despite that turbulent and licentious independence which ever suggests revolt against the ruler. His mental torpidity, founded upon physical indolence, renders immediate action and all manner of exertion distasteful. His conscious weakness shows itself in overweening arrogance and intolerance. His crass and self-satisfied ignorance makes him glorify the most ignoble superstitions, while acts of revolting savagery are the natural results of a malignant fanaticism and a furious hatred of every creed beyond the pale of El-Islam. Hence, he virtually says: 'I came into the world without having applied for, or having obtained, permission—nay, more, without my leave being asked or given. Here, I find myself hand-tied by conditions, and fettered by laws and circumstances, in making of which my voice had no part. While in the womb, I was an automaton; and death will find me a mere machine. Therefore not I, but the Law —or, if you please, the Lawgiver—is answerable for all my actions.'"

With this as part of our framework, we begin our historical survey of the sexual culture of the East.

I

WOMAN:
Passive Creature

In the West, ladies first;
Ladies last, in the East.

1. CONCEPT

The Oriental conception of woman was at times highly ironic. At one moment of defeat, the Arab would growl: *"Women are made of nectar and poison."* Later, in triumph, he would announce: "Praise be to Him Who fashioned her from semen-drop!"

A lovely female was much idealized and the ideal was stereotyped, from Egypt to India. She, a veritable slice of the moon, bore the wantoning eyes of a gazelle; her sleepy languorous glance was a potent charm, an incitement to love. Silken black hair, with coiling ringlets, adorned her head; teeth were of pearl and lips carnelian. "She hath breasts like two globes of ivory, like golden pomegranates—beautifully upright, arched and rounded, firm as stone to the touch—with nipples erect and outward jutting."[1] Three exquisite creases

[1]Sir Richard F. Burton, *The Book of the Thousand Nights and a Night.*

1

scored her stomach, the pride of a slim waist. Her hips were wide and heavy; her back-parts, like the revolving heavens. "She hath thighs like unto pillars of alabaster; and between them, there vaunts a secret place, a sachet of musk, that swells, that throbs, that is moist and avid."[2]

The Arab word for woman, *orett,* bears a double entendre: *shame* and *nakedness.* Woman was always from ancient times thought to be highly impure because of her apparently insatiable capacity for love and her periodic ailments.

Women, like camels and elephants, have their spells of rut, declared an eminent Persian physician.

> In torrid climes, man has need to be a demon to satisfy the lust of an unquenchable woman. He has need to be jinn-mad! A handsome gentleman is not safe at night in the bazaars of Persia and Afghanistan. In Cabul, the feminine population attack and maul him. In Hindostan, learned Brahmins have the erotic zones of these she-wolves well charted: beginning at a cold portion and progressing in intensity. When the fever reaches the genitals, she is raving wild; and then, digital friction can ease little. A gentleman must produce the real thing; and it had better be ample and enduring or he is laughed to scorn, spat at and kicked, scratched and bitten, as a beardless boy who emits even before he enters.

"Man's shame extends from his navel to his knees; woman's, from the top of her head to the tips of her toes." This was popular medieval Arab lore. "Who can stem a furious stream and a frantic woman? When in her recurrent frenzy of heat, man cannot appease her. It is like trying to stuff a bladder, with the essence oozing out the other end."

Her passion, supposedly ten times that of a man, was likened to that of animals. In India and Persia it was given the appellation of *must* (the annual excitement of elephants and other quadrupeds). In Egypt

------

[2] *Ibid.*

and Arabia it was termed *shogeh* (a condition when she-camels raise their tails in rut). Among the African nomads, woman was compared to an old she-hyena, shunned by all sensible male hyenas, who roams the desert in perpetual heat.

But while the misogynist damned woman as a tool of the devil, there was the romantic who fervidly burst: "Laud to the Lord Who adorned the virginal bosom with breasts, and Who made the thighs of women anvils for the spear-handles of men!"

Moslem ladies, facetiously termed *zewwah-el-fur-ooj* (the slit ones), were apostrophized by Arab bards who extolled or denounced them in limitless verse.

Women, for all the chastity they claim, are offal cast by
    kites where'er they list;
This night, their talk and secret charms are thine; that
    night, another 'joyeth coynte and kiss:
Like inn whence, after night, thou far'st at dawn—and
    lodges other wight thou hast not wist.

Another poet, analyzing the feminine qualities from youth to maturity, composed the following:

When a maid owns to ten, her new breasts arise; and like
    diver's pearl, with fair neck she hies;
The damsel of twenty defies compare; 'tis she, whose dis-
    port, we desire and prize;
She, of thirty, hath healing on cheeks of her; she's a
    pleasure, a plant whose sap never dries;
If, on her in the forties, thou happily hap: she's best of
    her sex, hail to him with her lies!

But our misognynist, ever alert, retorts:

Rely not on women, trust not to their hearts:
Whose joys and whose sorrows are hung to their parts!

Of all Eastern peoples, the mild, compassionate Hindoos display the most tolerant attitude toward their womenfolk. They regarded the feminine sex philosoph-ically, accepted its frailties, and shrugged away its riddles and intrigues. One Hindoo sage even had the courage to remark: "A woman is pure in all her limbs,

while the holy cow is pure only behind." Another, viewing womankind less appreciatively, merely commented:
"Women are the ploughed field, and men the seed."

Not only in literature but in everyday usage, Moslems generally addressed their women in the masculine
gender, young boys in the feminine, to avert the evil
eye (*eyn-el-fessaud*). In the case of boys, this led to joc-
ularity and sarcasm; but it was held in all strictness
with womankind, and bore not the connotation of les-
bianism as much as that of pederasty. A man addressing a lady in any other gender save masculine—or often neuter—was considered highly outlandish.

This relation of the evil eye with women and, because of their innocence, children, grew from the belief
that the frail sex was innately diabolic. "Man is fire
and Woman is tinder" wrote one inspired Hindoo; and
another:

> It is more easy to discover flowers on the
> sacred fig-tree, or a white crow, or the imprint
> of fishes' feet, than to know what a woman has
> in her heart.[3]

The Arab concluded laconically, "Consult females
and do contrariwise."

Just as the passive sodomite was looked upon
with scorn, so woman, as a passive creature, was regarded with distaste. She afforded ecstatic pleasure, and
yet she was unclean and lustful. This incongruity of
feeling tormented every ancient civilization from
Greece to Palestine.

For proud, selfish man to assume a passive role in
life was hateful and debasing. Even with regard to carnal intercourse the universal warning was: "Cursed be
he who maketh woman heaven and himself earth!"

2. Virginity and Marriage

The feelings toward the undeflowered virgin varied
in Moslem and Hindoo areas.

---

[3]Abbé J. A. Dubois, *Hindu Manners, Customs and Ceremonies.*

In India, the maid (*kunyah, kumaree*) was handled with the utmost delicacy; she was a frail willow, easily shivered by a coarse wind. But in the Moslem world man asserted his vigor. With gusto, he related of how he "rent the veil, broke the seal, and pierced the forge wherein children are hammered out." Softly, the fastidious Hindoo spoke of "breaking the hairless peach"; robustly, the fiery Arab said of taking a maidenhead: "I tore open a skin bag." Thereafter, he employed the crudest language to describe the night's work:

Ekheddo-enneh demm-bintee-heh (I bled her of the hymeneal blood and,) *y'zeggeh w'zeggeh fee ferj-heh* (thrusting and foining at her cleft,) *beyn-enneh fersee-heh w'ed-demmee-heh* (I was between faeces and menses).

This allusion to his position emphasizes the point of woman's alleged impurity; thus the instinctive aversion to the feminine sex, its premarital virginity, and its postpubescent menstruation.

Zehreh (flower) is a girl who has not menstruated; she is, next to a postpubescent boy, the purest of creatures. Legend tells us that Faut'meh, the Prophet's daughter, thrived in such a condition all her life. Next to Es-Seyyideh, the Blessed Virgin, she was the most honored of women.

Coition during the menses was forbidden to all Moslems, for such action was said to have bred *juzaum* (leprosy). *Sebeel* signifies the beginning of the flow, the period of *nejis* (ceremonial impurity). A child born out of congress during *heyzeh* (menstruation) was destined to become a sorcerer; girls born thus were doomed to be witches. In fact, the menstrual discharge was regarded with such horror that Egyptian women, at certain phases of the moon, compounded it with other ingredients to form a deadly poison that had no antidote, attacked the body like scurvy, and destroyed it within a year.

In ancient Persian belief, the rules of their prophet Zoroaster are severe:

A menstruous woman is the work of Uhremaun, the devil. A woman during her periodical illness is not to gaze upon the sacred fire, sit in water, behold the sun, or hold conversation with a man.

In fact, a menstruating woman was considered both dangerous and defiling by the Worshipers of the Sun; and such a woman was thought to be the bearer of illness and death.

In the Koran, we find:

They will ask thee also concerning the courses of women; answer, They are a pollution: therefore separate yourselves from women in their courses, and go not near them, until they be cleansed.

Hindoo lawbooks and the *Code of Menu* are just as rigid:

A woman, during her menstrual period, shall retire for three days to a place apart. During this time, she shall not look at anybody, not even her own children, or at the light of the sun. On the fourth day, she shall bathe.

However, in a land where Indree (copulation) was deified, the *Law of Menu* and the strong procreative disposition of the Hindoos clashed. The Indian Trimoortee (triad or Trinity), Brahma, Shiva, Vishnu, symbolized both massive propagation and destruction. Thousands died yearly; to preserve the race, thousands had to re-enter the world. Therefore, ironically, *ritoo* (period of fertility) was adored in womankind. In honor of the gods, particularly Vishnu, Lord of Preservation, all women were compelled to copulate for progeny at this time. Such in its natural course led to child marriage so that the first period of menstruation, the advent of fertility in a young girl, would not go to waste but be utilized in the cause of Vishnu.

The menstrual fluid, therefore, came to be regarded as hallowed, pure, and auspicious as Ganges water or *soma* (nectar of the gods). *Gulaul,* a gaudy red dye, was to the accompaniment of strident chorusing and thunderous drums squirted about the streets during religious festivals and smeared everywhere and upon everyone, as symbolical of the menses of fertile womanhood. Yellow dye, later mixed with red and tossed during the Hoolee (spring fiesta), came to represent the consecrated merde and blood of Mother Cow.

The primitive awe of and aversion to human blood manifested itself in the significance accorded to the blood drawn in devirgination and circumcision. From ancient Egyptian to surviving cults in modern India and Persia, a ritual of purification had to be observed. Among these sects, every virgin before wedlock was made to sit upon the golden phallus of the Sun-god so that it ruptured and bled her. Hymeneal blood, otherwise deemed foul, was thereby hallowed; and no decent youth would marry a girl who was not thus consecrated.

The taking of maidenhead, regarded as porter's work in many parts of the East, was inconsequential to certain haughty Egyptians. They would sooner penetrate the bride with an iron rod or command a black slave to deflower her than defile themselves in the act.

Modern Persian sects, reverted to the ancient sun worshipers who practiced this rite, were on the whole a celibate group keeping a modest community of women with whom they systematically generated their kind. Such were the adorers of Mithra or Mehr-Eezid (the Sacred Orb), symbol of light, purity, and creation. To them the sun represented the male principle; the moon, the female aspect. An eclipse (*khusoof*) signified their union.

The dogmas of the Mithra sect embraced asceticism and abstinence, austerity and penance, allowing sexual intercourse only at prescribed times, according to the lunar phases. One select group, honored for their youth and flawless beauty, were chosen to sacrifice their seed to the sun.

Each, nude as upon his day of birth, filed out into the blinding white haze of noon. Settling themselves down, murmuring their occult formulas, they focused upon divine communication with the pulsing orb;

whilst the heat and masochistic sensations provoked
by the thrill of self-immolation drew upon their organs
and caused a palpitant swelling that mounted in in-
tensity. Reaching a crisis, the devotee convulsed and,
in sacrificial ecstasy, his semen was cast to the sun.
After thrice discharging his libation, he descended into
a swoon and was borne away.

The youth of this sect was less than a man if he
could not achieve this, and his punishment was ex-
pulsion from the group. The sun served only as the
inspirer of male power; the imagination must conjure
the orgasms. This association with natural power pro-
gressed through the years, and love and worship of
Mithra supplanted attraction to a beautiful woman or a
comely youth. After prolonged adoration, the adherent
acquired a formidable hyperesthesia and would sacrifice his fluid on the slightest provocation in honor of
the sun. But if this happened in darkness, as if in involuntary and blasphemous veneration of night, the
doctrinal source of evil, the individual must make
atonement through painful torture, signifying the conquest of light (*uhremuzdeh,* good) over darkness
(*uhremaun,* evil). This penitential torment, flagellation
by nettles, was inflicted upon the genitals.

Therefore, in dimness, the Mithraist must play the
ascetic and never allow his mind to revert to thoughts
of the glories of day. Such was the awesome test of
devotion.

Another sect, the Mutawaulees, fervidly worshiped Seyyideh-ul-Kubeereh (Venus, Great Mother).
The women sacrificed their virginity in the shrouding
darkness of aromatic groves. Hymeneal blood was as
sacred to them as semen to adorers of the paternal
principle.

Squeamish Arabs in Egypt and the Sudan, who
reacted with aversion to defloration and the unclean
aspect of virginity, usually hired an individual known
as El-Muftah (The Key). El-Muftah was a young bull
of an Abyssinian, wealthy as a sheykh, who made a
thriving business out of defloration by proxy or unlock-
ing the obstinate orifices of brides for fastidious
grooms, or grooms who had tried and failed. El-

Muftah then, for another price, sold the nuptial sheets
so that the groom could boast in the coffeehouse that
he had drawn blood and was now a manly husband.

El-Muftah vaunted a sexual organ that was wrist-
thick, measured eight inches in length, and was so
powerful that, thus he bragged, it was capable of striking a person unconscious. The most famous El-Muftah
was killed by a shell that exploded in his residence
during the ill-fated defense of Khartoum by Gordon
Pasha. A number of Sudanese women, it is said, committed suicide when they heard of it, and a rich Arab
matron bought the dead man's phallus for a high
price. It is the most vaunted relic in the Sudan next to
that of El-Mahdi, whose measurements were and remain a matter of consecrated secrecy.

In the mania of purism and male superiority,
misogynous cults were swift to form. In Persia and
Iraq, particularly, many embraced an indifferent bisexuality.

A pair of early nineteenth-century Afghan adventurers, exploring the ruins outside Cabul, stumbled
upon a peculiar decayed temple that aroused their
curiosity. Descending into its dark moist vault they
found the stale air heavy with incense and a wraithlike
glow flickered from brazen lamps. Bats shrieked and
fluttered away.

As they reached the bottom, the eldest drew his
dagger, cautioning his brother to stand behind him.
They crept forward in amber dimness.

Sepulchral but tender, a voice alerted them: "I
welcome thee." A ghostly figure loomed out of the
haze. The two adventurers stared hard, discerned it to
be a young man with long black tresses and garbed in
a single loose mantle of white. He offered his hand. The
eldest brother, Ushruf, sheathed his dagger.

"I am Peer Nooraulee," the young man said, smiling.

The adventurers thought him to be an extremely
handsome Persian, with penetrative eyes and bland
lips. But his emaciated look indicated that he was ad-
dicted to keen excess.

The eldest newcomer touched his breast. "God so

willing, I am Ushruf Khan Ghilzye, and this be my brother, Uleem Khan."

The young man acknowledged this with a kindly smile. "Very good," he said. "Follow after me, and we shall be seated in comfort. I am master of the Chiraugh-Kushee, Lamp-killers of Cabul. We call ourselves by that name because our aim is to extinguish the light of procreation. We are diffused throughout India, Afghanistan, and Persia, but the tenets vary slightly from area to area. We of Cabul are the most strict in our disposition."

As a matter of sectarian custom and humility, Peer Nooraulee removed his chogha to display a lithe wiry body. The brothers were somewhat startled to note that his carnal instrument was tinted a deep crimson, and that red lines streaked from either groin to converge at his navel. Peer Nooraulee thus described his sect:

> Unlike the Hindoos and Mussulmans, our sect, like that of the Yezdee, the Mughwar, or the Aly-Ilahee, holds procreation as an abomination to mankind. Something must be done, lest the world overflow with people. India is smothered by life, much of it wretched and superfluous; and there is little food to care for such numbers. Soon the entire world must starve. And excessive numbers breed crime and enmity, and encourage filth and disease.
>
> We of the Chiraugh-Kushee take pride in destroying our virility, so that we may not revert to women and have issue. We feel, as do many men who are bound in wedlock, that there is nothing more evil than a woman; that she harbors an evil spirit in her bosom. When woman was created, the devil exalted; for she is his tool. She is voracious in the embrace of a man; and when he is insensate with exhaustion, she beats and abuses him playfully that he might continue to gratify her.
>
> Every week, thousands of people flow north and south, east and west. We are fortunate to initiate many fresh adherents, who carry our doctrines to other parts of the East. A goodly por-

tion of these are men, young and old, unwed or
with families, who have tired of the hypocrisy
of mankind, have been ill-treated by greedy, base
life. They have seen the falseness of established
religions, have abjured the unnecessary hell encircling masses of people. Our women have their
own rites, which are practiced in the Kuzzilba-
shee Chundhole Bazaar.

From earliest days of youth, our male adherents learn the processes of manipulating their
secret parts. We believe strongly in circumcision; it destroys hateful sensitivity, which dooms
a man to sexual convention. Our rituals for
youth become more intensive as years pass by;
and when the lad reaches puberty and can
achieve ejaculation, we must then be cautious
to guide him into a strict code averse to the
evils of feminine flesh. And this, to be sure, is
an arduous trial of mind over matter. From
puberty, thereafter, the youth must come to
recognize erection and emission as spontaneous;
thereafter, he is freed of dependence upon
women.

With the arrival of puberty, the rituals increase to every night of the week. Night when
man senses his greatest desire is free for diversion, and he is apt to seek women. As a rite of
our ceremony, the organ of each adherent is
artfully wielded by his companion until the seed
is exhausted, and even beyond, until he can
tolerate no more. After a number of years, when
the adherent arrives at twenty or thirty years of
age, depending upon his endowment or when
he pledged fidelity, he has by then destroyed
potency; he can no longer fecundate or enjoy
women. He is adapted to our sect and now as-
sumes the duty of instructing others. He can
never revert to women for progeny or pleasure,
merely because he has either obliterated all fleshly desire or has attained hypersensibility, preventing penetration. The slightest provocation,
the vaguest thought, must induce irritable throbbing; but frustration will foil every feeble attempt. Many have sought to break away, but have
met defeat; they are incapable of abandoning
the faith.

Ushruf, with the hint of a grin, said: "Would it not be easier, God so willing, for thee to just introduce the act of emasculation?"

"Ah! but then, the will is weakened; we aim for self-control and ascetic discipline."

"How must ye feel about sodomy?"

"We abhor it. That is not our purpose. In answer to nature, our adherents seek but superficial gratification, centered in the sexual apparatus. But from that point our only concern is to depopulate the earth, now smothered and debased by mankind."

"God be praised! it needs a strong man of principle to cling to such belief. And what of thyself, yah Huzoor?"

"As officiating Peer, I must represent the evils of procreation and exemplify their control. That is why I daub my phallus with *laul-rung,* and outline the seat of lust and sensuality in the human body.

"One night in every month we are allowed freedom with our community of women, to recognize and affirm their baneful lusts and deceptions."

Uleem Khan said: "We have often seen holy men whose implements are stained a bright red, or even green and saffron. In a bathhouse at Tehran, I remember a *soofee* (Moslem mystic) whose carnal member was dyed orange; and every catamite there who solicited our attention was similarly painted."

Nooraulee replied: "Many of these individuals have nought to do with our sect. Some tinge their parts by law of caste, or for special reasons touching upon pride and vanity. The Kuzzilbash and debauchees who frequent public houses are wont to decorate their tools. Others seek to impersonate Lamp-killers, and thereby deceive us by practicing sodomy. But the true Lamp-killer keeps his instrument hidden at all times save in ritual, and is to be distinguished by the peculiar manner in which he tints the glans [rounded extremity of the penis]."

The Chiraugh-Kushee, allied with the Yezdee devil-worshipers and Aly-Ilahee heretics, was but one of a dozen such cults infesting Persia and Afghanistan. Many of them had by the close of the eighteenth century abandoned their strict tenets and resigned themselves to senseless unbridled debauchery, both hetero- and homosexual. Masochistic flagellants performed self-mutilation of their sex; the Sheeah Persians, in exaggerating the glories of martyrdom as experienced by the Moslem saints, Hessen and Hosseyn, slashed, beat, and flayed their bodies; and a group in India, primarily Rajpoots, promiscuously copulated with a community of women every night of the week and, when children were born, destroyed each in sacrifice.

Eyyaum-en-nifaus refers to the forty-day period following childbirth during which a Moslem woman, considered ceremoniously unclean, may not cohabit with her husband.

Some Hindoos, Moslems, and Jews held nearly the same beliefs in regard to women and impurity. The Bible testifies for the Israelites; in Hindoo custom, a mother's pollution extended forty days in the birth of a girl, thirty days for a boy (the latter being more highly prized). No sexual intercourse was to occur during this time, under penalty of defilement. "A woman, following parturition, will destroy all her clothing and purify herself in cow's urine."

Thus, because of her inscrutable monthly courses and the belief that her carnal need was double that of a man, woman was looked upon as inferior. Her status was nothing more than that of a drudge who labored for the man and also served him for pleasure and propagation. The Koran and Old Testament clearly state these precepts; and womankind, knowing little else, accepted bondage.

The women of India, restricted as they were, nevertheless enjoyed the greatest freedom of any in the East. In some rituals they were obliged in the name of the Preserver to yield their bodies to any man willing to lie with them. This was one of the earliest and most innocent forms of prostitution.

"A man without a wife is an imperfect being." So reads the *Code of Menu*. The Koran teaches that "when a servant of God marries, verily he perfects half his religion."

Most Hindoo women, as well as Moslems and Jews, married soon after puberty—often long before—unless guided into a singular profession such as dancing, priesthood, or prostitution. Mohammed directed:

> Take in marriage—of the women who please you—two, three, or four; but if ye fear that ye cannot act equitably with so many, take only one.

Poverty restricted men of poorer classes to a single wife if, indeed, they could afford a wife at all. The wealthy were well able to go the limit of four and even beyond. But any female exceeding the fourth was considered a concubine (*abdeh,* she-slave), half-wife, or mistress. The keeping of slave girls was regarded as a mere peccadillo, because Mohammed was not explicit; he only voiced a preference that accorded with the reality for most men—that he have and prefer one woman to several. That one woman was generally for the Arabs, a man's first cousin. If she desired someone else, the law forbade her to marry another without her cousin's permission.

In explaining or excusing the need for more than one wife, the shrewd Mohammedan would reply:

> One wife demands equality; she answers back, acquires pride and hauteur. Two wives are forever quarreling; they are given over to vicious jealousy and are a danger to the children. With three wives, two of them usually end up by going against the one who is slightly different from the pair. But four wives are good agreeable company, able to quarrel and settle their differences; and a husband enjoys comparable peace. Anything in excess of four adds spice to what is already there for the eating.

In spite of certain restrictions that exuded the odor of bondage, the Moslem wife enjoyed at intervals certain rights of which many took advantage. She might be allowed a month's absence annually, without telling her husband where she was going or why. He was obliged to trust her. For man, very often, had only a faithful woman to rely upon when all others turned against him; and it was certainly worth his while to remain diplomatic and not witlessly accuse his spouse of infidelity unless he was absolutely certain of it. Though she was not educated in the scholastic sense, the Moslem wife possessed ample tact and wisdom. As long as her husband treated her civilly, though he showed her no love, she was bound to honor and serve him; but she also took advantage of his weakness or good nature. Moslem men were often henpecked, an example of the irony of custom, where one aspect inverts itself to form another.

According to the best Hindoo authorities, the "ideal wife is a nurse in illness, a drudge in housekeeping, a wise counselor in calamity, a mother in tenderness, the earth herself in patience, and a harlot in bed."[4]

In the *Code of Menu:*

> There is no other god on earth for a woman than her husband. The most excellent of all the good works that she can do is to seek to please him by manifesting perfect obedience to him. Therein should lie her sole rule of life.
>
> Be her husband deformed, aged, infirm, offensive in his manners; let him also be choleric, debauched, immoral, a drunkard, a gambler; let him frequent places of ill repute, live in open sin with other women, have no affection whatever for his home; let him rave like a lunatic; let him live without honor; let him be blind, deaf, dumb, or crippled; in a word—let his defects be what they may, let his wickedness be what it may—a wife should always look upon him as her god, should lavish on him all her attention and care: paying no heed whatsoever to his character and giving him no cause whatsoever for displeasure.
>
> A woman is made to obey at every stage of her existence.[5]

[4] P. Thomas, *Kama Kalpa.*
[5] Dubois, *op. cit.*

Eastern races generally held close to this ancient philosophy, and nothing more was thought of it. It was the accepted pattern: in India, *Dustoor hey!* (It is the custom); in Egypt, *El-audeh kiddeh!* (It is the custom). Where the man exercised his traditional authority, the woman had to take care. One disagreeable word and off might come a wife's nose, her tongue, her breasts, or there might be some ghastly mutilation between the thighs.

The conventional wife respected her husband, would not presume to eat with him, speak to him in public, nor walk anywhere but behind him. She had her friends and he had his. Often the only thing they had in common was the occasional need for gratification and the breeding of heirs.

It was a dog-eared saying that the Moslem wife, though confined in the harem, controlled her husband's mind, if only on the copulatory couch. There, true enough, man yielded to the ecstatic sorcery of incomparable woman; but outside, no manner of temptation, persuasion, or mesmerism could sway his judgment.

> Verily, a woman should grant her lover all of which she is mistress: by way of excitement, and rare buckings and wrigglings, and passionate movements.

Such a woman, the ideal wife or concubine, was called *Looloooh* (pearl of union).

> He who desireth to take a female slave for carnal enjoyment, let him take an Abyssinian; if he need one for the sake of children, let him have a Persian; and whoso desireth one for service, let him choose a Hindoo.

So the saying was in India.

Arab verse also explored the values of Eastern women:

I love not white girls, blown with fat, who puff and pant;
the maid for me is young brunette, embonpoint-scant.

I'd rather ride a colt, that's dark upon the day of race,
and set my friends upon the elephant.

Once the young buck had found the proper mate,
he set to work to show her just what sort of a man he
was. And the Oriental maiden, especially the impassive
Hindoo, demanded great impression ere she completely surrendered to his will.

The enamorate pair generally indulged from the
first in a form of sport known in Persia as *bosah-
bauzee* (kissing and toying) or *naumzud-bauzee* (pet-
ting, betrothed play, amorous dalliance). It consisted
of the girl rubbing her body over the young man until
she reached a climax. All varieties of groping and handling were allowed, without the least bit of self-consciousness or restraint. They so disported fully dressed,
and it was primarily the duty of the male to stimulate
the female, though the situation was sometimes re-
versed, when the man delighted in a passive role. But
he had to be cautious not to defile his clothing with
seminal emission; if he did so, the game was over and
a bath was in order. Any indecent display of the body
was also the signal for one partner or the other to
retire. The sport (or science) involved overcoming
such handicaps, through which greater pleasure and
respect were achieved.

Once a youth kissed his maid between the eyes,
the pact was sealed. Carnality was cooled. She immediately became chaste and delaying; she could well
afford being decorous and aloof, for she recognized her
triumph and was his to espouse. Respecting this asser-
tion of purity, he did not touch nor lay eyes upon her
again until after the wedding ceremony. During this
time, the suspense in awaiting her naked body was almost unbearable. Negotiations were carried on between the two families and, meanwhile, the affianced
spent the time undergoing lengthy preparation and
ceremonious visitations and receptions.

It is reported that by the regulations of caste in
India, should a betrothed pubescent girl die before the
ceremony, she had yet to be penetrated by her husband before disposal of her body. This was performed

in the groom's house in the presence of the village priest just before cremation. Such a custom (intended to free evil spirits) may be traced back to ancient Egypt where virgin corpses were deflowered by priests or embalmers.

Following the modest ritual in the bride's house and a clamorous wedding procession through the narrow streets, a nuptial feast (*weleemeh*) was held in the groom's abode where *gurbaun-el-bintee*, the libation of maidenhead, was to occur. Among the wealthy who could afford to prolong the *weleemeh*, there was often before consummation a week's delay spent in celebration in honor of the bride's family.

Upon the seventh or eighth night, the groom went in unto his bride and found her seated upon the hymeneal couch, surrounded by the various ladies-in-waiting and elderly matrons. At this time he paid *jelweh* (lustre, the tax of unveiling the bride) to the *sheykheh* or governess. Having done so and stripped the first of seven veils to reveal the face of his bride, he watched the attending ladies depart.

Stiff, composed, with downcast eyes the virgin wife anticipated her husband's gentle touch: gentle until she lay back, glowing naked olive in the pale light—and then there erupted the ceremonial *gurbaun-el-bintee.*

> Breaking a maiden's seal is one of the best antidotes for one's ills; cudgeling her unceasingly, until she swoons away, is a mighty remedy for man's depression. It cures all impotence.

So the Arab medical books expounded.

The ritual commenced with the husband's praying to Almighty God that their union should be fruitful, that this very night be auspicious in his bride's womb. Then, from the foot of the bed, he approached her chanting:

> I am the sky, thou art the earth; I am the semen, thou art its bearer. In the name of God the Compassionate and Merciful, the Glorious and Great!

In other chambers members of the family and guests awaited the virginal cry. It had to be heard by all or misfortune would descend upon the young couple. To elicit a cry vibrant and loud enough, the husband attacked unmercifully. A frightened sigh ("O beloved of mine heart and vitals! I am bètween thy hands and my body is your body; I give myself up to thee") was barely uttered, when the instant of glory shattered all illusion.

In India, upon the moment of hearing the bride's voice, a coconut was broken over a red stone *lingam* (phallic emblem) by the local priest, to signify the taking of her virginity. The unveiling tax (*sulwa'ee*, price of perforation) was then announced to one and all.

In the Moslem home a crescendo of drums and cymbals and jubilant chorusing proclaimed the sacrifice. Such rejoicing, thundering throughout the night, was meant to drown the sacred *zeghareet:* the shrill piping of the bride as she approached and reached her climax (*aulee-derjeh*). Thereafter,

> he spent the night with her in embracing and kissing, plying the particle of copulation in concert and joining the conjunctive with the conjoined.[6]

Such a jocose rendering of this solemnity is typically Eastern, an attitude mingling robust appreciation with ceremonial reverence. Witness one portrayal of the sublime moment:

> He clasped her in his arms and strained her fast to his breast and sucked her lips, till the honey-dew ran out into his mouth; and he laid his hand under her left armpit, whereupon his vitals and her vitals yearned for coition. Then, he clapped her between the breasts and his hand slipped down between her thighs; and she girded him with her legs, whereupon he made of the two parts proof amain and crying out: "O

---

[6]Burton, *op. cit.*

Father of Virility!" applied the priming and kindled the match and set it to the touch-hole and
gave fire and breached the citadel in its four
corners—so there befell the mystery concerning which there is no enquiry—and she cried
the cry that needs must be cried.[7]

Addressing the penis (*zekker*), offering it respect
for the duty it had to perform, was a necessary part of
the ritual. Were he not to do so, the husband exposed
himself to the punishment of humiliation during his
manly performance. The usual title employed was *Yah
Sheykh Zekker* or *Yah Eboo-ez-Zekker* (O Father of
Penes! O thou who canst take her maidenhead whilst
my tongue obliterates the chastity of her mouth!)

Among the Hindoos the membrum virile (*soot,*
or stamen) had a twofold duty: to ravish the virginity
of mouth lips and vulva lips.

Another Arab, less aggressive than most, offered
the following autobiographic sketch in relation to his
wedding night:

She (his eager and audacious bride)
stripped off her outer gear, and she threw open
her chemise from the neck downwards—and
showed her parts genital, and all the rondure of
her hips. When I saw the glorious sight, my desires were roused; and I arose and doffed my
clothes. Whereupon, she drew me to her and I
did likewise. Then, I took her into my embrace
and set her legs round my waist—and point-
blanked that cannon placed where it battereth
down the bulwark of maidenhead and layeth it
waste. And I found her a pearl unpierced and
unthridden, and a filly unridden; and I abated
her virginity and had joyance of her youth in
my virility. And, presently, I withdrew sword
from sheath—and then returned to the fray right
eath—and when the battle and siege had fin-
ished, some fifteen assaults I had furnished. Then,
I laid my hand under her head—and she did the
same—and we embraced, and fell asleep in each
other's arms.

_____
[7]*Ibid.*

Moslems were of the strong opinion that, if she try, a bride would conceive on the wedding night; and to this purpose went the preconsummation prayer. Pure maternal imagination prompted the bride on the morrow to boast to her family and friends that she had conceived by him; that the seed of her husband was thick, copious, and fertile. Everyone normally anticipated hearing this, or suspected the groom as being impotent or timid.

Notwithstanding, the stained bedclothes and sheets were almost invariably hung over the entranceway of the house; and thoughtful scrutiny by visitors seemed to convince them that consummation had taken place in spite of the manifold tricks of elderly matrons, substituting bird blood for hymeneal blood when necessary.

Marital customs greatly varied from country to country, tribe to tribe. Among certain Berbers of North Africa, the young buck must display to the father of his prospective bride the generative organs of slain enemies. Were these organs large, indicating formidable foes, the father deemed this youth a courageous man worthy of his daughter and heartily accepted him into the family.

In parts of Persia, custom did not permit a man to marry unless he could satisfy the female in bed. Certain ancient Greeks had an analogous custom. And among some Arabian tribes, women examined the groom's private parts ere the fateful decision. The Arabian Sheeahs observed this tradition primarily to determine if the betrothed male's penis were hardy enough to endure a wife's voraciousness and the rite of nuptial circumcision.

Since popular Arab belief proclaimed that woman is insatiable, man alone suffered shortcomings. Where the prospective groom was elderly, the semen was often examined. In perfection, the *karooreh* (water-doctor) declared it as being *ark-el-hellaweh:* essence of sweetness. When it appeared too thin, and required thickening for impregnation, the water-doctor recommended various restoring drugs, usually opium and hasheesh. These also aided in energizing the membrum virile which, in its proper state, was termed *gedheeb-es-sukker* (sugar-stick).

It was contrary to law to examine any woman except a slave to determine if she were a virgin. Money-hungry fathers, marrying their unchaste daughters off to wealthy old ignoramuses, prestained the hymeneal chemise with pigeon blood, the nearest in resemblance to human claret. For in Moslem and Hebrew custom, previously alluded to, the stained nuptial sheet was proof enough of virginity. Western excuses such as pleas of injury incurred in athletic activity, were unheard of.

In Constantinople some adhered to a tradition whereby the Turkish groom (*melauzim*) offered his bride to all friends before his own exploration. An incident in the long and sordid history of the Turkish Army describes how a *melauzim*'s young wife underwent intercourse with one hundred men of his regiment in a single night. The custom was styled *Opening the Cabinet*. The private was allotted a single orgasm, but officers, according to their rank, double and triple. By the time our *melauzim* entered, no appreciable response from Mrs. Turk, but great applause from his gratified fellows. He was held in due esteem and promoted to captaincy by a gratified colonel. His relations with his wife, until she could conceive again, often terminated with assurance of her pregnancy, as he reverted to the homosexual brotherhood of his colleagues. Homosexuality was life among the Turks.

3. SEXUAL DIVERSIONS

Eastern languages are peppered with singular and descriptive words which, often enough, have no equivalent in the West (particularly in relation to kinship). One of these, *seyyib,* denotes a woman who, having suffered brutality during consummation, abandoned her groom in a state of shock. More than one *seyyib* was never found again. Other brides, unfulfilled, got rid of their burdensome virginity in the arms of other men.

Thus might a bride, *de facto,* divorce an unsatisfactory husband. But the riddance did not become legal until the disgraced husband, uncovering her, declared: *"Entee-dauligeh!"* (Thou art divorced), with the usual addition of: "By Him Who fashioned thee from dirty water: I will cut out thy tongue and stuff it up thy coynte, O thou city-filth!"

Such procedure applied at any time in marriage. All a Moslem need do to divorce his wife was to say to her: "I divorce thee." No arguments, no supplications; she understood and left. But, if she loved him she could be sustained by the hope that he would summon her back. For the Mohammedan could divorce her twice by tongue. Then, if he desired her again, and she were willing to submit to legality, the custom was to hire a *mustehhel* or *mohellil* (one who renders legitimate, an intermediary), generally a prepubescent black slave boy. His duty was to wed, bed, and then divorce the woman, thereby making it lawful for her previous husband again to embrace her in matrimony.

Thus the saying: "A thousand lovers rather than one *mustehhel!*"

Many women, especially among the Sheeah Persians, to avoid the humility of divorce preferred *muta'eh* (morganatic marriage), a system that sanctioned flagrant concubinage, and was favored by fickle and licentious royalty.

The East, innately vengeful, delighted in the rare occurrence of shotgun matrimony. In countries where rape (*zinnah-bil-jebr*) was a crime almost unknown and where premarital chastity was a staunch religion, this infrequent delight, when grasped, was duly inflated and taken full advantage of—but at the risk of castration. For if vengeance was exacted the shotgun marriage ended in the rapist's emasculation. In the presence of four witnesses, the couple were united at sword point; and the bride, just as vindictive as her outraged family, demanded legal consummation, then separation—and payment of the penalty.

It is needless to remark upon the feeling of the guilty groom, naked and bleeding after the ordeal that followed. An Egyptian victim relates his experience, which occurred during the period of the Mameluke Empire:

> She arose and cast off her clothes—trousers and chemise—and seized my hand and led me up to the couch, saying: "There is no sin in a *lawful* put-in!" She lay down on the couch, outspread upon her back and, drawing me onto her breast, heaved a sigh and wriggled by way of being coy. "All I need of thee is that thou do with me even as the cock doth." Choking up response, I said: "And what doeth the cock?" She laughed, clapped her hands and squirmed. "O light of mine eyes: gird thy loins, and strengthen thy will, and futter thy best!" Then, she pulled up the shift above her breasts; and when I saw her in this pose, I could not withhold myself from thrusting it into her. Despite all my fear and hatred, my prickle was swollen and eager for combat. After I had sucked her lips, whilst she whimpered and shammed shame, she seized it and aimed it at the muzzle of her sheath. "Drive home, O my beloved!" And sobs and sighs, and amorous cries, well marked my second penetration. Truly, this night was glory high above all ravishment. But at sword point I divorced her, and I have long since regretted the vain precipitance of my youth.

He does not honestly tell us why he lamented his lustful haste; but no man deprived of his instruments of pleasure following shotgun-ritual feels at ease in discussing unpremeditated misfortune.

The majority of cynical Mohammedans felt that there is only one sure way to keep a wife virtuous: to sew up her vulva. Few laid trust in her loyal heart. Woman was considered foul and evil because she was weak, a slave to temptation.

> The ignorant European sets his woman upon a pedestal, leaving her open to seduction; and, if she fall, he blames and takes vengeance on the seducer,

wrote a prominent Indian judge (*Moonsiff*).

But in the East, where sensible men abide, an individual guards his jewel with great care; and, by chance, should she go astray, he cuts her down like a common street-cur and—rightfully —thanks the seducer for showing him exactly what caliber of feeble being he had married.

Arab philosophy held the same view:

'Tis wiser to keep a precious gem locked safely away, than leave it about for someone to take. The prostitute vaunts her beauty; the virtuous woman conceals it.

In the event of sexual offense, particularly fornication and sodomy, four witnesses, demanded by the Prophet, had to testify. When the judge (*el-kaudee*) leaned forward and rasped: "Didst thou see the needle in the kohl-pot?" they must all of them reply in the affirmative, or the case was thrown out of court. Thereupon the *kaudee* eased back, tugged at his beard and passed judgment: "The babe to the blanket and the adulteress to the stone!"

Such was the usual punishment: for the woman, public stoning or flogging and, for the man, a painful pepper-stalk thrust up the rectum.

But in many cases the adulterer did not escape so easily. Blood was upon his hands; he had cast the dust of disgrace into the eyes of the adulteress' family. Divine Vengeance (*Ilahee-intigaum*) was in order. One evening, a shadow amid shadows would seize him, amputate his genitals, and tie him to the back of a jackass. Thence, he was paraded about the darkened streets until he bled to death. Finally his corpse was taken down and tossed onto a steaming dung-heap to join the remains of the stoned adulteress.

In the Punjab province of northern India where fornication was notoriously flagrant, a law was enacted by the British Raj against vengeful husbands beheading adulterous wives and flinging them and their hacked paramours on village dunghills. But a month after this decree passed into effect, all professional courtesans rose up in arms against the district commissioners.

"Respectable" women, free with their favors, were taking bread out of their mouths. The Government, to avoid another Indian Mutiny, sheepishly rescinded the law.

Moslem magnates and potentates, scrutinizing the bed sheets of their women for signs of semen, could be convinced by their guilty wives or concubines that it was the seed of bats (popularly resembling that of man). After one lord had ordered all bats in the palace to be exterminated for fouling the harem sheets, the resourceful women alleged that they had been possessed by *jinn* (incubi), which absolved them of wrong, since popular tradition held it impossible for amorous spirits to be resisted.

Djezzar Pasha, the Butcher of Syria, wearying of harem infidelity, murdered all *memlooks* (white uncastrated slaves) in the palace and, after taking a concubine's maidenhead, slew her to insure her chastity. He was truly likened to King Shahriyar of the *Arabian Nights,* who bedded at dusk and beheaded at dawn.

In Egypt this led to a notorious racket. Where an adultery was suspected in Cairo, teams of four male rogues (legal witnesses) came upon the clandestine lovers demanding blackmail and carnal knowledge of the woman or they would report to the police. This became so prevalent at one time that, after a few weeks, every garden in the city was deserted after sunset and every locksmith was sold out.

Among the Hindoos, adultery, premarital fornication, sodomy, and other sexual diversions were sanctioned if practiced within the caste. If carried on outside, excommunication and blistering disgrace were the reward. Endorsing no manner of violence or retribution, the philosophic Hindoo laid trust in the vengeance of hell (*Nurrukeh*) where the fornicator is embraced by a white-hot image of a woman. Adulteresses, staked to the ground, are tormented by demons who thrust red-hot phalli into their vaginae.

The Hindoo, unlike the Semite, regarded the love-child with tolerance. The divine principle of massive procreation outweighed that of intersexual fidelity; and

any living being was in the light of Brahma the
essence of pure beauty. Thus, to prevent harmful in-
terference with the delicate and unending cycle of
reincarnation, the Hindoo was forbidden the destruction of anything that breathed. Hindoos believed that
if the taking of life were not forbidden, the obliteration of mankind would result.

Throughout the East incest was rare, being severely prohibited except in some congested cities or in the
harems of depraved royalty. A young prince who had
not seen his sister for many years might take a fancy to
her, attacking and bleeding her of her virginity. The ac-
cusation of incest in Moslem lands demanded the customary four witnesses; and the usual punishment was
rejem, death by lapidation (stoning).

As dissenters and heretics some Persians, mainly
those of the Ukhsheeyaun sect, encouraged incest on the
premise that it, through continuity, purified man unto
eternity. But it led to the spawning of regal abortions
such as plagued the country on the Tehranian throne
for many years.

Pishauchee-vivaheh or *raukshusseh* (marriage by
rape) was a tradition amongst the Rajpoots of northern
India. It took its name from the variety of incubi and
succubi who, according to popular belief, invaded one's
body at night. The wonted procedure was through *mun-
trum* (incantation), mesmerism, or drugs, performed
with the aid of a sorcerer by the youth desirous of a
particular maiden. Such a girl was generally above the
age of puberty (*j'waunee*); therefore, to lift disgrace
from her family and appease the angry gods, she had
to be taken by conjuration and rape, which acted as
a sort of sacrificial purifier. Any postpubescent girl un-
married was looked upon as being unclean and under
suspicion.

Widowhood was a particular affliction of Mother
India. Men of seventy could purchase and wed girls of
twelve. After the British abolition of *suttee* (self-immolation of widows upon their husbands' funeral pyres) it
became the custom for a bereaved woman, following her

husband's cremation, to proceed on a pilgrimage to one of India's many holy places. At such shrines they frequently fell prey to lecherous Brahmins claiming to be the embodiment of amorous Krishna or libidinous Lord Shiva.

In Persia, Moslem husbands were facetiously divided into three distinct categories:

Behr: married for love;

Dehr: married for defense against the world; and

Mehr: married for marriage settlements (money).

Marrying for money was the Persian ideal, and his means of effecting lucrative divorce was by unnatural use of his wife. But oftentimes he was startlingly victimized, having wed an oversexed female who relished venus aversa.

The ancient Hindoo was allowed four legal wives; in certain communities polyandry was the rule: four husbands per woman, all brothers, to insure harmony.

In polyandrous custom, the female entertained each husband successively in one night; but if there were only three, she was capable of gratifying each simultaneously by lying on her side and offering fellatio (sucking of the penis) and vulvar and anal coition. Hence, the popular feeling that woman is insatiable.

In polygyny, each wife or concubine had her own private night. "Thou mayest postpone the turn of such of thy wives as thou shalt please, in being called to thy bed," advises the Koran; "and thou mayest take unto thee her whom thou shalt please, and her whom thou shalt desire of those whom thou shalt have before rejected." It was unseemly for a man to enjoy more than one female in a single evening except in Egypt, where promiscuous orgies and the use of artificial phalli were common.

> *Kubbeh-e-khushee,* Prostitute for pleasure, *wuseefeh-e-khidmutee,* concubine for service, and *kubeeleh-e-turbeeyut,* wife for breeding.

This, in Persian, was the general code throughout the Moslem world.

T'remmeh-el-mehhremmeh (tossing the handkerchief) was the practice in the harem, as the master reviewed his women each night ere retiring. The woman on whose shoulder or head the cloth fell was honored for the night. In a very large seraglio, where discrimination outweighed fairness in choice, the concubine with the most handkerchiefs was the envy of all until, mysteriously, she was one morning found smothered to death. Then someone else bore the burden of fame. Notwithstanding, the entire harem suffered during the installation of every new slave girl; for the purchaser was granted three days' trial by the slave-dealer before paying the balance.

> Deyvedheenum yuggut survum;
> Muntredheenum t'deyvutteh;
> Tun muntrum Bruhmunnedheenum;
> Bruhmunneh mummeh deyvutteh:

The Universe is under the power of the gods;
    The gods are under the power of magic formulas;
The magic formulas are under the power of the Brahmins;
    Therefore, the Brahmins are our gods.[8]

The Kuleen Brahmin was, in native parlance, *utchee-motah* (beautifully fat). Indeed, this was a compliment. Obesity was a charm in women, and a cause for envy in men. The Kuleen Brahmin, a nobleman, was of the highest order. Among other distinctions, he had many wives. And, being of the most eminent caste, he was often a sodomist as well.

> But who can account for taste? I am a Kuleen Brahmin; who dares to question my actions? To be sure, I exist not in anything; nothing exists in me; I, myself, exist not! Alcoholic spirits, anal and oral coition, are the perpetrators of the most prodigious and lethal of external and internal pollutions; but curdled milk diluted with water, and tiresome women with their bottomless clefts, are most vapid. Therefore, I must hazard external and internal pollutions. When I am miserable, I damn all the gods in Indra's

[8]Dubois, *op. cit.*

heaven and beg that Lord Shiva's heavenly
spouse might only pass my door. Then, to assert
my disdain and defiance, I would pounce on her
and throw her upon her stomach and ravish her
unmercifully. But when I am gay, I praise all
the gods in Indra's heaven and lay trust upon
the fidelity, safety, and morals of Lord Shiva's
celestial wife. Hence, to be sure: *A whole
Brahmin when amidst those of my own caste,
half a Brahmin when seen far off, and a Soodra
(low caste) when entirely out of sight.* Is that
not an end to it, ey Hurreejee!

After India had long discontinued customary po-
lygamy, the Kuleen Brahmin remained staunch in sanctified voluptuousness.

In the East, where men and women were known
to fall passionately in love with a shadow, a footprint, or
a vivid description, marital love was rare except among
the poorer classes. The licentiousness and vanity of
the rich outruled all self-denial and spiritual affection.
Sensual gratification by any means became tradition;
and the seraglio leveled love to its gross physical aspect.

However, exceptions are recorded. One case, involving an Egyptian *wezeer* (minister-of-state) is told
by his body-servant:

Ah! blessed be the Martyrs of Love. Khaleefeh Yezeed—may God grant him an eternity
of orgasms in Paradise, reclined amid thousands
of *hooreeyehs* and *welleds*—he, my sire, had
two favorite wives, both of them seventeen, with
whom he remained undisturbed for one month.
They sang, danced, recited, instructed him in the
complex art of love—every aspect that included
the kiss, the caress, the embrace, the ecstatic postures—and they reveled in wine and perfumes,
not knowing day from night. At length, he grew
so exhausted that he could not satisfy them. He
fell into a swoon and, out of feverish anxiety
and desire, the lovely pair took poison to relieve themselves, preferring death to infidelity,
for they were oblivious of any other man.
Khaleefeh Yezeed—the Compassionate and Merciful preserve his soul!—would not believe that

they had died, but sought for hours to caress
them; and even long after they were interred,
his demonic passion drove him to exhuming the
bodies, decomposed as they were, and, seeing
nought but beauty, tenderly embracing them.
Soon realizing that they were gone forever, he
lost his speech; and Khaleefeh Yezeed sank into
a state of mortification, until he wasted to a
mere skeleton. And he died.

And he concluded piously, "It was the will of God.
So saith our Lord Mohammed: *He who dieth of love,
verily he shall enjoy Paradise.*"[9]

Eastern potentates have been notorious for their
teeming seraglios. But Occidental notions of fabulous
harems and amorous skeykhs, derived from rosewater
versions of *The Arabian Nights* and a highly imagina-
tive Hollywood, are far from reality. The harems saw
little of passionate love between the lords and their
women. Neglected women there reverted to vicious and
maniacal tribadism, (the homosexual practice in which
a woman plays the role of a man), and most sheykhs
were avid pederasts[10] (those who indulge in anal intercourse with boys).
    The Mahdi of Allah, a False Messiah who
scourged the Sudan in the latter half of the nineteenth
century, fought in the name of abstemious piety but
wasted of luxurious debauchery.
    Because of his reputation for sanctity, the Mahdi
succeeded in uniting tribes that had warred for years.
He united them into one cause: that of Holy War
(*el-jehaud*). His dung, urine, and the water in which he
cleansed his feet were used as medicine by his adherents. Any tree under which the Mahdi sat was reverently
stripped of bark which, when boiled in Nile water, was
said to have marvelous properties as an unguent. Once
a week he spilled his seminal fluid into a gourd shell,
and barren women shrieked and clawed to obtain it.

---

[9]Edward William Lane, *The Arabian Nights' Entertainments.*
[10]Burton, and the testimony of numerous other travelers, primarily
French.

People kissed, preserved the ground upon which he trod, for this secured everlasting health.

El-Mahdi's harem was crowded with females of from eight to twenty of every Sudanese tribe. It even boasted a few white and numerous Egyptian women, who practiced espionage and won the confidence of the eunuchs. Were one to catch the apparently ascetic and pious Mahdi unawares in his seraglio, he would perhaps find the concubines anointing their Expected Messiah with jasmine, sandalwood, and other aphrodisiac perfumes. They kissed, stroked, and kneaded him, fondling and mouthing his love organs. The Mahdi underwent this bodily shampoo every day for several hours, which stimulated his virility and increased the size of his sacred parts. He wished to represent the ideal Mohammedan: lecher and saint.

When in the presence of his emeers, El-Mahdi imbibed a mixture of date syrup and ginger; but alone, he was full-steam for wine. Since white (mainly Turkish) women were considered unwholesome and overheating, he bedded them only in cool weather, belaboring the Negroes and Arabs in the hot. And to think that, as a rebellious youth, crowds had jeered him and gnarled withered old hags, grimacing like hyenas, had yowled every foul word of abuse at him, and his own instructors had turned him out as a heretic—and, in the end, he made these people lick the dust at his feet!

The Hindoos adopted *purdah* (seclusion of women) from the Moslems, just as the Children of Allah adopted caste prejudice from the Valley of the Ganges. In India, the term *zunauneh* (zenana, seraglio) was naturalized from Persia. But from Turkey to North Africa the common designation for the women's apartment was *hhereem* (harem).

Throughout the East the largest of these which, in places like Baghdad or Stamboul, housed thousands of women, were frivolous sinks of luxurious stagnation. Tuberculosis, poison, and sheer ennui were the chief killers in the harems. Woman, a passive creature, knew little more than lustful servitude in the East until the advent of Western civilization. Then the Orient learned that woman is no more an impure human being than the egocentric man who molds her and then passes judgment upon her.

In Afghanistan and Sindh, during the Persian War and the Indian Mutiny, when Indo-British troops penetrated the harems of Cabul and Bushire, Lucknow and Delhi, women young and old fell upon them like wolves, storming their tents and clinging to them night and day. Princess, matron and slave, for painful want of affection, demanded to be used as common prostitutes. General orders and righteous padres directed the soldiery to respect the zenana; but Moslem ladies of the most delicate breeding cast off their veils and gave themselves to the victors.

Life and death in the harem or in a village street were indifferently regarded in the necessitarian Hindoo philosophy. For the Hindoo the principle of reincarnation (*avatareh*) eliminated the need for grief. The soul of the dead, be it virtuous, would enjoy such bliss that compared to it the pleasures to be found on earth would seem insipid. Thus, too, the Mohammedan Paradise (*El-Genneh*) had no earthly counterpart. The soul was the "seminal principle from the loins of destiny."[11]

4. CREATION

Praise be to thy Lord, Who hath created all things; Who hath created man of congealed blood.

Let a man consider, therefore, of what he is created. He is created of seed poured forth, issuing from the loins and the breastbones.

Was he not a drop of seed, which was emitted? Afterwards he became a little coagulated blood, and God formed him and fashioned him with just proportion.[12]

Brahminic concept is closely allied with that of Arab scholars:

The human body is a mansion: with bones for its beams and rafters, with nerves and ten-

---

[11]David Shea and Anthony Troyer, *The Dabistan.*
[12]*El-Koran.*

dons for cords, with muscles and blood for cement, and with skin for its outer walls. It is filled with no sweet perfume, but loaded with impurities. It is a mansion infested by age and sorrow; it is the seat of malady, harassed with pains—haunted by the quality of darkness—and incapable of standing.

Life starts in the womb and is brought about by seed and blood, mixed with excrement and water, and fouled with the impurities of blood. Thus, man—born of woman—is an unclean being.

Moslems hold that Lord Jesus (Seyyidneh Eeseh) was the only creature born in purity; even Mohammed, the Most Gifted Intercessor, was fouled by sin. The Miraculous Conception (*Roohullah,* Breath of God), in Moslem belief, evolved from the Almighty's breathing into the Virgin's womb; thus, Jesus is often referred to as *Roohullah.*

The Koran makes it perfectly clear that the only truly virtuous woman is a mother:

"When a woman conceives by her husband," expounded Lord Mohammed, "she is called in Paradise a martyr; and her labor in childbed, and her care for her children, protect her from hell-fire."

In the East childbirth was a sheer case of the woman stooping, leaning against a wall and spreading her legs, or getting down on hands and knees and concentrating her thoughts upon the deity. Thoughts of self or abnormal fears seldom hindered the mother from a tolerably easy delivery. Desire for the child offset all ignorance and dubiety. When difficulty arose, it was considered, like miscarriage, the result of evil spirits entering and clogging the vagina. Only concentration upon the deity could counteract the evil.

In wealthy Arab homes, the *kursee-el-wilaudeh* (birthstool) was employed. Upon delivery, the severed naval string of the babe was carefully hidden to protect it, the child, and its mother from the ever-present evil eye. Were the umbilical cord (*zebr*) to fall into the hands of a wicked *sahhir* (sorcerer), he could make use of it in conjuring destruction of the child's generative apparatus. Hence, in severing the string, "By the navel cord of Mohammed!" was a prescribed ejaculation that counteracted evil spells.

In India, where a village *da'ee* (professional midwife) often delivered the child, it was forbidden for anyone to break a coconut in the presence of an expectant mother. Being the symbol of miscarriage as well as defloration, in fact of any catastrophe, breaking the coconut was considered gravely inauspicious and the witchwork of a sorceress (*donehee*).

The wife who died in pregnancy was looked upon with especial honor; she was shrouded in bright red and borne to the ghats (consecrated places, usually on river banks, where the dead were burnt). Her fetus, carefully removed and wrapped in sable cloth, was burned separately on another pyre as a unique soul worthy of everlasting existence.

Abortion (*gurvhusrauv* or *dhaul-hutteyah,* manual destruction with an artificial phallus) was a heinous, unpardonable sin in a land that forbade the wilful annihilation of any living soul. In Egypt, however, it became a science that among other practices was taught in the harem. There, it is also recorded, lusty black slaves sometimes aborted women by violent penial thrusts.

The women of Turkey, Persia, Afghanistan, and Cashmere, following or sometimes before parturition, early lost the beautiful symmetry of their breasts, which assumed a pendulous form. This was scarcely climatic but racial, much as some females (Hindoos) possessed large bosoms and others (Arabs) small. This peculiarity of physiognomy, found also in Africa, seemed most prevalent among so-called bastard races, such as those of Turkey and Afghanistan. There were corresponding racial differences in the size of masculine genitalia after puberty. Mahratta women, though abiding in the hot and humid area of the Bombay Presidency, were celebrated for high firm breasts even following lactation.[18]

----

[18]Burton, *op. cit.*

Mata-deyvee or Mahama'ee, Hindoo Goddess of Creation, was depicted squeezing milk from her spherical breasts, whereby mankind is daily nourished. Maternal milk (*doodh*), sacred to the Hindoos, was also esteemed by the early Arabs who made constant reference to it in conversation. "Do according to thy mother's milk," meant *"Act according to your nature."* A stock interjection was: "By the milk we have sucked, and by that which is graven upon the seal-ring of Solomon—on whom be peace!" Another, even more common—as most execrations are—declared: "I spit upon thy mother's milk!"

Since ancient times, Arab children were often weaned at as late an age as ten years. This gave rise to the saying: "If one of you reproach his brother for sucking the dugs of a bitch (wet-nurse), he also shall suck her." This, in opprobrium, frequently bore a double connotation: relating to dogs, upon whom nomads and thirsty travelers in the desert were wont to suckle.

There were many charms against barrenness in Hindostan and throughout Asia. They were nearly as numerous as those worn against the evil eye, to which sterility was often attributed.

When amulets failed, the Hindoo woman might yield her body to a Brahminee priest who, impersonating the specific god of her sect, had his will of her. Husbands desirous of offspring fain agreed to this holy union. Then the chastity of his wife took second place to the birth of a son. Other women who sought children, moaning fervidly, rubbed their pudenda against the consecrated *lingam* (phallic image), invoking the blessings of Lord Shiva and Mother Parvuttee and praying for productiveness and marital felicity. A few drank the seed of holy men or, as was the tradition in Moslem lands, reverently handled and kissed the erect organ of an inspired mendicant devotee. In many parts of India, midday was the signal for certain holy men, *gooroos, saddhoos,* and others, to leave the temples, ringing bells and beating drums and blowing conch shells, summoning barren women to come to fondle their privy members in order to become fertile.

To be childless was to the Hindoo not nearly as

disgraceful a state as to have begotten daughters but
no sons. Only a son (*pootreh*) could save his father's
soul from *Pautaul* (hell). This belief gave rise to infanticide of girl children.

A female child, already considered impure, was
not to usurp precedence in the Brahmin family by
living before the glorious birth of a son. Until a newborn
son released his sire from hell, females might be sacrificed to *Kalee,* Goddess of Destruction. This custom
was rife among the austere Rajpoots, a martial tribe of
the Kshatriya (middle) caste in northern India. The
Rajpoots also formulated and were the last to give up
the practice of suttee (widow-burning). The natural
result of female infanticide was massive polyandry
and sodomy amongst the Rajpoots, originally a proud
and sober clan. But infanticide was merely one of several conventions that gave rise to endemic sexual perversion.

If after successive attempts a Hindoo could not
engender a son, he had one of two courses to follow
in eliminating this disgrace: he could remarry or adopt
a male child. For only a son could light his funeral
pyre, could pray for his soul, and salvage it from
eternal damnation.

Man took the responsibility for nothing. If the
woman did not produce that which was so prescribed by
law, she was held at fault. Her alleged impurity and
feebleness were affirmed and cast in her face. She was
debased and spat upon, and another, perhaps doomed
to a similar fate, took her place.

Ego, not the will of God, ruled in the relationship
of Eastern male with female; for man was heaven,
woman was hell.

II

GENITALIA:
Symbolism and Reality

Three things are insatiable:
The desert, the grave, and a woman's vulva.

1. FEMALE

So spake an Arab philosopher.

But in spite of all the unsavory things that Eastern men said of their woman, one aspect transcended the rest: without woman, there was little pleasure in life for most men.

Therefore, from earliest times man deified and represented in symbol not only his own organs of pleasure and procreation, but the woman's. The golden crescent of El-Islam denoted the vulva (*hheshoom*) from the mons veneris to the anus. The triangle, with significance dating back to ancient Egypt and called *el-herrem,* pyramid, also exemplified the vulva. The sycamore (*gimmeyzeh*) and sycamore fig (*gemeez*) came to symbolize the female pudendum and the virgin uterus (*rehm*). El-Mehraub, the arched niche in the wall of a mosque, and the sacred Black Stone of

El-Caaba in Mecca are symbols of the female genitalia (*hheshaushim*). The bulbous cupola extensive in Eastern architecture was clearly representative usually of the mons veneris, though sometimes of the male testicle.

Yonee-Tuntrum (Vulva Worship) dispersed its tenets throughout India. Women were sacrificed upon the altar of dark Mother Kalee; their hymens were pierced by priests and their virginal blood consecrated; and sometimes their vulvae were excised and offered as sacrifices to the Black Goddess.

Where Sheyveh-Lingayuts worshiped the *lingam-yoni* (male and female principles in conjunction), the Veyshneh-Shuktehs worshiped only the *yonee* (vulva, maternal power). For the adorers of Vishnu, the *shaul-graumeh* (saligram: a naturally flat, round, jet-black stone) emblemized the vulva. If the saligram, often found in the beds of streams, were discovered with a slit or crack, it was regarded as being more sacred. Peaches, beans, and seashells were also adored as symbols of female pudenda.

The Vishnu-bhukteh sect wore an emblem known as *naumum* upon their foreheads. It was trident-shaped, with one vertical red and two oblique white lines, the apex at the junction of the eyebrows. It symbolized the rich vulva of a menstruous woman. The priests of the sect painted this emblem upon their limbs, chests, stomachs, buttocks, and penes.

In antiquity, man and earth were closely identified. The fertility of the soil seemed connected with the fertility of human beings. Hence the belief that if man spilt his semen upon the earth, something must grow. This belief was prevalent in Assam and other parts of the East. Travelers in those countries, several centuries ago, noted men and boys stooping in the fields, discharging their seed over freshly broken soil. One origin of this singular custom is the legend that Vishnu hacked Parvuttee, Shiva's wanton celestial wife, to pieces. Her *yoni* or vulva is said to have fallen in Assam (where Shukteh or nature worship in its maternal aspect was first prevalent).

It was also the wont of Shivites to spray their

fields with the sacrificial blood of man and beast, as a means of fertilization. Seminal fluid and feminine secretion, compounded with the macerated testicles of bulls and tigers, were also employed. Among the Vishnuites, however, there was no substitute for menstrual emanation (*phool,* blossom).

The sacred lotus became symbolic of the fruitful womb (*peyd*); its pistil, the fetus. As a bud, it represented the virgin cunnus; when in bloom, the yawning labia of a productive woman.

Meru, a mythical mountain revered by the Hindoos, symbolized in their belief the mons veneris. In fact, every sacred mountain, such as Abu in Rajpootana or Annapurna in the Himalaya, bore a genital connotation. Nearly all of nature from the palm tree to the golden mango fruit supplied phallic or womb symbols.

In early 1857, when Anglo-India sensed the murmurings of the Devil's Wind (the discontent that led to the Sepoy rebellion), ominous *chupatties* (flat, circular, unleavened bread cakes) were borne by Bengal's watchmen and couriers from village to village, city to city, cantonment to cantonment. Few grasped the significance of these cakes. Modern historians of the Sepoy Rebellion fail to understand why they were distributed. An exciting shroud of mystery is cast over the incident, and Mother India remains fantastic and inscrutable. But these *chupatties* were just as symbolic as *pudmeh* (lotus buds, denoting rebirth and revolution, the vulvae and erect penes of mankind). The round, flat, unleavened cake represented the female principle. Lotus and *chupatty—lingam-yoni,* penis-cunnus—emblems of regeneration.

In Benares, in May of 1857 the secret rites of *Shukteh-Poojah,* propitiating the *lingam-yoni* and supplicating strength to destroy the East India Company incited the people to hysterical fervor. The ancient observance of *nurmeydha* (human sacrifice) was revived.

Once the devotees entered the great vault, they were no longer man and woman, husband and wife. The flesh was considered dead but their souls fierily alive. The fleshly integument was cast off like the skin of a snake, so that the glowing soul, naked and flaw-less, could rise to a place with the gods.

Descending more deeply into the earth, the ter-rible darkness becomes impregnated with dim eerie light. The air is stifling, sickeningly pungent. Persian camphor, rotting flowers. Cockroaches, bat excrement, lamp oil. Rancid ghee and human perspiration.

The walls, cut through limestone rock, are smeared with cow dung and *chunam,* painted and splashed with cow's urine and *gulaul* (the symbolic red dye). There is a monotonous dripping of water from the ceiling.

Soon the pathway becomes less slippery and cold. There are niches cut in the walls, and clay idols with gruesome expressions glare hateful, menacing. Willowy limbs entwine about the waist of a smiling god, smiling because he had penetrated an avid, unquenchable god-dess. She too was smiling, her lips throbbing. His fin-gers touched swelling breasts.

It was ecstasy, bliss; and a provocative, insistent throbbing, like the pulse of the sensuous enveloping warmth, beckoned ahead.

The roaring tide recedes; now but a hollow vibra-tion as though through a shell: *"Ome! Ome! Ome! Kalee-Ma'ee! Kalee-Ma'ee—a'ee—a'ee-e-e-e-e—!"*

Drawing nearer the sound, following the writh-ing passageway down, down, into the very bowels of the earth, sinuous light seems to palpitate portentously upon the walls.

Vibrant, doleful chanting; and then, the tide ebbs. A lone wail echoes: *"Ome! munnee pudmeh hum— Ome! munnee pudmeh hum—munnee pudmeh hum—!"* And the thunder increases, gorging the hol-low vault, then fades away in sibilation. (*O hail! the Jewel in the Lotus.*)

A great, hazy, incense-glutted chamber, and a dream fumes into frightening reality.

> *Ome!*—earth, sky, heaven!—
> *Ome!* thou art excellent vitalization!
> The Light Divine, let us meditate upon,
>   Which doth illumine our comprehension . . .

The *lingam* impales the *yoni*. The *lingam* is a huge, polished, columnar, basalt stone, crimson-splashed. It impales a black circular stone, the *yoni*. Conjoined, they symbolize the phallus of Lord Shiva and the cunnus of Goddess Parvuttee.

The interjections of hallowed mystery cannon hundredfold in the womb of the earth: *"Ome! Ome! h'home—h'rhoom—sh'hroom—sho'rheem—rummeh-yeh—nummeh'heh—!"*

And Kalee-Ma'ee, the Dark Mother, is there. She is luminous-black. Her four limbs are outstretched and the hands grasp two-edged swords, tools of disembowelment, and human heads. Her hands are blood-red and her glaring eyes red-centered; and her blood-red tongue protrudes over huge pointed breasts, reaching down to a rotund little stomach. Her yoni is large and protuberant. Her matted, tangled hair is gore-stained and her fang like teeth gleam. There is a garland of skulls about her neck; her earrings are the images of dead men and her girdle is a chain of venomous snakes.

She is there gloating sadistically over the scene, all-observant, expectant, demanding. The goddess Kalee stands stanch and powerful above the *lingam-yoni* and beside *ling-sungums,* which are images of Shiva and Parvuttee in a heated embrace. From between her thighs, daubed a bright crimson, there exudes a ruddy sap, and it drips down upon a great livid rock with a deep cleft in its center. And this yoni is counterpart to the many crimson *lingams* adorning the tremendous vault, heaped with garlands and glistening with poonga oil.

In here must lie the answer born of devotion, the torment, the hopes and dreams of centuries.

"Jey Mah-Kalee! jey Mah-Kalee!" (Glory to our Dark Mother; hail! O Goddess of Death.) And the drums begin to pulse and thunder.

The corpulent *poojaree* (priest) is there in the center. His acolytes form a circle like a great yoni around him. He is the *lingam* and he trembles in his devotion.

On a basil-covered slab below him lies a man. He is naked and strapped to the stone He is an untouchable (*mleytcheh*), but he is free of bodily blemish. And he is stiff with masochistic abandonment, rigid in a sacrificial delirium. This untouchable is of praiseworthy significance, for he has been blessed with a six-inch member. Now that magnificent phallus and all its consecrated fecundating force are being yielded to Mother Kalee.

A *chitrinee* (art-woman, prostitute, exuding the odor of honey) rushes forward. She presses her opulence against him. The art-woman shields his eyes with her palm. She moans, sibilates, rubbing scented breasts against him and digging her nails into his flesh. She seizes his lower lip between her teeth, then gently strokes it with her tongue. The muscles in his thighs begin to tighten; his fists clench taut. The groin swells, pulsates. And when her hot steaming hand closes round, the moment of conquest and exaltation bursts, and the phallus yields its treasure.

The waiting *poojaree*, swaying with vibrant power, captures the libation and drinks it greedily.

The *yoni* convulses, shrills. The *lingam* convulses, shrills. The victim bellows triumphantly. Feverish drums rise and fall; then the drums hush. The *lingam* ceases to throb; the *yoni* constricts. And there is silence, deep and heavy.

In the quavering hands of the *poojaree* are the *waughnukh* and *kuttaur,* sword and trident of Shiva. Droning prayers, he falls trembling before the image of Kalee. Then the corpulent *poojaree* swings round to gouge out the entrails of the untouchable. As he does so his acolytes spring forth, shattering the *yoni* to saturate everything with wine, screaming: *"Jey Kalee! jey Kalee!"* They devour the outcast flesh, sanctified in sacrifice, so that the luminous soul might cleanse it, freeing them of alien defilement.

The corpulent *poojaree* flourishes the intestines, the powerful genitals, before an exultant Mother Kalee. He shrieks his virtues, and prays that she might be pleased with their offering. For Mother Kalee subsists on human blood and human flesh; there is dancing and gluttony.

Presently, the *poojaree* casts himself before the great *lingam* and, lifting garlands of lotus and holy basil (*tulsee*), heaps them on and splashes it with the sacred libation.

"*Ey Somenaut! Somenaut!*" he says, raising bowl after bowl of hallowed soma wine (*umritteh,* milk and nectar of the gods). Then he twists round the salubrious *bilva* leaves, and secures them with *tulsee* vine, all to suppress the burning excitation felt by the great *lingam* in its union with the *yoni.*

"*Ome! munnee pudmeh hum; Ome! munnee pudmeh hum,*" he chants, pouring on the sacrificial blood. "*Ome!—vhur! vhoomeh! svurgeh!—Ome!*" He offers incense, sandalwood, colored rice, burning lamps of gold and silver.

The lamps flicker, the light wavers, the poonga oil glisters.

> We are here to placate thee, O Most Omnipotent God—and thee, O Most Noble Mother —for thou art surely wroth with the evils of man. We offer thee sacrifice, in thine holy and most exalted names, in anticipation that ye might only see fit to make the knees of the wicked tremble. We supplicate thee: turn their spleens to water! dissolve the hate in their eyes! cause them to flounder in their exertions! drive them hence, into the angry blackness of the ravenous sea, *forever! Eyvemustoo!* (so be it), O Mahadeva!

Then the corpulent *poojaree* begins to moan, crawling on hands and knees before an incredibly lifelike image of the goddess Parvuttee. Her eyes are green flames: mesmeric, all-knowing. The arms are open, the legs splayed—and waiting.

"*Ey Parvuttee! Parvuttee veyshyah-sey sumvhaushun punyeh hey, paupeh nushow hey!*" he says, lifting his arms before her. (*O Thou of Mountainous Breasts! To have carnal intercourse with the goddess Parvuttee is a virtue which destroys all sin.*)

He touches the image: huge, almighty. The arms move. The *poojaree* quavers: "*Sungum! sungum! sungum!* The orifice and the sheath, the lance and the power in the lance!" The arms embrace him, the legs close about him; he hears the maniac drone of the image as his chanting body begins to sway.

In a few seconds, the arms streak back. The shuddering legs open with mechanical grace. The corpulent *poojaree* draws back, closing his crimson-stained robe. "I have offered and consecrated my seed to the Goddess," he cries.

The moments throb, feverish. There is painful stillness, expectancy. The chamber seems to wax dimmer, more sensuous and unearthly, terrifying in its aspect.

The Chosen One is a temple priestess (*pudminee*, lotus-woman) a wife of Lord Shiva, slave girl to the Abode of Mahadeva with the phallic emblem tattooed on her breasts and groin. She is young and slender, with heavy hips; and she is yet a virgin, especially selected from all the temples for her choice body.

They kneel across from one another on soft woven mats, and the *yoni* encompasses them. The corpulent *poojaree* heaps aromatic garlands upon her, and the *yoni* hums and vibrates. Then he feeds her with sweetmeats. They imbibe toddy, and arrack, and soma wine. They recite and sing the sacred hymns and dogmas to one another in passionate resonance. And then they begin to disrobe one another.

"For those who adore the young and lovely Shuktee," the *poojaree* cries, "revealed to none but the few." He leans forward, seizing the tissuelike garments of the timid *pudminee*.

> Keep it concealed, like the rosy lips that pout between the recess of thy thighs, O Goddess. Hide this creed—so pure, so excellent—as closely as you hide your vulva cleft. Oh! hide this code of bliss from vulgar eyes.

Glazed, swollen eyes—intense, sagacious—probe into the Chosen One.

> Let the fuel of sacrifice be her incense; let the altar of sacrifice be her middle. The pit of her navel is the hearth, and her mouth the ceaseless fire; the south point her rich breasts, her

gentle hand the bowl. Let her graceful thighs be
the two sides of the altar. The holy flame is the
moist vulva; the fuel is collision; and the Lord
Lingam is the grand high priest. *I, Lord Lingam!*

He casts off his robe. Like a serpent, she clasps
him; and the Chosen One, wife of Lord Shiva, squirms
in a fit of rapture.

The corpulent *poojaree* whispers:

Relive, woman, the sacred ecstasy of Parvuttee when her husband, Mahadeva, seized her
and played the virile stag mounting the eager
doe. Relive a moment when the fabulous generative power of Shiva and Shuktee burst from
their loins, and the result was mankind. In trib-
ute and thanksgiving, we do as thee, O Mahadeva! O Mahadeyvee! so that the duty of man
be fulfilled: that a powerful race be engendered
in honor of thee and to thy purpose.

They are close and tight; and he glares into her
eyes as she murmurs and strokes, and digs with keen
fingernails. Then he assails her, unrelenting. She
screams and writhes. The corpulent *poojaree* gaspingly
recites:

Who is this timid gazelle? Why has this gazelle—with a
   burden of firm swelling breasts,
With roving glance and slender waist—gone forth from
   the frightened herd?
Drunk with love, unsteady of steps, she totters as if fallen
   from the temple of a rutting lord of elephants.
Beholding this divine form—adorned with beautiful, well-
   shaped limbs—even an old man becomes youthful as
   Kama.
Who is this beauty, her face shining like the full moon,
   advancing along the path in the anthesis of youth:
Inebrious with love and sleep—her eyes rolling, her lips
   full and red like the ripe bimba fruits—
Her locks in bewildering disofder: wounded by her lover's
   nails, and torn to pieces by his teeth?
Has this fair maiden been loved by a demon; and has he,
   imitating tiger-sport, enjoyed her?

Has this maiden been ravished, and then let go? With
     wandering glance, and garments clinging to her per-
     spiring limbs,
She flits—at dawn—like a fawn: coy and frightened.
     What bee has sipped the nectar of her blossoming
     lips?
By whom has Paradise been enjoyed today? Whom has
     Kama, once slain by Shiva's eye, blessed today?
With her hand holding her heavy hair, embellished with
     flowers crushed in the game of love—
Her upper garment and loose girdle gathered in her right,
     her hair disheveled and face swollen and languid, her
     passion sated—
Here she comes from the private chamber, having yielded
     to the power of love, longing for the breeze.[1]

     The Chosen One faints. The *yoni* breaks and
sways, deluging the floor. This is the moment of exulta-
tion.
     Various names are given the male and female
genitalia. French and Italian abound in metaphors for
them but are not the equals of Arabic and Sanskrit.
Among the epithets are *stalk, wand, wedge, bough, eye,
worm, thorn, wrapper*—and a thousand others.
     Futooh, opening, refers to the Gate of Victory
(*bowaubeh-en-nezr*, vulva). *Mooweffek* (well-
notched) was a flattering eipthet applied to an Arab
lass; and *erooreh*, little clitoris, is a common term of
endearment. *Zemboor* (wasp, pincer) was so named
because of the manner in which the fully developed
clitoris firmly presses against and rubs the upper surface of the penis in sexual congress. *Derfeh* (shutter,
clitoris) *w'sheffa'if* (labia) together signify the parts
genital; and *ereereh* or *zubbeeyeh* (little sprout) the
clitoris alone. The most vulgar word, *ferj* (slit), is
analogous to the raw Persian *kuss* or *durz* (machine,
hole, cleft).
     Sanskrit, more elegant, chose *nullinee* (pipe, flute,
lotus) and similar words derived from the word *nullee*
(sexual organ). The word is inverted to form the masculine *nullah* (reed, penis). *Dunteelee* (notched) is a

---

[1] P. Thomas, *Kama Kalpa*.

facetious Hindostanee term for a woman. In the masculine, *dunteelah,* it inverts itself to form the connotation *yarded* (with a large penis). Concerning elephants, it is applied to their tusks. Arabic and Persian are very similar, as witness *zubb* (prickle) and *zubbeh* (little prickle, clitoris).

Arab literature frequently extolled the aspects of the female pudenda:

> When he beheld them stripped of their clothes, his cord stiffened for that looking at them mother-naked he saw what was between their thighs—and that of all kinds—soft and rounded, plump and cushioned—large-lipped, perfect, redundant and ample—and their faces were as moons and their hair as night upon day.
>
> He cast a glance, seeing her mother-naked; and there was manifest to him what was between her thighs: a goodly rounded dome on pillars borne, like a bowl of silver or crystal.
>
> . . . parts softer than silk, smoother than cream—pink, white—plumply rounded, protuberant—resembling for heat and moisture the hot-room of the bath.
>
> "O my mistress: by God! thou hast not grassed me by thy strength, but by the blandishments of thy back-parts; for I so love a full-formed thigh and crystal-mound, the delight of prickle thick and strong."[2]

In Arab verse are to be found such crude but honest gems as:

> Perceiving me, she had hidden it; but 'twas too plump
>   for fingers fine;
> Would to Heaven that I were in it: an hour—or,
>   better, two hours—li'en.

She hath those hips conjoined by thread of waist: hips
    that o'er me—and her, too—tyrannize;
My thoughts, they daze whene'er I think of them—and

---

[2]Sir Richard F. Burton, *The Book of the Thousand Nights and a Night.*

jewel between, that fain would cause prickle to up-
rise.

The veil from her shoulders had slipt—and showed
her loosened trousers. Love's seat and stay—
And rattled the breezes her huge hind-cheeks, and
the branch whereon two little pomegranates lay.

Boylike of backside: in the deed of kind, she sways as
sways the wandlike boughs a-wind.

If I liken thy shape to the bough when green, my
likeness errs and I sore mistake it;
For the bough is fairest when clad the most, and
thou art fairest when mother-naked!

Her bosom is a marble slab, whence rise two breasts like
towers on lea;
And on her stomach shows a crease, perfumed with rich
perfumery;
Beneath which, same, there lurks a Thing: limit of mine
expectancy;
A something rounded, cushioned high—and plump, my
Lords, to high degree;
To me, 'tis likest royal throne: whither my longings wan-
der free;
There, 'twixt two pillars, man shall find benches of high-
built tracery;
It hath specific qualities, driving sanest men to insanity;
Full mouth, it hath, like mouth of neck—or well-begirt by
stony key;
Firm lips with camelry's compare, and shows it eye of
cramoisie;
And draw thou nigh, with doughty will, to do thy doing
lustily:
Thou'll find it fain to face thy bout, and strong and fierce
in valiancy;
It bendeth backwards every brave, shorn of his battle-
bravery;
At times imberbe, but full of spunk, to battle with the
Paynimry:
'Twill show thee liveliness galore, and perfect is its raillery;
The sweetest maid it is also like, complete in charms and
courtesy.[3]

---

[3] Ibid.

Eastern erotology, artistically refined, has typed and categorized the human body with a certain degree of veracity. Arabs and Hindoos in particular were connoisseurs of physiognomy. The Arab, generalizing, expounded:

A maiden's mouth shows what's the make of her chose;
Man's mentule one knows by the length of his nose;
And the eyebrows disclose how the lower bush grows.

But there were exceptions. A Deccanee Mussulman, saw woman only as a sexual devourer and man as her prey.

Surely, how ironical is life; how enigmatical is God. The Mussulman woman is gifted with an enormous cleft, a fathomless sheath; but we men are less endowed. It is disheartening. Is it any wonder that we revert to boys, in order that we might obtain gratification. How very great is the number of my wooers—but how small the size of my furniture. Fair, sleek gazelles have by wantonness emaciated my body. I am laughed to scorn. There is a saying: *A mouse feared that her carnal part was not sufficiently wide; the other mice thereupon introduced an iron pestle.* Such a thought turns my blood to water. It insults less fortunate men, smearing their faces in dirt. *Thou kissest thy lover, and tearest out his teeth.* It is as horrendous as all that. Opium, arrack, hasheesh: they are of little use save for the imagination. And the imagination works like evil *jinn* that come in the night and steal the precious seed of virile men, being jealous of their power. Even datura, which makes a man ragingly lustful and exuberant for an entire night, is of little avail. It deceives one, robs him of true courage in lieu of false; and when he possess reality of manly vigor, he is hopelessly lost in an abyss of bewilderment.

This is exaggerated but it appears that Eastern women *were* sexually overendowed. The pudenda, desire, and capacity for love greatly exceeded those of most men, for sexual immaturity, common and scarcely regarded as abnormal among females in the West, was rare in the Orient. This, among other things, led to the intense masculine fear of impotence. It made man hyperconscious of his genitals, their size and power; and harrowing self-condemnation resulted from any acknowledged deficiency. The Oriental woman was, however restricted mentally and socially, nearly always above her man sexually.

Hindoo erotologists, after careful survey of feminine types, classified their women as follows:

Pudminee (lotus woman), the perfection of womanhood. Every sweet and delicate quality belongs to her. *Pudminee*'s breasts are small, firm, and spherical; her hips narrow but ample; her waist thin; her vulva smooth and tiny, resembling the lotus bud; and her love-water (*kama-sulileh*) is perfumed like the newly burst lily.

Chitrinee (art woman), the perfection of courtesans. Her beauty is equal to that of the lotus woman, save that it is not innocent but worldly. *Chitrinee*'s lips are slightly wider, and her vulva a trifle plumper. The down is thin about her *yoni:* the mons veneris being soft, raised, and round. Her love-essence is hot, bearing the perfume of honey and producing from its abundance a distinct sound during coition.

Sunkhinee (shell woman), the common variety. She is the ideal wife for labor and breeding. *Sunkhinee* is highly sexed, and as capable for love as the artwoman. Her breasts are fuller and slightly pendulous; her hips wide and waist thicker; and her vulva, ever moist with *kama-sulileh* and covered with thick hair, much larger.

Hustinee (elephant woman), the most undesirable of the four types. She is of little value for work, but her sexual capacity is that of a rabid *mustee* (beast in rut). Coarse and indelicate, *Hustinee* is the bodily extreme with thick protruding labia and clitoris: pudendum which suggests the condition of genital elephantiasis. Her vulva is nigh to impenetrable because of hair, and

her copious love water bears the savor of the juice that
flows in spring from an elephant's temples.[4]

2. MALE

Indian castes were originated not only out of occupation and wealth but in relation to bodily charm. Genital
proportions were also a basis for classification and
men were rated by the size of their *lingams,* from in-
significance (*tussoo,* inchlet) to greater length and
thickness (*lumbah,* yard). In accordance, Hindoo
males were thus categorized:

Shushah (hare man), the beau ideal of manhood.
He is lithe and strong. Being the counterpart of
Pudminee and a Brahmin, his penis corresponds in
erection with the *yoni.* It is small (two or three inches),
and proportionately thin.

Mrigah (buck man), the perfection of warriors.
He is fleet and graceful. Being the counterpart of
Chitrinee and a Kshatriya, his penis is slightly thicker
and longer, four or five inches.

Vrishubha (bull man), the tough muscular
artisan type. Being the counterpart of *Sunkhinee,* his
penis is (for a merchant) from six to seven inches in
length or (for an agriculturalist) from seven to eight.

Ushvah (stallion man), the most coarse and vulgar of the group. He is worthless and indolent save for
propagating his kind. Being the counterpart of *Hustinee* and of the servile caste, he has adorning his body a
nine- to ten-inch, wrist-thick tassel; and his seminal
water flows like the Ganges in flood.[5]

The Hindoos believed that there is a Jack for
every Jill; and keeping company and propagating with
partners of the proper type and caste were supposed to
insure fulfillment of desire and perfect harmony. Nothing seemed more incongruous or defiling than an elephant woman mating with a hare man, or a lotus wom-

---

[4]*Ananga Ranga.*
[5]*Ibid.*

an coupling with a stallion man. Each normally held the utmost contempt for the other.

As an appendix to this classification, Hindoo eroticists taught the following:

> Long penis, poverty;
> Thick penis, sadness;
> The man who is called to high
> things and good fortune has a
> thin short member, a smooth
> prepuce, and hanging testicles.

Arab physiologists, in examining the subject, generally agree in their writings. Sheykh-en-Nefzawee, author of *The Perfumed Garden,* supplies this example:

> Praise be to God! Who has placed the source of man's greatest pleasure in woman's natural parts, and woman's greatest pleasure in the natural parts of man.
>
> A woman's religion is in her vulva. God has given this object a mouth, a tongue, two lips, and a shape like unto the footprint of a gazelle on the sands of the desert. When a desirable woman walks, her natural parts should stand out under her clothing; and when she is in heat, they should become turgid and moist—and grip, and suck firmly upon, the male organ.
>
> When a worthy man is in the company of woman his member grows, becomes strong, vigorous, and hard; he is slow to ejaculate and, after the spasm caused by the emission of semen, he is prompt at re-erection. His member must be well developed; it should reach to the bottom of the vagina, in which it should be a snug fit. He should be slow to ejaculate but quick to erect.
>
> For a virile member to be pleasing to a woman, its length should be—at most—three hand-breadths and, at least, one hand-breadth and a half.

The conventional Arab rather bitterly said: "The Moslem woman prefers an additional inch of penis to anything this world or the next might offer." In accordance, an Abyssinian slave girl once told her prospective buyer: "I desire a man whose penis is not in *his* belly, but in *mine*." This, audacious but true, clearly affirmed the feminine aversion to fat gentlemen with tiny organs, called *filberts,* hidden between their thighs. Common among wealthy Aryans and Semites, such an anatomic peculiarity was unknown to the African Negro, whose genitories were of imposing proportions.

In Greek painting and sculpture, the small pointed (uncircumcised) twig and diminutive testes were the standard of genital beauty. A sizable portrayal with large glans exposed was granted the Egyptian hierarchy in scenes depicting Hercules and Busiris. The Egyptians are given Negroid characteristics. They are shown with robes tucked into their belts above the pubic region to display proudly their thick, pendulant genitals.

Since tiny pudenda were deemed subjects of beauty, constriction of the genitals (infibulation) was often resorted to. Artificial phimosis (elongation of the foreskin and constriction of the orifice) in Spartan and other Greek warriors and athletes was achieved by the use of metallic locks and clamps. Erection in public was considered unseemly and grotesque; and the young athlete, exhorted to abstinence, found no other means of mechanically allaying desire. It was not until the advent of Syrian and Turkish culture and the triumphal rise of libertine Rome that the large phallus erectus became fashionable in depraved society. From Egypt to India, the statues featured conspicuous genitals. Shiva in India and Osiris in Egypt were seen testimonially clutching enormous phalli. And from China humorously refined pornography depicted an Oriental Hercules with gigantic member strongly erect, shattering a copper pot with one blow. Another favorite, an adventure tale, related the voyage of huge-membered gentlemen who, intent on demonstrating their singular manliness, sailed to and conquered the Isle of Women to return impotent and with mighty organs shriveled.

From earliest times, the most reverential regard was accorded to the organs of generation. Mohammed in his teachings said:

Truly, the men who guard their privities and the women who guard their privities: for them, God hath prepared a rich reward.

In time of danger, declared an eroticist,

. . . persons lay their hands on what they most prize. A pregnant woman will place her hand on her belly, for she is with child; a nurse will place her hand on her bosom, for she is suckling; and a third will cover her parts with her hand, proving that she is a virgin.

Another declaration, concerning married women, said:

When caught unawares, the European will shroud her implements of procreation. An Eastern woman will cover her head.

Once her virginity was gone, woman's concern was veiling her face. Below she was now avid. Man, however, had forever to guard his genitals. Such was proved one day by a shrewd Moslem who tossed two wooden balls at the stomachs of a man and a woman. The woman opened her knees in trying to catch it; the man closed his tight.

The very manner of Eastern dress served the male genitalia for comfort and for decency, to conceal their proud—or modest—aspect. When a stranger facetiously inquired of an Egyptian what he kept hidden under his robe, the Egyptian said wryly: "It is hidden so that ye may not know what it is."[6]

When Napoleon invaded Egypt in 1798, the most depraved Cairenes were shocked at the mode of European dress: tight breeches clearly outlining the buttocks and genital organs. After viewing this, philosophic Arabs were not surprised to learn that tailors took measure of the Infidel apparatus and that *braguettes* or *brayettes* (artificial phalli of leather) were sometimes used. But, in a land where virtuous women were

---

[6]Michel de Montaigne, *Essays.*

forbidden to show their faces to or consort with men,
perhaps nothing must have startled the Arab more than
beholding apparently shameless females with heads un-
veiled and breasts partially exposed to masculine scrutiny. Hence Orientals in all innocence generally regarded each and every European woman as being
promiscuous.

The original Arabs, unblemished by corrupt civilization, assumed a loose flowing system of garb because of their small protruding members (*shoke:* thorn,
twig). Women, having little need for unconstrained garments and more anxious to flaunt their shapes, wore
tight pantaloons and vests.

For a man to wear trousers was considered a
breach of etiquette and immoral, whereas in the Occi-
dent it was considered a disgrace for a woman, not a
man, to wear "fast" clothing. Only certain Asian races
were customarily suited to tight raiment, or a single
swath bound firmly round the middle. For the others,
tight garb was as ludicrous and revealing as a Scots-
man's kilt on an untrained Londoner.

Wealthy Hindoos, adopting taut cotton trousers,
added for the sake of decorum the *ungurkha* (tunic)
that extended to the knees and even below, in imitation
of the Mohammedan *jamah* or gown. Lower and poorer castes, verging in skin hue to black, generally wore
the simple *dhotee* (loincloth) and arranged it in the
most comfortable fashion. Many were obliged to drape
it down about one or both knees in accordance with
taste or class tradition for necessary concealment, while
affording natural comfort. Others, with only a *lungodee*
(G-string) to tie about their loins, trussed themselves
up and mastered the art of ascetic muscular control. A
few tribes in hill and forest solved the whole problem
by adopting the unornate condition of nakedness.

The instinctive respect shown the genitals of man
is first recorded in the Book of Genesis:

> And Abraham said unto his eldest servant
> of his house, that ruled over all that he had:
> Put, I pray thee, thy hand under my thigh;

And I will make thee swear by the Lord,
the God of heaven, and the God of the
earth. . . .

And the time drew nigh that Israel must
die; and he called his son, Joseph, and said unto
him: If now I have found grace in thy sight,
put, I pray thee, thy hand under my thigh, and
deal kindly and truly with me. . . .

In Latin the words "testicle" and "testis" are derived from the roots *testiculi* and *testes,* meaning *witnesses* (of generative force). To bear witness, testify,
or swear called up the image of the testicles in Latin,
for that was an ancient significance of the organs among
tribesmen; a man swore by his procreative power, his
fecundity.

The Arabs in all seriousness pledged: "I swear
upon the cullions of Lord Mohammed!" Each man
would then touch his secret parts and murmur: "O
Father of Virile Organs, bear witness to this solemn
oath!" or, more simply: "I swear upon mine own genitories!" Even today, offering pledge upon the penis is
the most solemn oath of the Bedewween.

When the nineteenth century Sudanese dervish
was clothed in the patched white *jubbeh* and red skull-
cap that identified him as a follower of El-Mahdi, he
grasped his instruments and said: "May my leg never
touch the saddle, may my body be smitten with the
lance that kills, and may I be consumed by the raging
fire, if ever I break the solemn oath of fidelity which I
now pledge to our Most Blessed Messiah." He then, by
law, clutched another's wrist. "Ye must take my seed
into thy hand, that the vow be sealed forever: until the
day and the moment I, in death, cast it upon dust."
This was known as the inviolate ceremony of *Zerreh-
en-Nutfeh-el-Emmaunee* (sowing the seed of trust).

The Hindoo practice was much the same, either
touching between the thighs or actually gripping the
testes (*foteh*) with the right hand of purity. Upon this,
each man would say: "We are bound together by the
Salt!" or "We, as brethren, are on terms of salt!"

European captives, on being brought before El-

Mahdi, were compelled to lay their fingers upon his privates while he guided them into the Faith:

> Repeat that which I say unto thee: *In the name of God, the Most Compassionate and Merciful—and the Unity of God—I pledge to God and His Prophet, and to thee, El-Mahdi, my allegiance; and I swear, upon the Unity of God, that I shall not steal, nor commit adultery, nor lead anyone into deception, nor disobey thee in thy goodness; and I swear to renounce this world, and look only to the future world, and shall not flee from the Holy War. There is no majesty, no might, save in God the Glorious and Great!*

Sudanese sheykhs by strict custom would tender their semen, carefully preserved in rosewater, as evidence of fealty and manly power. Under their sheepskins, one need never fear; for desertmen were of honorable word and disposition. But in treacherous defiance, to assert his infidelity, the inconstant Turk discharged his stone upon dust. Hence he was no longer bound; the Salt was not in his loins.

The Oath of the Circumcised Penis (*Yemeen-ed-Dehhereh Gedheeb*) was that ceremony wherein men grasped one another's, or their own virile member and swore allegiance. Warriors and noblemen offering fealty to King Solomon performed this sacred ritual as alluded to in the Book of I Chronicles:

> And all the princes, and the mighty men, and all the sons likewise of King David, submitted themselves unto Solomon the King.

To signify homage, the oath of fidelity was pledged upon an organ sanctified by blood covenant (circumcision). Sacrifice of the foreskin made all men brothers in truth, honor, and purity. Anyone who had not shed the blood of impurity was considered a barbarian.

In greeting, the usual respect paid a man was to recognize his virility. In Afghanistan, when one traveler said: "May thy shadow never be less!" the other replied: "May thy pintle never be less!" which, like most ironical Afghan salutations, could be interpreted two ways. Other volleys of phrases, familiar in Persia and Arab lands, were:

> May thou live, yah Khwaudjeh!
> May ye not be tired, yah Huzoor!

> May thou not become poor.
> May God keep thee prosperous.

> May thy abode flourish.
> In front of thee may good appear.

May the Compassionate and Merciful endow thee with many years of ardent virility; and, He so willing, may thine offspring be numerous.

May thine organ never flag in the moment of conquest, yah Huzoor!

Inshallah! God grant thee the everlasting manliness of Paradise.

God so willing: inch by inch, may thy firm stalk increase in power and sensitivity!

Yah'llah! might thine own implement progress, that with it ye might ensorcell the most unwilling of damsels.

God willing, our implements shall thrive.

> In the name of God: may He keep thee.
> Peace be unto thee.
> And unto thee, peace, by God!
> O God!

Then, as in greeting, each touched the fingers of his right hand successfully to chest, lips, forehead, and, to show greater deference, laid his palm upon the generative organs. Thereupon each went his way.

In the Sudan, when saluting another who was of rank and prestige, the Arab tribesman touched his hands between his thighs to affirm humility. He always embraced a sheykh, kissing his beard or the hem of his garment and, if he chose, allowed the patriarch to acknowledge him by genital examination. If venereal erection were thereby effected, honoring the sheykh, the patriarch was under obligation to entertain him that night with concubines and catamites. Erection (*muk-neh,* firmness) indicated manliness, and manliness had always to be esteemed. *Rekhoo* (flaccid) denoted little more than a eunuch.

The names bestowed upon the male genitalia are as diverse and vivid as those granted the female. In Arabic, the stock term is *gedheeb* (rod) or, vulgarly, *zubb* (prickle). Politely, the membrum virile is *adho-et-tenausul* (limb of generation). One-eyed (*el-a'awer*) was an Egyptian favorite, particularly in the opprobrious expression: *"Yah ibn-el-a'awer!"* (*O one-eyed; O son of a yard*). A fortunate man was styled Ed-Dew-weel (the Long) or Es-Smeek (the Thick).

In Persia, the member masculine was popularly dubbed *zukkur* or *zurduk* (carrot) and, jocosely, *keer* (worm). *Ney* (reed) is as familiar in Turkey as in Persia and Afghanistan. *Khusseyaun* or *beyzetaun* (eggs) signify the testicles, but the more euphemistic term is *kees-el-bedn* (scrotum, bag of one's belly).

In Sanskrit, equivalents of our Latin word *penis* (tail) range from *lingam,* mark, sign (of masculinity) to *dhundh* (rod).

Phallic cults found their origin in the East, primarily Egypt and India, where the gods Osiris and Mahadeva (Shiva) symbolized the male principle.

Mahadeva, Great God of the Hindoos, was given the appellation of *Linganaut:* the Heavenly Root, Celestial Penis, the Phallus Lord. His irradiated *lingam* was so large that neither Brahma nor Vishnu could reckon its extent. He, God of Destruction and Rebirth —for they were that closely related—was the omnipotent symbol of drunkenness and debauchery: his usual disposition in Paradise (*Kailasa*) where he drank and copulated to the point of insensibility, shaming all the gods with his incontinence. Thus, in sculpture, his *lingam* was ever crimson-daubed, to signify its perpetually engorged and irritated state of excitement.

Several related sects worshiped Lord Shiva under the aspect of *Sheeshum-deva* (Phallus God). The greatest body of *Lingayuts* or *ling*-worshipers were the Veereh Sheyveh (*Yungummeh:* stanch, virile men dedicated to the procreation of mankind). They were distinguished by a single red perpendicular caste mark (*ling-teekah*) upon their foreheads, and their chief precept taught that the *lingam* equalized mankind and destroyed the bondage of social distinction. About their necks they wore a silver-encased phallic emblem, and smaller ones, usually of gold, were attached to their arms and genitals. These acted as defenses against the evil eye (*drishdeh-dosheh*), as preservatives of vital manhood, and as extollers of Vatoo, a guardian spirit of the sexual organs. Many Shivites also wore signet rings upon which were embossed irradiated *lingams*.

The priesthood of the Lingayuts, often more properly termed Shiva-bhukteh, were embellished with phallic amulets. These hallowed men, presiding stark naked in the temples, were given over to unbelievable excesses. Upon the foreheads of the higher priests was daubed the *trisooleh* (trident) emblem. A single dot, *bindee,* represented the seed of creation. Their scepter of office was the trident, the head of which symbolized the sensitive tissue of the glans, and the rod, the ejaculatory canal. Two significant egg-shaped tassels were frequently suspended from the *trisooleh,* with the *svusteekah* (swastika, emblem of life) painted thereon. Not a few of the Shivite *poojarees,* in honor and emulation of Mahadeva, sought to sustain their members in constant erection; for Lord Shiva, God of Sensuality, possessed a *lingam* forever turgid and of the most exquisite sensibility.

The other extreme was to be found in groups of celibates who dismembered themselves in laudation of Shiva or, by affixing heavy stones to their members, destroyed their erectile powers.

From the *sunnyasee* or *yogee* came numbers of total abstainers from physical contact, achieving sexual tension and release by mental power. With the aim of uniting the senses and achieving divine ecstasy, they practiced a mode of sitting called *maha-ausunneh.* The heel of the left foot is placed at the orifice of the anus; the heel of the right foot is raised to the pubic area, then to the breast. The eyes, without blinking, are directed to the middle of the eyebrows. The membrum virile is mentally raised, in palpitant stiffness. Wind is then forced from the throat and rectum, sperm is ejected, and incantations are intoned. Thus, all evil is expelled from the flesh. A veritable feat of concentration!

Others, less sacrosanctly sensuous, indulged in the art of *sunyum* (sexual restraint) in the face of temptation. Without mechanical means, the sensitive genital muscles were subdued by sheer divine concentration upon the ideal that nothing really exists, nor has shape or perception. Convincing himself of the nothingness of life and the human body, he obliterates temptation and desire by way of self-anaphrodisia.

The Veyraugee, an austere type of Shivite holy man, is a sect of mendicant priests. An early traveler to India[7] thus described a Veyraugee:

> I have seen a fanciful Rascal, seven Foot high with a large Turband of his own Hair wreathed about his Head, and his Body bedaubed with Ashes and Water, sitting quite naked under the Shade of a Tree, with *pudendum* like an Ass.

This same individual retailed rumors concerning Brahminee priests "who observe *heathenish* customs."

> They have a yearly Feast—but the time of its celebration is only known to themselves—wherein, after much Mirth and Jollity, each Sex withdraws to a Room. The women take each a Handkerchief and go in the dark promiscuously among the Men.

A native of Tehran, an eighteenth-century Persian mercenary, observed a Hindoo monk in Hurdwar:

> The Veyraugee's tool must be sufficiently long so that, when he is seated, it touches the earth. Otherwise, in its proud state, it has not shown its utter humility as an evil and worldly phenomenon.

---

[7]Captain Alexander Hamilton, *A New Account of the East Indies.*

The children of the Shiva-bhukteh were also adorned with amulets, generally of gold or silver, called *lingum-kuvuch,* attached to the glans penes of boys and the wrists of girls. A small shield (*dhaul*) was worn by girls to conceal the pudendum. It was the ritual in love-play for them to remove the charms. Digital manipulation, fellatio, and cunnilingus were usually pursued; or the boy rhythmically massaged his organ against her vulva without entering her vagina. Upon marriage, the *lingum-kuvuch* and *dhaul* were permanently removed, signifying the loss of virginity.

Worship of the *lingam* also led to sundry cults that deified snakes and tortoises. The cobra, deadly as syphilis, was adored as the embodiment of Kalee; and Seyshnaug, the hydra-headed serpent-king, represented genital power and its destruction (syphilis) united. This symbol was depicted in sculpture by the image of Lord Shiva with Kalanaut, the Snake-Lord, twined about his neck and arm and swallowing his enormous member. This cult, notorious for its masochism, practiced heterosexual ritualistic masturbation to the point of hysteria. Amongst the Vishnuites, the tortoise (*koor-meh-avatar,* embodiment of Vishnu) was glorified as a phallic symbol because its head, projecting from the folds of a long slender neck, resembled the erect penis with retracted foreskin.

The famed Hoolee and Dewalee (spring and autumnal fiestas) inflamed the normally mild, sober Hindoo to a lustful satyr. Two- and three-foot, red-daubed, wooden phalli were strapped to men's waists. Rushing and shrilling about the streets, they clutched and wielded them, brandished them in the motions of coition, poking them at people right and left, and chanting obscene ballads.

During the festival of *Shiva-Rautree* (Night of the Lingam), men and women flocked to the temples in order that they might participate in the ceremonies honoring Mahadeva. In emulation of Lord Shiva, these rituals invariably terminated in indiscriminate and frenzied coition.

The Indian supposed that consecrated venery between Mahadeva and Mother Kalee would not alone replenish her needs, assuage her lust, glut her seething desire. *Blood*. Streams of blood. She must subsist on human life. Late at night, during the Hoolee and just before the torrential bursting of the storm in 1857, fanatical Hindoos rushed from their houses. They moved frantically, ere time caught them dead. Down they stampeded to the banks of the Ganges, where they stripped themselves, and rubbed their bodies and foreheads with ashes of cow-dung. They feverishly molded foot-long *lingams* of red clay, and they fell prostrate before them.

Some shook violently. There were tears in their eyes. They dreaded the insidious, bloodthirsty power of the Black Goddess. They cleansed their idols with holy water, fondled them, kissed the sand before them and pressed their foreheads into the coarse yellow loam.

Not a few sat moaning in fetid shallows. Some submerged themselves. Many offered their own seed in libation to Mother Ganges, then abandoned the hallowed stream to smear clay over their bodies, caking it especially round their secret parts, for purification and protection! protection against Kalee, Mistress of Castration and Impotence.

Naked, fearful, earnest before their gods, they took up the sacred *lingams* and tossed them into the glittering black womb of Holy Mother Ganges. It was ended. Shiva grant them peace.

In the Shivite temple of Ishwara at Benares, the Brahminical hierarchy claimed that they possessed a lifelike image of Lord Shiva. It was an ingenious mechanical device, cast and painted to perfection. A large graven brazier rested directly beneath it and, as the temple priestesses writhed before it in naked dance, the idol achieved a succession of orgasms from a monstrous *lingam* that moved and palpitated as if in the copulatory act. This image, performing before all worshipers, was obviously thus designed to stimulate procreative desire. The viscid substance that jetted into the brazier was then mixed with the fresh blood of goats, the testicles of bulls, and the intestines and genital organs of tigers, and drunk by incoming devotees. Each thereupon retired amid the priestesses, who awaited them like hungry wolves.

The mighty syndicate of *poojarees* (priests) also erected a machinelike image of the goddess Parvuttee in the principal Hindoo bazaar at Benares. It was constructed for the use of young boys and elderly men, who sought its virtues to hasten or restore manhood by inserting their organs into a moist compressing cleft. The idol, like that of Mahadeva, excited passion by embracing with spindly limbs and artfully clasping and constricting upon the penis. A young girl, secreted within, operated it, moaning heatedly and lubricating the artificial pudendum with sandalwood oil.

Thus the Brahminee priests of Benares reaped a fortune from the all too susceptible devotees. Those who did not pay up risked instant defilement and a threat of eternal perdition.

In defiance of the hateful Europeans, grotesque images of Mother Kalee were erected everywhere, especially along the Grand Trunk Road and at its forks. Sometimes the cannon of the Europeans were set up on end and used as phallic images. The stone phalli and other stone creations, depicting all forms of sexual congress, were stained a deep crimson. The phallic symbol and lotus buds were painted and strewn throughout Hindostan, indicative of approaching reincarnation of maternal India.

In regard to symbolism, the minaret, sleek and white-hot in crystal sunlight, is like most architecture phallic in origin. The aureate Star of El-Islam, like that of Judaism, is representative of sexual conjunction. Several Islamic societies, dedicated to the propagation of the Faithful, wore silver *khautims* (seal rings) embossed with the ancient Key of Life (*ankh*). In India, the ring was termed *ungoodhee* and it portrayed the familiar *lingam-yoni:* an erect phallus with a circular vulva symbol as its base.

The apparently enigmatic formula, *Ome! munnee pudmeh hum* (*O hail! the Jewel in the Lotus*), bears several connotations. *Ome,* the sacred interjection preceding prayer, signifies the Trinity (Brahma, Shiva, Vishnu); and the *Trimoortee,* emblemizing the trinity, also signifies the generative organs. Shiva, in the charac-

ter of Linganaut, is representative of the penis; and
Brahma and Vishnu, under the titles of Lokeputtee
and Juggernaut (Lords of the World), symbolize the
testicles. *Munnee* (jewel) can denote semen, penis, or
embryo, depending on its relation with *pudmeh* (lotus), which indicates womb, vulva. Different sects chose
different forms.

By the Veyshnuvees, worshiping the maternal
principle, the formula is thus translated: *O hail! the
sperm (or fetus) in the womb.*

To the Sheyvehs, worshiping the paternal principle, the formula bears a different connotation: *O hail!
the penis in the vulva (lingam-yoni), or O hail! the
sperm in the penis.*

Eastern languages are so cluttered with metaphors
—some not in the least euphemistic and quite natural
and vivid—that it requires careful scrutiny to conceive
what is intended. Many writers, seeking to analyze this
formula, claim that in Buddhist usage where it is now
most prevalent the Jewel signifies Buddha, who is often
depicted sitting meditatively in a blossoming lotus flower. But this is not what was intended.

The entire formula is ingeniously constructed and
crammed with phallic symbolism. Lord Buddha at rest
in the lotus blossom is merely an imposition of symbol
upon symbol. The extensive history of religion is based
upon phallic symbolism, from the Christian Cross (*lingam-yoni*) to the Moslem Crescent. Without it, no form
of religion could possibly have survived; for man, desiring partial understanding, had as the demand of vanity and human nature to cling to materialistic as well
as spiritual principles in his adoration of one or many
gods.

3. ASPIRATION

Some of us be hawks—and some, sparrow-hawks—and
    vultures, some, which at carrion pike;
And maidens deem all alike we be; but, save in our tur-
    bans, we're not alike.

So sang the Arab; and the witty Persian, with less euphemism, would chant to a skeptic:

> Every round thing is not a walnut,
> And every long thing a banana is not.

How sad the lament of the merchant from Lahore:

> Unfortunately, many of us Punjaubee-Mussulmans are not blessed with members that are both thick and long. We must employ artificial means.

And how blatant the chorusing of ragged urchins in the streets of Cairo:

> Short and thick is never quick;
> Short and thin has little in;
> Long and thick well knows the trick!

From Khartoum to Hyderabad, the aged Mohammedan said to his brother:

> "Who among us, pray, can boast that his prickle be as straight as the letter *alif?* No man in our decrepit midst can now jog his comrade in the coffeeshop and utter, tormentingly: *I am the thick one and thou are the thin.* Now, we are all of us El-Mugheffef (the Shriveled)."
>
> "God so willing: weep not, *yah ekhooyeh,*" his brother would sigh, touching his shoulder. Then, beaming: "Recall, thou, the day when we were as the long-necked gugglet (*el-ezwaunee*) because of our proud instruments? Then, *Inshallah!* we could convert any woman in the world to El-Islam and the Truth. A single night was all we needed; by God's blessing, the Converters failed us not. But now, alas! we may as well shave our whitened beards, for all the virility they denote."

The topic of anatomy and manliness was a great favorite amongst the Arabs; it gave rise to jocular tales and chaffing. One of them found in the *Arabian Nights* relates of a king's son, a shrewd masquerader, who entered a public bath:

> When the young man put off his clothes, the bath-keeper saw not his yard; for it was hidden between his thighs, by reason of the excess of his fat, and there appeared thereof but what was like unto a filbert.

Feeling sorry for the apparently unseasoned youth and distressed with his condition, for he had seen nothing like it before, the bath-keeper sent for his wife, expecting that she, stripping naked, would arouse the lad's organ into normal prominence. His wife, as licentious and dull-witted as Egyptian women come, agreed to the experiment. Stripped, she was locked in the bath with the young man. The bath-keeper mounted the roof to observe the reaction, peering down the skylight. But what he saw overshot his expectations. The youth approached her and she, grinning baldly, approached him:

> He took the damsel in his arms and pressed her to his bosom and they embraced; whereupon the young man's yard swelled and rose on end, as it were that of a jackass, and he rode upon her breast and futtered her: whilst she sobbed and sighed and writhed and wriggled under him.

In his agitation over his wife's infidelity and the young man's deception, the bath-keeper stumbled and fell headlong down the skylight and was killed.

> Who can find a virtuous woman? for her price is far above rubies.

This sort of tale, with its "presumption begins in ignorance and ends in ruin" moral, always aroused great applause from the coffeehouse clique. The wiles and weaknesses of women, well told by any spinner of yarns, invariably caused the gravest of Arabs to vibrate with glee.

The ever-looming decline of virility (*koowut-e-*

bah) was the Moslem's greatest worry, if there were
any others besides. Nothing appeared more contemptible to a rich-blooded Son of the Prophet than a passive
castrato or an impotent old man.

To admit impotence (*zooa'af*) was to open oneself to abuse:

> O thou tailless, hairless one! thou hast not
> the prick of an ant. Free women display their
> faces to thee; for they think nought of thee but
> that thou art a stripling, a eunuch—to be sure,
> anything but a man. Pluck out thy beard, thy
> mustachios, thine eyebrows, and we shall make
> of thee a fine sodomite.

In Persia, to call one a thin-beard was to call him
a eunuch. If a man wished to praise another, the proper
epithet was *khush-reesh* (handsome beard). Combined
with *koozeh* (flask), in the phrase *koozeh-o-khush-
reesh,* it became a designation of praise, relating thick
beard with thick penis: thus metaphorical eulogy of
manhood.

In Arabic, the parts genital are allied with whis-
kers in the term *mehhaushim* (merits): the singular of
which, *ma 'ashoom,* indicates either beard or penis.
Esh-shoosheh (topknot, whereby Mohammed draws the
True Believer into Paradise) was just as important as a
well-clipped beard to the proud Moslem. The Turks
and Tartars, among others, almost unconsciously identified the topknot with masculinity and a large phallus.
Thus, symbolically, the horse-tail emblems acquired
phallic significance attesting power and virility in a warrior. A one-tailed pasha's organ was to have measured
four inches; a two-tailed pasha's, five inches; and a
three-tailed pasha's, connoting supreme rank, six inches
in length.

Hair has since the days of Samson and Delilah always implied manliness. And, as the Persians say: "A
kiss without mustachio is bread without salt!"

Fear of becoming impotent (*inneen* or *ze'eef,* weak
in venery) obsessed the aging Oriental. This pride demanded remedies, of which there were many.

In Persia, when the gray-beard appeared before

the beady-eyed sinister *hakeem* and lamented, "My sperm is weak and watery, and impregnateth not!" the omniscient doctor would concoct a restorative of two parts *tukhm* (semen virile) and one part Shirazee wine.

The scarab beetle (*gooraun*), worshiped in the Sudan, was thought to be bisexual and self-reproducing. Women wore its sable image on their yellow scarfs as a charm against the evil eye. From such a beetle a fabulous potion was made by crushing the live insect and compounding the mash with liquid hasheesh. Imbibed as a matter of daily routine by men, women, and children, it was thought to preserve, intensify, or restore sexual power.

Reverend Father Nile (Eboo-en-Neel) and Holy Mother Ganges (Gungah-Ma'ee), held in great veneration by Moslem and Hindoo, were regarded as having magic powers of rejuvenation. Mixed with the seed of bulls, tigers, stallions, and holy men, the waters of these rivers were employed as aphrodisiacs.

In all sections of the East, *hhesheesh-el-herraufeesh* (rascal's grass) acted as a stimulant. The favorite of Hindostanees for provoking wild illusions and satyriasis was hemp (*bhang*). *Dhuttooreh* (datura), sap of the thorn-apple seed, induced nearly the same sensations as alcoholic drinks and narcotics. *El-hheshaush* (hemp-eater) would experience fantastic visions of Paradise, desirable nymphs and catamites; and such dreams were said to make men potent who had psychologically lost their manhood. The Hheshausheen (Assassins) habitually indulged in this drug-induced form of delusion. Under the power of the drug they convinced initiates of the glory of death, which released them into paradise.

Aphrodisiacs were administered with art in India but with poisonous effects in Egypt. One private soldier, a *fellah* (Egyptian peasant) sluiced with barbarous potions, ran amuck and raped nearly all his company in barracks at Cairo. He had to be shot down like a rabid dog, but such cases recurred, and with such violence, that men preferred to oblige rather than resist.

For immediate excitation, the Persians were notorious for their use of the *m'yaujung* (anointed battle-root, or artificial phallus). This, generally made of wood, was first dipped in olive oil, then sprinkled with fine pepper and ground nettles. Worked into the anus, it produced instantaneous results.

Among the Hindoos, mutual masturbation and fellatio were common especially between man and wife, along with urtication (scratching). The stomach and pubic region received especial flaying which, satisfying masochistic tendencies, procured the desired condition. Cowage (*kewaunch*), a hairy pod known for its aphrodisiac effects, was the delight of Hindoos seeking such stimulation. When rubbed upon the penial skin, it provoked a prurient itch accompanied by swelling and throbbing. Sometimes the skin twitching, intensified by friction, reached such an extreme as to drive witless users of the drug to suicide or self-mutilation. Virgins going to sacrifice were said to rub it upon their vulvae to counteract pain. Hairy insects and strange varieties of plants were also used for similar purposes. Frequently these aphrodisiacs proved toxic and brought on frightful skin afflictions which, in time, spread over the entire body and ended in death. In some individuals, the furious priapism it induced lingered even after death.

The Persian *pushmee-hulkeh* (hairy ring), affixed between the glans and prepuce, was popular throughout Asia. In India it was called *rome-choorree* and was produced in several varieties. One type of caoutchouc (India rubber) was smeared with powdered hairs; another, a metallic sheath, was studded with fine titillating points. Other devices, intended to equalize the organs of the man and woman, were of bone or wood. They consisted of slender strips, disposed in the skin around the shaft of the penis in such a way as to increase its girth and reinforce its hardihood so that, in coition, it would congest the vagina which, in turn, would bring greater pressure to bear upon the male organ, drawing it inward, expanding its length and, with the increased friction, its width. Such proved a practical remedy for inequality, if the man were willing to incise his member.

Some masochistic Brahmins provoked a bee to sting their virile part before engaging in copulation, not only benefiting by increased turgescence but reveling in the, to them, pleasurable pain.

In the mid-nineteenth century, when French and English troops occupied parts of China, those quartered in Peking, found many curiosities in the harems of that city. Among them were small bulletlike devices that females inserted between the labia, causing the slightest movement on their stomachs to produce pleasure. There were also aphrodisiac pills and applications, causing erection of the shaft and swelling of the glans penis; rubber penial bracelets; artificial phalli of rubber, ribbed horn, gold, and silver; and artificial feminine pudenda (*cunni-succedanei*), familiarly called *merkins* in France, which were employed by men.

The gleaming, hairless Sudanese Negro, with a filthy strip of linen between his thighs, was a hardy warrior, inured to hardship and pain, and, indeed, taking enjoyment thereby. He could undergo thirst and privation, and no more cared for pain or death than if he were of stone. A favorite sport among Sudanese youngsters, designed to stimulate masculinity, was the test of the lash. One after the other they submitted to flogging with the hippowhip (*kourbash*) to see who could bear up the longest.[8] In many Sudanese tribes, too, a lad was not considered a man until he had proved that he could penetrate a virgin without the use of a knife or his fingers. In preparation for this test, long ere puberty, the blacks strengthened their erectile muscles through proper dieting, cold-water applications, and systematic mutual masturbation. Meanwhile, to increase their labia, girls resorted to similar practices.

Needless to say, Moslem women preferred Negroes because of the unusual size of their parts. According to Arab slavers and eroticists, the average Negro organ in a quiescent state measured not less than six inches. This, though rare among Semites, was their ideal in a man.

Indian *saddhoos, dervishes, fakeers,* and *gooroos*

[8]Major General C. G. Gordon, *Journals at Khartoum.*

were masters of *maya* (deception). Aside from religious rape and fornication or even holy intoxication, they deceived old men by making them believe that they could restore virility. Taking the flaccid organ in their hands, they whined *muntrums* and artfully rubbed an aphrodisiac solution on the meatus urinarius (orifice of the penis). In only a few seconds it scourged the urethra (canal), provoking instant erection and wild sensations. The old man, blessing both deity and holy man, heartily paid; but the holy man, pocketing his money, made himself scarce. By the time the old man reached his wife or the courtesan he admired, the effect had worn off and he was as incapable as before.

One seventeenth century Arab traveler noticed the following peculiarity in the Deccan of India:

> Hindoos on the Coromandel coast straddle themselves over the poisonous milk-hedge, which engorges their privy members to immense proportions. Then, they are deemed saints by ignorant women.

Sexual overendowment is a rarity in the East where it is supposed that man was never manly enough for the woman. But Hindees (Indian Mussulmans) had devised cures for priapism and hyperesthesia of the sex organ. Most of them destroyed virility and converted one into a pederast which, according to many cynics, the majority of Moslems are at one stage of life or another. Hindoos regarded priapism (*punyautmah-kurraupun*, holy inflexibility) as highly praiseworthy, the blessed gift of virile Lord Shiva, whose mighty *lingam* is ever erect. According to legend, he was the first god to be affected with satyriasis, a condition of sanctity granted to *saddhoos* and other fanatics, who operated even at the entranceways to temples. Because of the eternal tumescence of his instrument, Shiva's title was Phallus Lord, and his stiff tremendous *lingam* by itself received the worship owed to divinity.

The literature dealing with impotence and its conquest is without limit, from the most concise and sensible (*Overcome thy fear, thy nervousness, and thy doubt*) to the most complicated and ludicrous. The following, in the sad cause of Lord Limpo, was a recipe common in the harem:

> If, upon rubbing and toying with it, the prickle will not stand at point, thy mistress must take dried aromatic herbs—such as are scattered upon corpses—a couple handkerchiefs, and a gugglet of water. Wash the prickle, as if it were a dead body, then shroud it with herbs and lament the untimely fate of such a young and vigorous yard; for such must ward away the Evil Eye, which has ensorcelled thy member. Verily, thy penis is buried so that it may soon experience resurrection.

Arab verse, more ardent and pathetic than facetious or obscene, has also examined the matter:

I have a yard that sleeps in base and shameful way,
    when grants my lover boon for which I sue
    and pray;
But when I wake o' mornings, all alone in bed, 'tis
    fain o' foin and fence and fierce for futter-play.

I have a froward yard of temper ill, dishonouring him
    who shows it most regard;
It stands when I sleep; when stand I, it sleeps; Heaven pity not who pitieth that yard!

She saith—sore hurt in sense the most acute, for she
    had proffered what did not besuit—
"Unless thou stroke as man should swive his wife,
    blame not when horns thy brow shall incornute!
"Thy wand seems waxen, to a limpo grown; and
    more I palm it, softer grows the brute!"

Quoth she to me—and sore enraged for wounded
    pride was she; for she, in sooth, had bidden me
    to that which might not be—
"And if thou swive me not forthright, as one should
    swive his wife, thou be made a cuckold straight:
    reproach it not to me.

"Meseems thy yard is made of wax, for very flaccid-
ness; for when I rub it with my hand, it softens
instantly." [9]

The bloody Indian Mutiny saw an extensive rebirth in Eastern philosophy and a rousing of dormant
nationalism. This fateful year of Fifty-seven was one of
festering discontent, revolution, and revival. There were
changes, even in sexual attitudes. From virtuous pride,
based on his scriptural literature, in having a thin,
short, and smooth organ of copulation, in 1857 the
fastidious Brahmin idealized a large organ. Young and
old, the Brahmin now aimed to be a stallion man. He
wished to increase the length and thickness of his member, and he employed everything from engorging aphrodisiacs to hairy insects and strips of caoutchouc. The
amulet was no longer used to insure abstemiousness; it
now called constant attention to an instrument which,
when daubed with a substance that activated the erotic
zone, kept it in a state of palpitant swelling.

The opinion became rife that the Brahmins were
not men, had not affirmed their power and vitality, until they honored Lord Shiva by seeking to achieve phallic enlargement. Having done so, successfully or unsuc-
cessfully, they were promised the aid of Mahadeva in
annihilating the puny Europeans.

Young boys were fed certain drugs and liquors to
hasten puberty, and their parts were subjected to continuous excitation. Old men, in order to regain their
youth, resorted to the priesthood and mendicant-devo-
tees who cast spells over them and chanted:

"Play the bull: blow, increase, and spread.
Let thy member swell and throb. With it, smite a
woman. I make thy shrunken member long as
the bow, taut as the bow-string, thick as the
quiver of arrows. Ye shall be as a fervid stag,
from whom the gentle doe must gain no rest."

Then, the supreme and sacred aim was massive
procreation, the strengthening of Mother India against
her unclean invaders.

---

[9]Burton, *op. cit.*

One clan of Shiva-bhukteh *saddhoos* incessantly
drank arrack infused with a hideous potion. Their private parts were thereby congested day and night, in
imitation of the phallus of Lord Shiva. In this way they
believed that they were asserting the copulative power
of their race against an impotent Christianity that
sought to engulf and defile them. They were to be seen
parading, completely nude, in the bazaars. Faithful
women were commanded to kiss their *lingams* and, if
so directed, yield their bodies to holy congress with the
Inspired Ones.

Indian Moslems, because of their imposing parts,
loathed the castrated Negro slaves imported from Zanzibar, to which the Hindee wife invariably alluded when
abusing her inadequate husband. Other Hindoos also
were made apprehensive by these enormous blacks who
could crush men in their embraces. The big blacks with
their impressive instruments were a great temptation to
the lascivious Hindoo women.

In early 1857, a few casual remarks were passed
by English officers in their verandahs to the effect that
the growing discontent in Bengal would breathe its last
were the East India Company to recruit Zanzibar Negroes and disembark them at Calcutta. Someone over-
heard; in one week, it swept like wildfire throughout
the entire Province: *The Sahiblogue are to send fierce
Hubshees to eat our children and violate our women,
so that we will not rise against them.*

Within a week a compact brotherhood linking all
of Bengal was established, to meet and withstand the
awaited army of blacks. And this massive fraternity,
patterned after those of Biblical days, locked away
every woman and child of its religion and joined arm-
in-arm in a strange but powerful band.

Who would wittingly dare to defy custom? Men
watched one another hour by hour in the *sepoy* (native
soldier) barracks, the streets, the market places. They
sought redemption, garbed in the pure white cloth of
Paradise. Mighty El-Islam, a volcanic mountain, patient, expectant, its men rising as one to obliterate the
uncircumcised Infidel. To the Moslem his strength lay

not in the massive procreation of the future but in the masculine brotherhood of the present. It was this union on the walls of Delhi and in the gardens at Lucknow that kept the Mussulman standing when the Hindoo fled. It kindled success as it has since the days of Marathon.

Twenty-seven years later, El-Mahdi revived the ancient fecundate principle long dormant in the Mohammedan world. He evoked it in the cause of Holy War against the Infidel and in doing so said thus to his emeers: "Behold, thou, *Rumh-el-Gooweh* (Lance of Power)." And for but a second they gazed upon the rod of flesh oiled and perfumed, large and glimmering as a spear. *"The Lance of Power, strength of El-Mehdeeyeh."*

The Egyptian soldier sent by the Khedive to destroy El-Mahdi presumed that the only way to insult or frighten or force a Dervish into submission was to steal and devour his *sejjaudeh* (sheepskin prayer-rug). But far above any *sejjaudeh* the Dervish of El-Mahdi held his private parts in especial reverence, scrupulously protecting them from injury and tinting them with bright colors to attract and fascinate Sudanese women. The only way to cause a fanatic to submit was to emasculate him; consequently no Egyptian *fellah* would dare get within ten yards of a Dervish.

The Mahdi, though he did not practice what he preached, talked of abstemiousness, ferocity, and virtue. The Mahdi forbade sodomy, pederasty, onanism, and fornication. The Mahdi was greatly feared in Egypt, land of these abominations. Every one of the Mahdi's Dervishes was considered a demon invulnerable who transformed the bullets of his enemy into harmless drops of water.

Lo, now, his strength is in his loins; and his force is in the navel of his belly.
He moveth his tail like a cedar; the sinews of his stones are wrapped together.

The Book of Job speaks in the true manner of the Oriental conception of figurative manliness. In Egypt it was an honor to be known as *Seyf-ed-Deen* (Sworder

of the Faith) or *Gedheeb-el-Kebeer* (the Great Rod).
The greatest and most illustrious of Iraqi Caliphs bore
the surname *Resheed,* meaning "guided on the right
path," (into a woman's vagina). In Persia, a man of
distinction styled himself Alee or Futteh Khan (Conqueror of virgins; Opener of vaginae). One of the
ninety-nine glorious Moslem epithets of God, the hun-
dredth of which only the camel knows, *El-Fetooh,*
the Opener, proclaims His divine command over the
vulvae of maidenhood.

    Hhuzaun (stallion), *Tore* (bull), and *Gaumoose*
(buffalo) are examples of names favored by the *Memlooks* (Mamelukes, Circassian slave soldiers), and
Abyssinian eunuchs in Egypt. These hulks of manhood, with impressive physiques, were responsible for
much of the harem corruption that blighted Cairo; and
the Arabs regarded them with utmost scorn. "A great
ugly black slave, with member long as a lance and
broad as a bench" was the usual manner of reference
to these "skunks of the human race."[10] Yet the core of
contempt lay not in their seductive strength—for to the
Arabs women are normally weak and lustful—but in
their unlimited genital powers. And Negroes, in vaunt-
ing their masculinity and twitting the less-endowed
Arab, would take the oath of fealty by saying:

    "I swear by the valor and honor of blackamoor
men, and deem not our manliness to be the poor manliness of white men!"

    Many of them, in emulation of Osiris and to add
insult to injury, conjured instantaneous erection and
swore upon their secret parts. Suffice it to say, the
dusky Arab turned scarlet with envy. But when he
beheld the brutish copulation of the massive black, he
waxed absolutely pale with scornful astonishment.

---

[10]*Ibid.*

III

CIRCUMCISION:
Blood Covenant

And God said unto Abraham . . .
This is my covenant, which ye shall keep, be-
tween me and you and thy seed after thee: Every
man child among you shall be circumcised.

1. Male

The Jews adopted circumcision (*meshookim*) from the
ancient Egyptian priestly ritual. As a sacrifice of sinful
blood and flesh, priests laid their organs of generation
upon the altar and severed their foreskins with a stone
blade.

The Hebrew rite, generally performed eight days
after birth, was presided over by the *mohel* (an official
of the synagogue). It consisted of three effectuations:
milleh, preyeh, and *mezeezeh. Milleh* (the cut) was
the simple process of abscission. *Preyeh* (tearing the
foreskin), executed with keen fingernails, involved lac-
erating the inner tissue to prevent retraction and produce a thin ring of cicatrice fitting snugly to the cervix
of the glans. *Mezeezeh* (applying styptics to the wound)

was effected by the *mohel's* lips, moist with wine; and this procedure was hastily performed until the slight flow of blood was stanched.

No mention of circumcision (*el-khutneh*) is made in the Koran; but Mohammed, following Hebraic practices rather closely, personally recommended it. Popular belief claimed that he, the Most Gifted Prophet and Greatly Praised One, was born circumcised as well as with kohl'd eyes; and when asked to comment on the rite of blood covenant, he said in reply, "Circumcision is an ordinance for men, and honorable in women."

Known also as *el-khitaun* (seal, covenant), *ed-duhoor* (purity), *et-tedheer* (lustration), and *es-sunneh* (ordinance of faith), circumcision was customarily performed between the ages of five and twelve; but it was lawful, though rarely observed, a week sequential to birth. According to many Oriental physiologists, who are today supported by not a few in the medical profession, this deferment of the ceremony until just before puberty was indeed wise: a humane score in support of Arab sagacity. For hereby, it is their contention, the male organ is able to achieve its proper form ere mutilation; the child and his delicate nervous system are able to muster strength in order to tolerate the obvious shock without ill effect; and, just as important, such delay enables the full development of the blood corpuscles essential in normal coagulation. The loss of life risked in the Jewish rite, with its early operation and impure manner of occlusion, was said to be high, whereas Moslem circumcision, when executed before puberty under comparatively sanitary conditions, caused few fatalities from paroxysm, hemorrhage, or infection.

Mutilation after puberty was dangerous in hot moist climes, where bacteria thrived rampant. Consequently it was infrequent save in cases of punishment or forced conversion. It was not required of proselytes, and those who insisted upon the operation generally suffered for it. Enacted prior to sexual awakening, however, there was scarcely the fear of harrowing involuntary erections tearing the sutures, causing suppuration, bleeding, rawness, and genital disfigurement, and accompanying damage to the patient's mind and nervous system.

Not as essential nor practical in northern climes and amongst civilized people, the virtues of prepubescent circumcision were many in the squalid East. Accurate circumcision facilitated cleanliness, the supreme prophylactic, and in many cases stayed the individual from intemperate excesses.

But the original design of circumcision, that of blood covenant, was soon forgotten, and the motive of cleanliness was replaced by apathy or sensual gratification. *"Inshallah-Te'auleh,* yah Khwaudjeh," exclaimed an eighteenth-century Egyptian to a young French convert in Napoleon's Army, "how does it feel to have thy precious hood removed? *Wehhyah-en-Nebee!* one cannot fully appreciate The Cut, adore the glories of El-Islam, unless he has been initiated at a later moment in life. How can an innocent boy, mutilated ere pubescence, know the value of natural prolongation of pleasure if he has not at first endured the frustrating hypersensitivity that plagues the uncircumcised?"

Prior to circumcision, the young *motahir* (one who is without stain) was dressed as a girl and, in great honor, mounted upon a richly trapped donkey. Were he to be mutilated on the same day as a prince or the son of an official, his esteem would be even greater and his gifts more lavish. So disposed, he was paraded through the narrow streets, accompanied by a raucous procession of family, friends, and musicians. All the while, for protection against the evil eye and so that harmful *jinn* might not enter his body and defile the consecrated ritual, he scrupulously covered his mouth, nose, ears and all other bodily orifices with heavy shawls. The Omnipresent Eye also accounted for his feminine attire.

Arriving at the establishment of the barber (*mezeyyin*) or physician (*hhekeem*), he was taken down from the donkey and borne upstairs by his male relatives. All females were barred from the hallowed ceremony. Stripped naked, he—sweating profusely—was laid upon a divan spread with white sheets; and, when ready, the surgeon came forward to amputate.

A true and lucid description of the general operation is given in the *Dictionary of Islam:*

> A bit of stick is used as a probe, and car-
> ried round and round between the glans and
> prepuce, to ascertain the exact extent of the
> frenum and that no unnatural adhesions exist.
> The foreskin is then drawn forwards and a pair
> of forceps—consisting of a couple of pieces of
> split bamboo, five or six inches long and a
> quarter of an inch thick, tied firmly together at
> one end with a string to the extent of an inch—
> applied from above in an oblique direction, so as
> to exclude about an inch and a half of the
> prepuce above and three-quarters of an inch be-
> low. The forceps severely grasping it causes a
> good deal of pain; but this state of suffering does
> not continue long, since the next thing to be
> done is the removal: which is done by one stroke
> of the razor drawn directly downwards. The
> hemorrhage which follows is inconsiderable and
> easily stopped by the application of burnt rags
> and ashes.

In some areas, especially among the Turks and
Egyptians, only a diminutive portion of the foreskin was
removed, leaving the glans covered though unhooded.
The purpose of this merely partial circumcision was to
preserve acute sensibility in the organ, yet observe religious ordinance. It was much despised by the Arabs,
who looked upon all Turks (*Toorks*) and Egyptians
as unclean for that, among other reasons.

In southern India, *ma'ajoon,* an intoxicating compound of hemp, milk, ghee (melted butter), poppy
seeds, datura (a plant yielding atropine and other
drugs), and sugar was employed in circumcision. Producing pleasurable stupefaction and causing the penis
to swell, it made the ceremony considerably easier and
preserved much of the foreskin. Tippoo Sultaun, the
Tiger of Mysore, practiced this method on captive Europeans to make certain that they survived and, by im-
proper mutilation, to brand them as only partially
cleansed, quasi-Mohammedans.

As in Biblical days, the slashed prepuces of the

Unbelievers, heaped into mounds following a great battle, were held as trophies of victory in the more illustrious days of El-Islam. In accordance with the rigid martial code of the Moghul Empire, a warrior rose in rank according to the number of foreskins (like scalps, heads, or entire genitals among other tribes) he brought in from the field. Some boasted of as many as a thousand. Later, when this custom ceased, captive Gentoos (Hindoos) were tortured by infibulation or artificial phimosis (*mohree,* muzzling), elongation of the prepuce, and constriction of the orifice, so that the glans of the penis could not be uncovered.

In *mohree,* the long prepuce common to many Eastern races was either sewn or cauterized over the glans, preventing growth in the child and erection in the adult. In dealing with Hindoo women captives, the Moghul conquerors chiefly resorted to the simple process of sewing up the vulva. Other practices involved mutilation of the uterus by means of iron prongs, searing of the breasts, declitorization, or labial excision. Following forceful circumcision and defilement, defiant Hindoo prisoners were accustomed to use weights and liniments in order that they might stretch and protract the skin to well-nigh its normal state. Were they caught in this, subincision, urethral splitting all the way to the scrotum was the general punishment, rendering them sterile and useless.

It was a popular Hindoo belief that circumcision not only destroyed sensitivity and induced impotence, but that it prevented desirable enlargement of the penial shaft—not only in erection and congress, but in normal bodily growth. Brahmin erotologists and physicians based their belief upon comparison of Semite genitories to those of Hindoo and Negroid groups. Retraction of the penis in quiescence was looked upon as indicative of sterility; whereas an organ that remained in a smooth, broad, suspended state was considered to be one quick to attain length and stiffness.

In some parts of Arabia, the bridegroom might be circumcised during the nuptials. This ceremony, which the bride carried out, involved utter flaying of the penis, prepuce and integumental tissue being literally torn from the penial shaft, leaving it with the appearance of a skinned eel. The sacrificial blood was sprinkled upon the bride's raiments. Admission of any pain whatever prompted a faithful but austere bride to denounce her groom as being less than a man. And if she could not thus accuse him during the circumcision, she generally had occasion to do so later that evening; for, in his wounded condition, the groom was called upon to procure firm erection and penetrate his virgin wife, however painful, however seemingly impossible. And many a brave man, withstanding the mutilation, did not endure the fateful wedding night in a state of consciousness despite the old Arab proverb: "There is healing in the vagina of woman."

A similar amputation at puberty was performed in the province of El-Eseer, lying directly south of the Hejaz. Lads from ten to twelve proved themselves men by submitting to *es-selkh* (the rite of scarification). Standing before the *hakeem*, the boy gripped firmly in his right hand a spear, with the butt resting upon his foot. This was done so that the point of the spear would reveal the slightest tremor. Men and other youths of the tribe surrounded him to judge his fortitude. The spear was not to move an inch. As the barber held a razor-edged *gembeeyeh* (dagger) in anticipation, the lad said: "Cut, thou, and fear not!" Thereupon, the *hakeem* knelt; the youth endured shallow incisions below the navel and down each groin, the epidermis and pubic hair being removed, then a swift flaying of penis and testes, in which the foreskin and integumental flesh were rent away in a succession of no less than six expert cuts. At the finish, the mutilated lad sighed: *"Ullah-o-ukber!"* (God is great) and staggered out of the circle. The further he walked before collapsing, the greater man he was deemed, worthy of the respect due any youth thus ceremonially purified. Upon his swooning, salt and heated sand were applied as styptics; the lad was buried to the waist in a fresh dunghill and fed on goat's milk for about a week. This ordeal was sometimes fatal. *Es-selkh* is often practiced even today.

As a prisoner in the Mysorean dungeons of Savendroog, Colonel Sir David Baird, a prominent Scottish officer of the 71st Highland Light Infantry serving in the war against Tippoo Sahib, was thus mutilated with many other Europeans. He watched not a few young subalterns bleed to death.

Baird and the others were seized by burly Abyssinian slaves, stripped naked, and tied to the ground, their limbs splayed wide. A lean white-bearded surgeon regarded each of them for a second or two and, with thin precise fingers, determined the extent of each prepuce.

"Praise be to God! thou art now to receive the ordinance of *El-Khutneh,* creating thee all True Believers."

The victims shut their eyes. *Hubshees* forced open their mouths, introducing astringent *ma'ajoon.* The frail old surgeon, with ratlike eyes, waited patiently. Then:

"Bismillahee-ur-Ruhmaun-ur-Ruheem!" (In the name of God the Compassionate and Merciful.)

As soon as the drug had taken effect, each victim, young and old, experienced masochistic stimulation. He grit his teeth, clenched his fists; the muscles tightened in his thighs, and the moment came.

"Uluzzmut-o-lillahee! Ulhhumd-o-lillahee!" (Great is God; God be praised.)

Working as on an assembly line, the *hakeem* seized and clamped organs, one after the other. The razor flashed once for each victim. Bleeding was stanched with hot oil, the wounds anointed with viscid balms. Vague through the numbness, they could sense the pincers being removed, the skin retracting. Their mutilated rings of flesh were then offered to the fire, as libation to Allah.

Destroying the amputated prepuce (*ghelauf,* sheath) was an essential practice in averting the evil eye. The Turks usually buried it for fear that some ungodly being or ghoul should obtain it, murmur incantations over it, and thereby disfigure the penis or cause the testicles to swell (orchitis). Thus, a house containing an unburied foreskin was believed to be doomed to the curse of sexual impotence. Notwithstanding, among Hindees and Persians, the prepuce was carried as a charm, either worn encased about the neck or tied to the male organ. This served to protect the boy until his penis was thoroughly healed. It is also recorded that barren Persian women were wont to eat the foreskins of freshly mutilated *motahirs*.

King Yoohenneh (John) of Abyssinia, notorious for cruelty, forced ill-fated guests not of his faith to change their religion, the conversion requiring circumcision. In accordance with the Book of Genesis, the rite was performed with a sharp stone or piece of flint, merely requiring the motions of grasp and slice. In this case, as a barbarous addition, the victim was made to swallow his own prepuce. To the orthodox Mohammedan this procedure involved instant defilement, since the foreskin and blood lost in circumcision were considered sinful and thus called for sacrificial obliteration. Swallowing the prepuce was as heinous to the Moslem as the ingestion of cow flesh to the righteous Hindoo; but King John, a descendant of Solomon and the Queen of Sheba, was, according to Gordon Pasha, "of the strictest sect of the Pharisees; drunk every night, at dawn he is up reading the Psalms."[1]

2. Female

In ancient Arab tradition a woman was regarded impure unless declitorized; and no respectable man would accept her in marriage until thus consecrated. *Ibn-el-bezzreh* (son of an uncircumcised mother) was a stock expression of scorn hurled at one; and its scandalous connotation of sapphism was equaled by other obscene ejaculations: *O thou biter and licker of thy mother's enlarged clitoris; O heathen sucker of thy sister's overgrown uncircumcised clitoris;* and *O thou son of a she-circumciser*.

But later, as Turko-Syrian corruption overspread the East, much more out of jealousy than desire for purity did the Arab circumcise his women. The operation lost its sacramental significance. *El-khutneh*, like

----

[1] Lord Godfrey Elton, *General Gordon*.

other ancient religious institutions, degenerated to a materialistic practice, generally serving selfish pleasure. Less endowed than the huge-membered Turk or Negro, the Arab felt that by mutilation his female would be more easily satisfied and less given over to wantonness. But he was often mistaken. Owing to the destruction of delicate sensitivity and erectile tissue found in the clitoris and labia pleasurable sensation was concentrated in the vagina. Therefore it often required large male organs to gratify the woman who thus became more lustful than before, seeking men with organs of the size necessary to produce sufficient vaginal friction.

In warm, humid lands, the female pudenda were singularly developed. The abnormal size and hyperesthesia of the clitoris (*zemboor*) necessitated its excision in prepubescent girlhood. Following clitoridectomy (*tebzeer*), the exterior feminine sensibility was of course restricted to the nymphae (minor lips of the vulva). But no two people made a more rational, loyal, and happily wedded pair than the circumcised Arab lad and the declitorised Arab lassie. The matter of size and its demand arose only when there was abnormality of passion and excessive nerve-esthesia, an indication, among other things, of acquired or hereditary neurosis.

Hence in this case female circumcision, rather than allaying, only increased lasciviousness. The deprived woman, sheared of her proud organs, unknowingly craved twice as much and selfishly demanded the largest male member for that complete gratification which she never attained. In contrast, the woman who retains all her parts, each capable of thrilling sensation, does not require size or girth, and is quickly brought to a succession of strong orgasms. But Arab theologians, surgeons, and eroticists, misconceiving feminine disposition, never realized that female circumcision, though reducing the physical area of prurience, caused something far worse: *mental nymphomania*. The Jews, from whom the Moslems adopted Blood Covenant, never mutilated their women, obviously realizing its danger to many individuals. The Arab resort to female circumcision resulted in disaster.

An Abyssinian woman whose clitoris and internal

labia were brutally removed did not necessarily desire intercourse, but would suffer a peculiar masochistic depravity of the mind. She could never really enjoy fleshly congress. Being a loyal wife, she would yield to bear offspring or, if a prostitute, she would yield for money. But another, rendered perverse, would pimp and procure, regulate sexual orgies, and delight in every type of pornography and obscene exhibitions. She would prove vicious and unrelenting every day of her life. Even the familiar union of two goats in a pasture must thrill her inconceivably. She might even marry or consort with eunuchs and other women, practicing inordinate homo- and heterosexual acts. Even animals appealed to her.

In the prepubescent girl the nymphae or labia minora (*sheffa'if-ezzugheyyereen,* little lips) were generally thick and fleshy: about an inch in length. At womanhood, at some time between fourteen and twenty years of age, the excrescence, resembling a turkey's appendage, might attain the length of four inches. In a fully developed female the clitoris and nymphae when in erection might become as conspicuous and measurable as a man's genitals.

Among several Negroid tribes, including those of the Egyptian Sudan, this morbid hypertrophy of the lesser lips of the vulva was greatly admired. But the Egypto-Arabs deemed it indecent and excised the nymphae to restrict erections in their women. It also reduced the prevalence of female masturbation and uncontrollable friction of the clitoris, which enlarged its growth and induced sexual morbidity.

The rite of *el-gellem* (nymphotomy) was performed in the Sudan by an elder matron (*sheykheh*) of the tribe or, in Egypt, by a she-circumciser (*dahireh*) who, like a beggar-woman, would roam the streets of Cairo shrilling: *"Yah dahireh! dahireh! meen lauzim-ed-dahireh?"* (Circumciser! circumciser! who wants a circumciser?)

The process of *el-gellem* comprised three deft slices of the razor, in which the labia and clitorial head were amputated; the wound was then anointed and sewn with a pack-needle (*miselleh*) and sheepskin thread. In some areas, a tube or thin hollow reed was inserted for the passage of urine. Many an Arab gallant in Aden beheld the scars of coarse mending on lissome Somalee prostitutes, who would not yield to a man whose privy member was anything less than wrist-thick.

IV

AUTOEROTISM:
Sterile Pleasures

1. DEMONKIND

Just as Moslem men and women believed that *jinnees* and *jinneeyehs* (good and evil spirits) invade the human body at night, superstitious Hindoos acknowledged the nocturnal power of *raukshehs* and *pishauchees* (male and female demons capable of conjuring a wet dream). This belief derived its strength from the rich Hindoo imgination, from the anxiety over potency prevalent in the East, and from the effects of climate, highly seasoned foods, and a generally sensual environment.

In Arabic, the term for demonic possession is *rekibbeh-b'jinn* (ridden by supernatural spirits). To one who has had intercourse with *jinn,* the appellation *Ta'areefeh* (noteworthy) is bestowed, particularly if the individual has just arrived at puberty (*bulooghee-yeh*) or, being older, greatly enjoys his chaste method of gratification.

Er-Roohaunee (spiritual magic) involves a study of incubi and succubi, the experts of which were a multitudinous species of sorcerers and holy men, weird celibates who copulated with all manner of metaphysical beings. In order to receive the homage of good and evil spirits, Egyptian *sahhirs* (conjurers) employed various drugs, among them hasheesh, which evoked a supposedly sanctified excitation, and thereby prepared them for the imminent union with the supernatural being.

The Bhang-eaters of India were a notorious sort, generally Thugs and *dacoits* (robbers), who might not only strangle and rob an unwary traveler, but might defile him with urine and faeces, in true sadistic character. In their unchecked drug addiction they were rarely to be seen in a normal state. Their condition of narcotic inebriation (*keyf*) often culminated in hysteria. In some cases it led to humorous incidents. A familiar Arab tale relates of a hemp-eater (*hheshaush*) who, going into the bath for a shampoo, sank into inebrious sleep while awaiting the masseur. In his dreams he imagined himself setting a beautiful woman between his thighs; but, just as he was about to weigh down upon her, he awoke abruptly. He was surrounded by laughing spectators. The towel had slipped from his waist, and he perceived that his membrum virile was at stand. More infuriated than ashamed, he growled hazily: "Would thou hadst waited till I put it in!" and nonchalantly turned over to resume his dream.[1]

Moslems, being highly emotional, despite their outwardly fatalistic temperament, could develop insane jealousy if they suspected their phantom lovers of inconstancy. Men accustomed to wet dreams or, as they imagined, supernatural amorous visitations, slept naked to avoid contamination of their clothing. When young and proud they rarely disclosed the sensations of their encounter. One, however, an ascetic mystic, described how he had kept up a lively affair with a *jinneeyeh* for over forty years. Not a few eccentric youths, finding the relationship agreeable, delayed marriage to prolong their nocturnal affairs with the amo-

---

[1]Sir Richard F. Burton, *The Book of the Thousand Nights and a Night.*

rous spirits. Nevertheless, a goodly portion did not allow matrimony to hamper them; they were quite virile enough to manage women and succubi with remarkable equality!

Among females, voracious incubi made for heated conversation in the bath-house. Some professed disappointment, others complained of utter exhaustion. Not a few remarked that the black *jinn*-semen caused an icy feeling in the womb. A young lady coyly but fretfully inquired if she could possibly become impregnated by spirits. M'lady was relieved to learn that *jinn* propagated their own kind, by stealing the seed (*nutfeh*) of living men, and that the cold fluid which entered her matrix was a sterile substance. But this explanation left much to be desired. Another pert lass, feeling certain that she could allay the virginal fears of all and provide a general answer to every question, proudly asserted that, in spite of her frequent nocturnal bouts with virile *jinn,* she had still retained her sacred hymeneal membrane.

An incident that helped to provoke a public massacre at Cabul in 1841 involved a troupe of very real incubi. When the bleak November day had ended, what was left of the Resident Commissioner, Sir Alexander Burnes, hung in shreds from the trees of his compound, his head being paraded through the bazaars. Shah Shoojah, the pitiable puppet-king enthroned by the East India Company, was dragged naked from the palace, slashed between the thighs and thrown into a ditch to die. Many people, European and Afghan, guilty and innocent, fell by the sword.

It all occurred when a restless band of sepoys (native troops) and British infantrymen, aching for the company of women, managed to bribe or bundle away the drunken guards at the Ameer's palace. Invading the harem, they sought to charm the apparently lonely and male-starved concubines with their marvelous appearance. It being night, the women at first thought them to be *jinn,* as no man had ever gotten into the Ameer's seraglio heretofore. But this delusion evaporated when these *"jinn"* began to speak English and Hindostanee. With their romantic notions of harems, these unfortunate intruders did not realize feminine hatred for the male sex, which caged them like animals. Nor did they know that most harem women, owing to their imprisonment and vapid life, were of neurotic lesbian passion. None of the men escaped without having their precious scrotums torn out. This scandal was all the nationalists needed for an excuse to light the petard of rebellion against the invading infidel.

A prevalent belief among many was that, during the first ten days of El-Mohurrum (New Year Festival of the Sheeah sect), *jinn* appeared to men and women at night. A boy who experienced his first nocturnal emission during this sacred time was considered highly fortunate (*mehmood*). This tradition had universal acceptance. *Mehmoodee* involved a simple involuntary and therefore holy libation of seminal fluid, consecrated by the spiritual world, upon the magic and powerful nights of New Year. The 10th Mohurrum (*Yome-el-Asherreh*) was the most propitious. Upon this night, it was believed that youngsters of wealthy homes were circumcised by the *jinn*.

The supernatural realm was held in awe by nearly every Moslem. Before entering an enclosure of any kind, a superstitious Arab begged permission of the *jinn*. In their veneration for the Unknown manifested in the incomprehensible experiences of night, the superstitious world of El-Islam was ready to grant *jinn* the hallowed power of circumcision and coition (*duhoor w'jimmah*). It was therefore no insult for one admiringly to address a buxom Arab lady thus: "May God copulate with thee! may a thousand huge-membered virile *jinn* have carnal knowledge of thee!"

In judging the matter of nightly relations, inscrutable and therefore hallowed, and their effect upon imperative ceremonial cleanliness, Arab authorities wrote:

> Emissions of spermatozoa in nocturnal pollution or at the sight of a strange and beautiful woman are not held shameful, but commendable. The Jinn have power over the body at night; in the day, man is worthy if his system

would sacrifice in honor of beauty. And these occurrences, so common, do not violate the fast of Ramadhan as must willful acts like drinking and eating, deliberate swallowing of saliva, masturbation, and carnal copulation.

Ehhtiraum (veneration, respect) was the term used to designate the young Arab's initial wet dream as signalizing the advent of manhood. Nocturnal emission was common in those climates of sensuality, spiced by belief in *jinn,* and they persisted past puberty and even in marriage. All healthy Sudanese experienced it. And many Egypto-Arab youths, proud of their chastity, adopted the appellation *mohhtelim* or *mooteleem* (honored, respected: one having a wet dream, one subject to nocturnal discharge). *Bole-megh-roor gedheeb* (morning erection, or what Anglo-Indians called "urine-proud pizzle") was also common among Easterners, in view of their extensive consumption of liquids. In speaking of erotic dreams, the word *menee* (semen) was substituted in lieu of *bole,* the popular word for urine. Thus, the Oriental was no less affected by periodic spermatorrhea (*ayyed-el-gedheeb,* weeping penis) than the Occidental.

In India, all nocturnal illusions were classified under *maya* (appearance) a philosophical term enwreathing the supernatural. The wet dream (*svupnah*) was thought to be a product of the deity, therefore explained by the principle of *maya:* that which has no substance, is neither good nor bad, and is not to be interpreted or understood. A Brahmin who believes in *maya* holds that nothing in the world really exists, and that he himself is God.

Demoniacal possession (*loottus,* plundering—i.e., the virility and semen, influence of spirits), when placed within the realm of *maya,* becomes a mode of existence. Hence, to the adherent of the doctrine of *maya,* every individual falls into one or more classifications that are free of moral labels and dedicated to the sublime elevation of human pleasure. A man is, therefore, either a copulator, a masturbator, a sodomite, or a relisher of nocturnal emissions—or all four!

Hindoo women were subjected to a wide variety of gruesome incubi, *raukshehs, bhootums, preyts,* whilst the men were fortunate in dealing with only a few, the most horrendous of which being the *churreyl,* ghost of a woman who died in travail. The most voluptuous and beautiful of the succubi was the *yukshee,* a ravenous and enervating nymph who taxed a man to exhaustion. Her favorite prey was the lone traveler who camped beneath a tree, where Hindoos believed she commonly haunted; and, according to legend, the only person able to turn the tide and thrash a *yukshee* into fearful submission was the indomitably virile Kokah Pundit, an eroticist and minister-of-state in the eleventh century.

Rape, formidable in the West, was rare in Asian lands, except in the palace and highly congested areas, simply because of severity in punishment (castration, decapitation) and the inviolate respect shown to women and the sacred veil.

> There is no shame in being a thief, a rapist, a swindler—anything corrupt, lawless, immoral— as long as one is not caught.

So believed the Turks.

Moslems, drooling over the tempting aspect of virginal rape and the vigorous male organ in all its savage capacity, described the flagrancy as "a brutal dispassionate penetration, the veritable stimulation of a fire-iron, a ruthless drill, sharp, burning, spasmodic." And, sadistically, enjoyable.

Easterners accounted for rape by demoniac bewitchment. The evil *jinnee El-A'awer* (one-eyed, penis-genie), patron spirit of the ravisher, is said to have expounded:

> To rape a resisting wench is like trying to sheath a sword with an unsteady hand. If she faints, there be no life in her vitals. The art lies in directly arousing her by friction; clutching her firm but tenderly, hending thy prickle in hand and rubbing its head against her slit until it becomes moist and avid for penetration. Who is

the brutish, ignorant man? It is he who vainly bellows: "I will piss my tallow into thy womb, unrelenting! Note, thou, the ardor of ripe fruit when impaled by a vigorous thorn." Rape is glory and guileful conquest! It is estimable seduction, subtle enravishment—not the coarse antics of lowly beasts. Be brave, be artful—and be almighty!

In men, succubi accounted for impotence. An Egyptian, lamenting this imminent condition to the coffeeshop clique, would utter:

Alas! I am growing so exhausted, the day shall be soon that I can but abuse the rump of a beardless boy. Night after night, all manner of evil *jinn* haunt me for my infidelity. *Yah Ullah!* they have sapped me to despair. Gluttonous insatiable *ghoolehs* and *afreetehs*, deceiving me in nightmares of brutal ecstasy, seduce me and give indulgence to my evil whims. *Ghuddars* lure me into darkness, and there they ply my implement of lust. The Jinn of Sensuality, Zellemboor and El-A'awer, drench me in reeking liquors and drugs and ungodly potions. And now I frustrate myself on virgins, and my wives laugh me to scorn. Ye must not even touch my body, lest my pitiable tool rear up its head and pollute me. As a youth, it served me well; now it is treacherous and vulnerable, giving way to the least indulgent thought. And so I retaliate by offering it hatred and abuse. Every morning I apply ice-cold water to my parts, trusting that strength and virility will soon return; but alas, I waste day by day. All prescribed formulas are of little avail; I am doomed to the love of hairless youths and shameless men.

The galaxy of *jinn*, bearing the blame for impotence, was also the cause of satyriasis and nymphomania (*gerrebeh-shehweh*, prurient lust).

Arabs consider the vast majority of all Turks and Egyptian *fellaheen* to be born irrational, of high-strung, inharmonious temperament. Along the lines of march during the Sudanese campaigns they were to be seen running stark naked in the blazing desert, screaming like banshees and clawing and beating their flesh. They came to believe that the sun meant to convert them into feeble women, by sapping their strength and causing their sexual apparatus to atrophy. The Arabs too believed this: man's being unsexed by the Desert. To be lost in the desert meant that one became sapless and dehydrated, mummified to a leathery pulp. Nothing mattered and death was welcome. Few ever recovered from the experience. It was monstrous to conceive, much less fully understand.

The Turk, in Arab opinion the embodiment of *jinn*-borne satyriasis and psychosis, was accustomed to crowded streets and dim alleyways. When he struck blistering wasteland, he disintegrated. Nevertheless, as before mentioned, it has been asserted, but as mere conjecture when regarding Turks as a whole, that a definite strain of atavistic emotionalism augmented this physical weakness.[2]

To the Turk, history tells us, there was nothing genteel or refined about sex. Whenever and wherever the impulse struck him, the average Turk did not hesitate to react. *Jinn* swarmed in his brain, his breast, his loins, his swollen penis, and tremorous testes. He sought release within the moment of demand. Not a few, unhinged with passion, slashed their bodies or, to defy nature and sacrifice the hateful flesh, castrated themselves. Masturbation, often practiced twice daily, was designed systematically to purge the body of evil spirits. Hence, self-relief assumed a ritualistic duty comparable to belching, coughing, sneezing, vomiting, answering the calls of nature, and breaking wind.

At the slightest provocation, upon grief or joyous excitation, the susceptible Egyptian or Turk ripped his garments, marred his flesh, and experienced sharp and often unacknowledged orgasms. The sight of running blood drove him to greater cruelty and pleasure, bred out of anguish.

Their women, like many among the southern Hindoos, often required mental and physical torment be-

---

[2] Burton and others.

fore they could respond. The Turks generally took them by the hair, rending them tooth and nail, mounting them like curs in heat, and then cudgeling until one or both of them fainted away. During the Crimean War, a Turkish prostitute naked and bleeding from self-inflicted wounds raged through an entire regiment of Bashi-Bazouks, then ripped open her womb because passion could not be sated in a moment of demoniac need. The Bazouks as a rule shot such a woman down like any rabid dog in periodic rut. However, in the case of men known as *welees* (saints) running sexually amuck, the Bazouks were by custom obliged to unfasten their cummerbunds and brace for the onset.

Any European woman having the ill fortune of being captured by the Turks was in for a shocking surprise. She suffered the violence of men whose emotions were primitive, whose pride in manhood lay in gross brutality. The pasha looked upon his virile limb as a sturdy spear that jabs and thrusts unmercifully. The man of shame was one who could not satisfy a woman until she swooned or supplicated mercy. Individuals were daily stoned out of the Street of Fornication for their strength in tongue but instability of body.

2. Masturbation

Krishna, Pan and Narcissus of India, was in ancient Hindoo mythology God of Self-contemplation. The symbol of autoerotism, Lord Krishna became the favorite of Hindoo youth. His practice, *hautrus* (manual orgasm), regarded among early Greeks and Romans as being devised by Hermes and Mercury, was deified as ritualistic.

Women of the Sheyveh and Veyshnuvee sects, worshiping the female principle (*yoni*), stimulated the clitoris (*muddun-chutree,* passion-umbrella) and labia in emulation of the maternal goddess Shuktee. Shuktee's symbol was a huge black stone, the *shaulgraumeh,* with a yawning cleft. In seeking to emulate the magnitude and strength of Shuktee's pudendum, Hindoo girls methodically masturbated. Forming a circle, like certain African tribes who regarded genital hypertrophy as an indication of beauty, women and girls kneaded, stroked, and pulled the labia and clitoris, exercising the muscles and delicate tissue, and seeking enlargement of the erogenous areas. Others in the temple rubbed their vulvae upon the *lingam* stone and prayed for maternal power.

Male youths also indulged rhythmically in the practice. From the cradle they recognized its pacifying qualities, as much a relief as passing water or evacuating. Their purpose was to achieve thickness and smooth suspension of the organ in emulation of Lord Shiva. The popular technique was known as *mudhun* (churning) and involved rotative agitation with open palms. A Hindoo enamored of this diversion was therefore styled *mudholeah;* his feminine counterpart, proud of her large pudendum and small breasts, was called *mudholee*.

The comparative truth of love being free throughout Hindostan bears little connection to the lack or prevalence of self-relief amid Hindoo peoples. It was more a question of what offered man and woman the most gratification. A woman's greatest pleasure lies in the clitoris; a man's in the frenum preputium of the penis, the fold of skin connecting the glans with the prepuce. Hence mutual stimulation of these parts by male and female, evoking acute sensations not experienced in coitus, was relished extensively. So for the Hindoos masturbation (and often fellatio) was esteemed far above genital intercourse, particularly in cases of incompatibility of genital size. Oriental man, wont to enjoy and quickly respond to vigorous friction, could not always adapt himself to the large, velvety vagina of a woman. Seeking to remedy this, Brahmin erotologists, like those of venerable Greece, made a science of prolonging tumescence and deferring orgasm. They taught man artfully to prolong pleasure for a half hour or more, avoiding all haste and thereby conditioning himself for harmonious wedlock. Only Hindoo women of the north, known for their frustrating impassiveness, were advised to stimulate the clitoris and thus realize the delight of successive orgasms.

In Egypt, the technique of massaging and squeezing the penis (*ferrek, firk*—stroking, churning—*bil'eed*, with the hand) and that of exciting the clitoris and labia (*meshh, sehhk:* rubbing) were imported from Turkey, Syria, and Persia where, respectively, autoerotism is called *istimneybilyet* (the practice of self-control of the stalk), *keyyiseh-el-'ezzeb* (penial rubbing), and *maulish-e-zubb* (shampooing the cord) or *dustee* (hand custom).

Throughout the Orient, where a strict moral code was imposed on the youth of both sexes, masturbation was just as prevalent as in Western lands, if not more so. In China and Japan it replaced or augmented extensive homosexuality; in Hindostan, it formed a part of religious observance and personal pride. In Arabia, where a boy might not be permitted to gaze upon a feminine countenance from the time he was weaned until he accepted a stranger in prearranged wedlock, masturbation (*zelleg, sehhauk*) served to allay desire. It was taught by *sheykhehs* and eunuchs in the harem, practiced extensively in early years, occasionally abandoned at puberty, and resumed, in mutual indulgence with hetero- or homosexual partners, during marriage and in later life.

In Persia the vulgar term for self-relief was *julk;* in the attempt to discourage it a brutal form of circumcision was sometimes employed—removing the entire preputial sheath. But the habit was usually replaced by fellatio or techniques stimulative of the glans.

Amongst some Turanians (nomadic tribes living in cold, elevated Asian climes) excitation in youth was cultivated as part of the sexual practices of a brotherhood. The Cossacks also were known from earliest years to handle unconsciously their secret parts, habits passed upon them by their elders, who thereby soothed them when in the cradle. When on forays with their women out of reach, they effected sexual relief among themselves, achieving greater joy from artful and prolonged manipulation, which systematically excited the most sensitive area, than in intercourse with women. In fact, they were thoroughly potent and responsive beneath a skilled hand, having from infancy identified sexual pleasure with masturbation alone. Women were comparatively tasteless and unattractive to them, often leaving them unsatisfied. They were used merely for toil and breeding. And centuries of this sort of treatment and philosophy rendered them cold and impassive.

Hence masturbation, thought by many European sexologists[3] to be a primarily Occidental practice, was in truth as normal and endemic in the Orient. The prime difference is that Easterners, because of psychological, physical, environmental, and climatic factors, adopted the custom rather early and responded favorably to it throughout life. In the West it is ordinarily regarded as a regressive practice characteristic of the adolescent stage, occasionally learned but unsanctioned prior to that stage. In the East custom demanded that masturbation (designed to preserve intersexual chastity) should be made a science and cultivated during early childhood or even infancy. Whether it leads to excess and impairment of health depends upon individual temperament and physiology.

---

[3]Foremost among them Paolo Mantegazza, who chose to stigmatize western men as a "race of masturbators."

V

FEMALE PROSTITUTION:
Luxurious Custom

And they committed whoredoms in Egypt; they committed whoredoms in their youth. There were their breasts pressed, and there they bruised the teats of their virginity.

1. PURPLE AND INCENSE

Long before the time of Aholah and Aholibah and of the reproof of their iniquities and the judgments upon them, the oldest profession in the world claimed holy eminence. The prostitute wore the laurels of womankind, for hers was an ancient and honorable position. She was sought after while other women were merely chattels. Educated, mature, and astute, she jealously held her superior rank. As priestess she sometimes stood next to the ruler of the land and might exceed ministers and generals in influence over him.

Among the greatest women in history were those who won power through their sexual prowess, whether as queens or courtesans. They were also usually famous for their shrewdness and wit. Cleopatra, the Serpent of the Nile, was said sometimes to have enjoyed the passionate assaults of over a hundred men in one night. And she could make sex a part of canny diplomacy, as Caesar came to realize.

In the East, men and women who earned their living horizontally often enjoyed esteem. They were invited to weddings, feasts, and public affairs. Particularly in India, the courtesan was associated with purity and respect. She was held to exert a potent charm against the evil eye. She, supreme mistress of the sacred science of copulatory gymnastics, became the envy of all.

Prostitution was not forbidden because it swelled the public revenue, kept officials and priests in prosperity, reduced fornication and adultery, and, because of its religious origin, retained a consecrated aspect. In several countries it became legalized under governmental control. In Japan the redlight districts, housing the Yoshiwara for licensed prostitutes, were handsome sections. Geishas, women trained to entertain men with music, dance, and intellectual conversation, rivaled the hetairas of ancient Greece and the courtesans of the Renaissance. Male prostitutes, depilated and perfumed, were elegant dancers and balladiers.

2. THE MOSLEMS

To the Arab, joyance lay in three things: *eating meat, riding meat, and putting meat into meat*. The Queen of Night, whose favorite offerings were ambergris'd coffee, a silver hookah, and wine, was honored above all women. "Glory be to Him Who created and fashioned them out of vile water!" said one young Arab scholar who, after a year of reflective abstinence, condescended to relish the deftness of a famous courtesan. In describing the evening, the young man said:

The lady was crowned with a diadem of pearls and jewels, her face dotted with artificial moles in indigo, her eyebrows penciled with kohl, and her hands and feet reddened with henna. When I looked on her, I well-nigh bepissed my bag-trousers for the excess of her beauty and loveliness.

When she saw me, she smiled and took me into her embrace and clasped me to her breast. Then, she put her mouth to mine and sucked my tongue; and I did likewise. Then, we fell to toying and groping and kissing and dallying.

Straining me to her bosom, she threw me to the floor; then, she sat astraddle upon my breast and kneaded my belly with her fingers, till I well-nigh lost my senses. And she said to me:

"My life on thee! harken to me: look upon the narcissus and the tender down thereon, and enjoy the sight of naked waist and navel, and touzle me and tumble me, from this moment till break of day."

She opened the bosom of my shirt, and bent over me and kissed me, and put forth her hand to me: pressing my breast. And, because of the smoothness of my body, it slipped down to my waist, and thence to my navel, and thence to my yard; whereupon, her heart ached and her vitals quivered and lust was sore upon her. And mad for me, she stripped my body and left none of me unkissed and unfondled.

"By God! no male hast ever filled mine eyes but thyself," she whispered; and she gripped me, with supple limbs, as a python must seize and clasp its victim. And taking in hand my prickle, firm to the utmost of its height, she nailed it into her coynte.[1]

Another Arab, claiming more experience and relating of the same courtesan, wrote:

Clasping her to my bosom, I sucked first her upper lip and then her under lip, and slid my tongue between the twain, into her mouth. Then I rose to her, and had of her amorous delight. I rained upon her cheeks kisses like the falling

---

[1] Sir Richard F. Burton, *The Book of the Thousand Nights and a Night.*

of pebbles into water, and struck with stroke
upon stroke, like the thrusting of spears in battle
brunt, for that she still yearned after clipping of
necks and sucking of lips and gripping of tress
and pressing of waist and biting of cheek and
cavalcading on breasts with Cairene buckings and
Abyssinian wrigglings and Persian sobbings and
Syrian nibblings and Nubian lasciviousness and
Hindoo leg-lifting and Bedewween moanings and
Turkish hotness and Alexandrian languishment.[2]

The women of Egypt flattered themselves that
their *ghoonj* (manner of swinging the buttocks, or passionate gymnastics in coition) was superior to that of
all other females in the world. *Ghoonj* was nothing less
than art, an essential phase of harem training; for to
please the male was woman's greatest honor. According to Burton, "in China (as in Egypt and India) there
are professors, mostly old women, who instruct young
girls in this branch of the gymnastic." Those who perfected *ghoonj* to a science made the most celebrated
harlots. Men journeyed miles, tendered fabulous sums,
to gain their favors.

A peculiar variety of uncircumcised Abyssinian
women, known in the Sudan as *hhelaubehs* (milkers)
and to the north as *kebbauzehs* (holders), were out-
standing for their erectile powers. In Egypt they were
famous and much prized for their *ghoonj*, especially
among wealthy Arabs and Turks, who paid dearly for
them. It was their custom to sit astride a man in venereal congress, and they were capable of provoking orgasm by tightening upon and releasing the penis
through singular control of the sphincter vaginae or
constrictor cunni muscles. Sudanese Negroes derived the
utmost pleasure from it; for it engendered an almost
unbearable sensation and prolonged the act. Many
young Arabs sought such women in order that they
might enlarge the size of their parts, which this convulsive form of coition sought to achieve. In the harem
it was always employed in conjunction with fellatio.

----

[2]*Ibid.*

The promise of night is spread with butter that melteth upon daybreak.

Warm, scented darkness but accentuated the artifices of a subtle bona roba. Mohammed, skilled in feminine witchcraft, sought to warn the Faithful against its insidious charm. In speaking of fragrancy, he said: "Perfumes for men should have scent and not color; for women, they should have color and not scent." His fastidious aversion to feminine fashion also prompted him to declare that "silk was invented so that women could go naked in clothes."

But dress, atmosphere, and aroma bowed low before the sensuous liquid voice, the ripe lips, the doe-like eyes, and the soft stroking fingers: "Coolth of mine eyes—fruit of mine heart—O eyes of me!"

Unable to resist, the utterly overcome male gasped: "There is no majesty, no might, save in God the Glorious and Great!"

Then did they suck lips, till the "taste of blood was as forbidden wine"; and then did they clasp limbs, in heat of demoniac furor. Others, in pure Arab jocundity, portrayed the moment as one of "toying, joying, biting, handling, groping, fingering, bussing, and bosoming, and playing the close-buttock game."[3]

Many courtesans, so enravishingly cunning in the technique of provoking in the male a furious orgasm, held a small musk'd pillow for him to seize in his teeth lest, in the crisis, he rend or mar their bland olive flesh. For once the artful harlot closed her thighs, springing the ecstatic trap, it was do or die!

Unsteadiness of gait, after the pains and pleasures of night, was the man's sign of satisfaction. The harlot's came on receiving her gold, when the wearied male sighed, jestingly: *"Heddullah-o-beynee w'beynekum!"* (God draw the line between me and thee.)

Following coition, *ghusl* (total ablution) was in order. For this purpose every brothel was equipped with a bathhouse. A popular saying was: "The *ghusl*-ablu-

---

[3] *Ibid.*

tion or one's feet"; meaning: *Wash thoroughly after lying with a woman, or no horse worth its salt will permit you to mount it.* Many an Arab came to verify the apparent truth in this adage when he encountered difficulty with his steed.

El-mendeel (handkerchief) was carried by all traveling women who, where there was no water, used it to wipe away the ooze of copulation. For the majority of Eastern women, highly sexed, experienced in orgasm a definite discharge of lubricating mucus from the vagina. Hence the pollution of clothing following copulation was just as prevalent among women as men.

Male wayfarers having no access to water would to avoid defiling their raiment rub fine pure sand upon their members until all viscid matter had disappeared.

In regard to the time and place granted fornication, there was a familiar set of rules:

> Have no connection with woman in the bath, for its consequence is palsy; nor do thou lie with her when thou art full or when thou art empty, nor when thou art drunken with wine, nor when thou art in wrath, nor when lying on thy side, nor when thou art under a fruit-bearing tree, for that it occasioneth swelling of the testicles. And avoid carnal knowledge of an old woman, for that she taketh from thee and giveth not to thee.

Youths in Egypt sometimes managed to gain entrance to the *hhemmaum* (hot bath) when ladies and girls were there bathing. They did so by impersonating eunuchs, having mastered the device of retracting the scrotum. For that purpose they applied cold stimuli, hot water, and steady frication of the testes, or methodically rubbed the inner thighs, inducing the cremaster muscle to contract the scrotum. Feeling that they would thereby reduce weight and facilitate contraction, youths on the previous night often masturbated until all their seminal fluid was exhausted. If by accident the testes decended, the fun was over, as the gouging fingernails of vicious matrons came into play. But if the ladies were young, innocent, and curious, a showing of

scrotums and several impressive erections brought a
merely momentary stir of fright and indignation. Thereafter, looks of fear or annoyance gave way to smiles.
Thoroughly depraved in mind, the ladies fell to teasing
and dallying. Yet the real eunuchs, insanely jealous of
virility, generally allowed nothing more than a little
oral or manual diversion, which was often the extent
of their harem pleasures. Soon, as occurred in ancient
Rome, the *hhemmaum* became a sink of assignation
and perversity (the lair of tribades, fellatrices, and
prostitutes). This certainly led the practical Prophet to
declare: "Whatever woman enters a bath, the devil is
with her."

Aside from numerous ergotic drugs, purgatives,
and mechanisms employed to effect abortion, courtesans
had in their possession many varieties of contraceptives. The India-rubber prophylactic, theoretically invented by a seventeenth-century Colonel Condom of
the Grenadier Guards, became an instant success
throughout the world. Among its sundry appellations
were French letter (*mektoob-el-Frensauweeyeh*), English capote (*kebboo-el-Ingleeze*), a bad umbrella
(*shemseeyeh*) that a storm can break or burst, cuirasses
against pleasure, and cobwebs against infection.

Originally of *baudruche* (sheep's gut) and fashioned
by the individual, in Egypt it was known as *el-meseer*
or *mizraun*. Well lubricated, strong, and adhering like
caoutchouc, it caused no irritation, literally molding the
flesh as a sheath. In medieval times, long before the
elastic condom, it was the Arab's only protection
against syphilis. Young gallants and debauchees frequently wore them at all times, for quick performance.
Others, wont to relish the visitation of succubi, bound
them between their thighs ere retiring in order that
they might avoid befouling the sheets. Old and young,
suffering from hypersensitivity or chronic emission of
semen, spermatorrhea (*tegdeer*, distillation), had need
to protect their clothing by application of *el-meseer*.

With the French conquest of Algeria, condoms of
gum elastic were shipped from Paris to North Africa
where, upon embarkation, they sold in the matter of a

few heated moments. But later, toward the end of the nineteenth century, rubber condoms were manufactured in Cairo and Alexandria.

India was a ready market for aphrodisiacs and contraceptives. Soon it produced the European condom (*neyaum*) in large cities such as Lahore, Calcutta, and Bombay. Kurrachee, den of iniquity, led them all with the caoutchouc *ghilauf* (sheath). Used by wenchers and sodomists alike, the *ghilauf* aided in reducing the formidable prevalence of venereal disease (*zozauk*) that annually scourged the coastline.

Syphilis, blight of Egypt and the endemic disease in the Sudan, found its origin not in female prostitution but in the sodomy and fellatio of ancient Syria (*Esh-Shaum*). Thence it was transmitted to Greece and Rome, infecting the entire Mediterranean region, and gradually ate its way around the globe.

The Egyptians struggled with syphilis ever since the Pharaohs. Mummies have proved that. The Arab contracted it from Europe; hence, the term *hhebb-el-Feringhee* (corn of Europe). And the Sudanese contracted it from the Arab.

In modern Egypt the general cure was through sand baths and sulphuric unguents until the blessed appearance of mercurials (*zeybeg*). Notwithstanding, many compounds injected into the urethra or vagina as measures against syphilis usually ended in creating sterility. Consequently, every man who could afford them purchased condoms and took especial care of his genitals, guarding them against abrasion, and before penetrating vagina or anus, he saw that his member was well lubricated against dangerous friction. The circumcised especially were vulnerable to infection.

Et-Tertoosheh of Alexandria and El-Hhoshe-Derbek of Cairo were the prominent quarters of prostitution in Egypt, analogous to the famed Yoshiwara of Japanese cities.

El-Hhoshe-Derbek (Street of Thine Open Hall) was the headquarters of gypsies and related tribes dedicated to entertainment and harlotry. The best known of these were the *ghewwauzee*. The male dancers and musicians, called *ghauzees,* were notorious sodomites; and the women, *ghauzeeyehs,* danced and sang clothed only in *shinteyaun* (petticoat-trousers of tinted gauze). El-Feyyoom, the delta in Lower Egypt, was during spring and autumn festivities overspread with their multihued tents. Therein, amidst dim, inebrious luxury —cushions, water-pipes, viands, lithe young men and girls performed in the nude.

During private orgies, it was the custom of the host and his guests to retire directly after the general entertainment and, allowing the dancers some moments for rest and preparation, eagerly await them upstairs.

Egyptian whoredom reached its acme of professional organization with the triumphal appearance of the *aulimeh* (learned in the arts of pleasure). She, like her counterpart in India or Japan, was the perfection of educated and desirable womankind.

Famed as supercourtesans and dancing girls, the *aulimehs* were mistresses of diabolic temptation. Governed and instructed by a staff of *sheykhehs* or *mowaulimehs* (skilled matrons), *el-aulimehs* owed their allegiance to Mowaulideh (she who bringeth forth, the Supreme Procreatrix). They, in conjunction with similar societies of men, were dedicated to the propagation of the Faithful; and each yielded her body in the name of maternal energy to scores of men daily. Abortion was forbidden, punishable by death; the sacred honor of being an *aulimeh,* with its consequential life of pleasure and reproduction, was passed on by inheritance. The price laid upon her holy virginity was tremendous; and so long as she remained young and fertile, her word was command to all True Believers. In later years she abandoned prostitution and took up the wand of instruction and, in some cases, taught her own daughters or grandchildren the voluptuous sciences.

Other tribes of itinerant strumpets and effeminates, dealing with the poorer classes, haunted the streets of Cairo and Alexandria, blackmailing men into lying with them. Any place where European males and females consorted, balls, picnics, parties, was considered a business opportunity for harlots, male as well as female. Custom even permitted these gypsies, when others were rigidly prohibited, to enter the coffeehouses.

There, taking a young man unawares, a gypsy trollop slid into his lap, twined her ropy limbs about him, and indulged in an amorous liveliness known in Persia as *nauz-o-undauz* or *nauzee-noozee* (wanton coquetry). She proceeded to fondle him with keen, flashing fingers, missing no part of the body. Rubbing her clitoris against his thigh, she artfully incited his penis, squirming and wriggling, until he finally bought her off. This flagrant practice, gross to the most depraved Moslem and averse to all public propriety, soon became so abused and obnoxious that, to allow men to drink and converse in peace and save shops from becoming houses of assignation, the police intervened and forbade such antics. The first to complain were those who had defiled their clothes as a result of *nauzee-noozee*. Seminal fluid, impure to Moslem and Jew, belonged nowhere but in impure women's matrix; therefore, in love-play Moslems were often accustomed to perfect nakedness.

Increasing with Egyptian debauchery, the *sher-moodeh* or *sherdoodeh* (punk, piece, rag) became as celebrated as the most exquisite and cultured *aulimeh*. They were hired to perform, stark naked, in public houses; and it was the mode for fast youths to stick tiny gold coins on their perspiring bodies as they writhed near, then before they could move away, pluck them off. The girls sought to shake them from their flesh, the usual places being the forehead, cheeks, lips, breasts, stomach, thighs, and mons veneris. Just before the performance, one or two were always inserted between the labia, reserved for men of choice later to probe for with their tongues.

Prostitution, originally inherited and confined to a particular tribe or caste, soon ate its way into staid and respectable society. Promiscuity, the bane of Europe and America, exploded in the Moslem world. The oldest profession lost its sacred and honorable aspect. Every female who sold her body was termed *kehbeh* (whore), whether she were *aulimeh* or gypsy. But women of the higher classes, possessing greater environmental luxury, were styled *deleelehs* (temptresses).

The holiness of whoredom fled upon the advent of monotheism, which forbade the worship of all Venuses and Aphrodites, and the divine teachings of the Prophet who condemned *zinnah* (fornication) as an act of the Unbeliever. But shrewd and wealthy Egyptian ladies, on the pretense of harboring orphans from the evil eye until their beards began to sprout, gathered all young boys, grimy and tattered, from the streets of Cairo. They housed, clothed, and fed them handsomely and, at length, used them clandestinely as pimps and catamites. Their tiny rumps pleased the enlarged clitoris and their small penes stimulated the hyperesthetic labia. As procurers of men or as ganymedes rented to the coffeehouse, they proved excellent. Kept until puberty, they were sold outright. There was, of course, never any danger of impregnation.

In El-Hejaz province of Arabia, women and boys flocked outside Mecca (Mother, Pearl of Cities) and El-Medeeneh, clamoring to sell their bodies to the pilgrims who, sworn to rigid abstemiousness during the fervid Hadj (pilgrimage), were thereafter allowed to revel in the debauchery as their reward.

Many youths in Egypt and India learned to solicit and procure for profit as soon as they could walk. Women, some of the most respected families, threatened to strip themselves nude and then blackmail for attempted rape if a passing male refused to appease them. In Cairo, women were known to drag men to the nearest and darkest alleyway, open their gowns, seize the man's turgid organ and use it to fricate the oversized, morbidly sensitive clitoris and labia minora.

Concubinage, scarcely a deterrent to prostitution and, in fact, but a legalized, marital form of prostitution, swelled the corps of panders (eunuchs and *memlooks*). Society, well aware of what occurred within the palace, adopted an indifferent air to propriety and assumed the grossness of royalty.

The *deyyoose* (a man who pimps for his own wife and daughters) became a reputable person of business, especially in Egypt and Persia. *Ez-zoke* (hedonist, voluptuary) waxed as notorious as *el-faujireh* (whore); and pimp and bawd (*ars w'arseh*), hand in hand, often gained most of their employers' wealth. What they were not paid they stole, enjoying fornication and adding the charges to their masters' accounts.

Procuration soon became a powerful, interwoven institution with local politicians and magistrates as its leaders. The palms of the priests were greased. Presently, the *olemmah* (Moslem doctors of divinity) became professors of procuration and swam in filthy lucre. Respectable Egyptians who had previously fallen upon their knees and kissed the feet of one of the priesthood now addressed him thus: *"Selaumun-aleyk, yah Kewwaud-el-Kebeer!"* (Peace be unto thee, O Great Pander).

Islam like the empires of Greece and Rome had reached its nadir of depravity; and the nucleus, as since Biblical days, was unsavory Egypt (*Bilaud-Mezr,* land of abominations).

"O foulest of pimps! Fetus! abortion! O whoreson, dogson! baseborn and obscene-bred!" . . . "Ho! sons of whores, spawn of adultery and nurslings of abhorrence!" (Such was heard from dawn till dusk in the streets and on the rooftops of Cairo between rival organizations.)

> A dog—dog-fathered, by dog-grandsire issued—
>   no good a dog, from dog-race bred;
> E'en for a gnat, no resting-place gives he: who
>   is composed of seed by all men shed.

"O thou foulest of harlots and filthiest of whores ever futtered by Negro slaves, who are hired to have at thee!" was a common salutation addressed to an emulous sister; and irony refined to an art created such fast-spoken gems as *"Ullah-yeneek!"* (God copulate with thee) for *"Ullah-yehenneek!"* (God pleasure thee). Girls barely arrived at puberty were accosted with *"Ullah y'belleghek mugsoodek!"* (God grant thee thy desire) which bore a double entendre: meaning the girl could then gain a decent night's rest, having been relieved of the burden of maidenhead. The most courteous salutation offered frail sisterhood, *"Ne'ametullah!"* (blessings of God), was replaced by "Urine alighted upon dirt. *Welcome, my friend!*" "God favor thee!" became "God futter thee!" There are similar examples, from euphemistically ironic ("Thou are pierced by the shaft of Fate!") to utterly obscene: "Ho! thou who would lick coins from the coynte of a rag."

> Whosoever believeth in God and the Day of Resurrection must respect his guest, and the time of being kind to him is one day and one night.

Guest harlotry, thus excused by the words of the Prophet, soon made its appearance. The custom of lending wives and daughters to guests, found in most primitive societies, proved lucrative to the lazy *deyyoose* who did nothing but entertain wealthy guests. And meanwhile his females gained unheard-of independence, which they abused excessively, not realizing the value of freedom in discretion. Competition became so keen and Egypt so tainted that wives and daughters seeking to equal and steal business from the professionals had to be brought under the restraint of the law; and the advent of a new and less indulgent potentate opened the gates to social reform. Such were the vicissitudes of Egyptian morality from era to era.

The prostitute, revered by one man, was loathed by another. But these diverse feelings rarely bore any relationship to a personal moral code. The greatest philosophers and theologians, like those of venerable Greece, thoughtfully regarded and accepted the fallen woman as an essential and indestructible link in the chain of society; and many of them, out of fatalism or misanthropy, became the slaves and victims of strumpets high and low. Writers and poets, decrying their lethal treachery and the paint of deceit in their books, nevertheless frequented them to excess.

The man who hated yet in his heart desired was he who approached impotency. A harlot had spit upon his feeble organ, called him *tailless*. Now, when passing a harlot in the streets, he would address her thus:

> "O thou extract of despicable water! thou art nought but a rag wherewith to wipe one's pizzle after making water. Verily, thou stinkest like a muskrat in heat and the seminal fluid of curs and jackasses gluts thy womb, oozing daily from thy slit!"

Her only reply—if any, besides a sneer or expectoration—was: *"Yah menyook!"* (O thou befuttered); to which the man responded in the feminine (*menyookeh*). The harlot, customarily without a veil, would then draw the end of her shawl across her face and walk on, haunches swaying rhythmically. She had little need to seek an apology; she was as much aware of the man's true feelings as he himself. Whoredom was, like many other things, only hateful and immoral when one at long last could not indulge.

Ghemz or *ishaureh* (the art of assignation) was of multiform and singular aspect. Among professionals, a mere glint, the vaguest motion of the lips or turn of the head, was recognized and reacted to. But the less perceptive or those unacquainted with the cryptic signals were attracted by gesticulations quite familiar throughout the East.

Sitting at her window above the Street of Fornication (Dereeg-ez-Zinnah), the public prostitute (*beghauyeh*) would thrust her forefinger into her mouth; others, joining index and middle fingers, would press them between their breasts. The vulvar sign, *ishaureh-el-ferj* (tips of thumb and forefinger touching) was replied to by the man's raising either his middle or index finger.

Once the assignation had been made, the courtesan despatched her slave girl to the street and the client was ushered upstairs. The nightly price according to each class was usually fixed and known, for the wealth of a man was not to be determined by his garb. Wealthy individuals deliberately dressed as vagabonds both to avert the evil eye, destroyer of opulence, and to elude ingenious thieves and pickpockets. If a man were exceptionally virile he got his money's worth; otherwise, he must resort to scum or beardless boys who, sadly enough, commanded as much as, or more than the most eminent courtesans. But Cairo had an abundance of vagrant orphans, and a wise man adopted a few and relished his pleasures untroubled by extortion.

In Persia and Afghanistan, lands of *facetiae* (erotic tales or jests), the courtesan was popularly termed inn-woman, *suroyeh* (from serai'inn) because everyone lodges within her. The *lolee* (dancing girl) was queen of Cabul, mistress of Bazaar-e-Huraumkaree (the Street of Fornication). Here, the *aubash* (rake) made his home, being *sirdar* (bazaar headman) and *tuhseeldar* (revenue collector) and, swaggering along with one of his chums to a fresh assignment, it was not uncommon for him to say:

> "Indeed, *Wullahee!* this girl is a fat piece of meat; there are good pickings to be had out of this job."

To the newcomer, he extolled the aspects of Bazaar-e-Huraumkaree:

> Here, yah Khawind, a single blow from one's lover is as sweet as the eating of a million raisins. Here, is to be found the most natural and effective method of achieving hypertrophy of the carnal implement. Gain cheer at Zeyghum Khan's Prostitute Palace, where there be luscious ecstatic women who grin wide and part their moist pinkish lips at both ends. In one another's embrace, frothing with rapture, man and woman faint straight away!

The Street of Fornication at Cabul was a gigantic clipjoint. Among its deceptions were those aimed at the prudish ogler who came to sate himself merely with cautious peeping. Sweetmeat sellers prodded him into buying *nukkle-e-pishkil* (dung-dragées), being the sugar-coated orbicular excrement of sheep and goats. This racket was even carried into the practical jokery

of society, and nothing tickled the Persian more than to
see an inexperienced stranger pop one into his mouth.

But Persian bonbons were mild in comparison to
what the credulous traveler encountered inside the
brothel. An elderly matron, the proverbial bawd, and
a lissome young creature came together to greet him at
the door. Inviting him in, they relieved him of burdensome garb, the young harlot all the while ogling and
squirming. Already aroused to white heat of enthusiasm,
the traveler could scarcely contain himself; but artfully,
winning his confidence and allowing him a liberal look
at her body, the harlot held him off.

Leading the drooling novice into a dim scented
apartment, she toyed with him, playing amorous, then
coy or indignant, the old bawd looking on the while.
Slapping and cuffing him, the frisky wench said to her
procuress: "I never saw aught nicer than this." Then,
to her victim: "Be patient, and thou shalt win thy wish."

"How much longer have I to wait? This slapping
hath made me feel faint."

The bawd replied: "As soon as she is warm with
wine, thou wilt have thy desire."

The two then doused him with rosewater; whereupon, he said: "O mistress mine, I am thy slave and in
the hollow of thy hand."

"Know, then, that God hath made me passionately
fond of frolic; and whoso falleth in with my humor
cometh by whatsoever he wisheth."

The bawd said: "She wisheth only to dye thine
eyebrows red, and pluck out thy mustachios, and rouge
thy cheeks. Be patient. She would do on this wise only
that thou mayst be as a beardless youth, and that no
hair be left on thy face to scratch and prick her delicate
cheeks; for, indeed, she is passionately in love with thee.
So be patient, and thou shalt attain thine object."

When they had performed all this, they made him
stand up and dance; upon which they pelted him with
pillows and cushions.

The bawd said: "Now, thou hast attained thy wish;
there are no more blows in store for thee, and there remaineth but one little thing to do. It is her wont, when

she is in her cups, to let no one have her until she put off her dress and trousers and is left stark naked. Then, she will bid thee doff thy clothes and run; and she will run before thee, as if she were flying from thee. And do, thou, follow her from place to place till thy prickle stands at fullest point: when she will yield to thee. Strip off thy clothes at once."

So he rose, well-nigh lost in ecstasy and, doffing his raiment, showed himself mother-naked;[4] whereupon the harlot stripped also, saying: "If thou want anything, run after me till thou catch me."

Needless to say, he pursued her in a rage of desire, in and out of chambers, up and down vestibules, until he almost lost her. It appeared that she darted through a row of curtains far ahead in the dimness; so, bracing himself for the kill, our traveler rushed headlong forward—and fell out into a crowded bazaar.

Naked, with swollen penis, shorn of beard and mustachios, with red-dyed eyebrows, cheeks smeared with rouge, he was lashed and kicked and spat upon, even carnally attacked, battered with fruit, laughed at, scorned, and finally hauled off to jail by the local police.

Of course, he never did get his clothes or money back. The house was routinely "investigated" by the police who were, of course, in collusion. Consequently nothing at all was found. This little badger game allowed law-enforcing officialdom to reap a share of the profit.

As long as Persia and Afghanistan could attract wayfarers by their myriad delightful perversions, Persia and Afghanistan used this as a source of wealth.

In 1878, only a few weeks before the British government declared war on Afhganistan, it was rumored that the sisters of Eyyoob, Yakoob, and Ibraheem Kahn, sons of the Ameer, descended into whoredom for the cause of El-Islam in order to entice the noblemen of Cabul to throw all their weight and capital in support and provision of Holy War. They were allegedly induced to such action by their brothers and other

[4]Burton, *op. cit.*

scheming ignoramuses, particularly the old *jehaud* (holy war) *mollah* (preacher), Meer-Wyze Mohummud Mushky-Alum Khan. The report was confirmed when British officials at Peshawar learned that the Imaum of Cabul had ordered every prostitute in the city to devote her riches and body to the Faithful, all in the cause of Holy War, a traditional procedure enacted at such times and sworn to by the testicles of the Prophet.

Not only eunuchs but fascinating respectable women as well as prominent courtesans were employed for espionage purposes. Their operations included poisoning, castration, and other gruesome activities. One at Cabul supposedly had a trophy from every man whom she had ever lain with. It inflated her ego to know that she was then the Ultimate; that after a man had knowledge of her, he need seek nothing more. And she made good that delusion by removing his private parts.

One explanation for general feminine cruelty and immorality in Persia was the result of their social status. They were regarded as having no souls, no place in Paradise, and were debased to the lives of impounded animals. Environment, hand in hand with distinct masochistic tendencies, led them to commit savage and hysterical acts of vengeful brutality. Hence, the moment she applied the knife to her paramour's body, the moment her fingernails gouged his scrotum, the Persian female relished orgasm. Sexual congress became vapid and ungratifying, meant little to her in comparison to the joys of sheer sadism. It was like the ineffable thrill exploding in a tigress as she claws to death the trainer who has long caged and maltreated her.

This physical and psychological phenomenon manifested itself in the feminine desire for coitus per anus. In speaking of the Parsaic courtesan, famous for her adeptness in the art of aversa venus (*zeyr-o-zubber*), the Arab erotologist said: "She is apt for two tricks: *raus w'mshegleb* (top and topsy-turvy)."

The Hebrews practiced it in the belief that it procured a clever child; the Hindoos so used their wives in emulation of Shiva, who never tired of experimenting with Parvuttee; and the Arabs, in justifying their inclinations, cited the Koran:

> Your wives are your tillage; go in, therefore, unto your tillage in what manner so ever ye will.

Nearly every Oriental eroticist, though not understanding its physical or psychological cause, mentioned the peculiarity:

> There are women who delight in anal coition, and can procure orgasm through no other means.

Such individuals, a few of them tribades, thrived well in Persian prostitution. The *ghulaumeeyeh* (girl cupbearer dressed as a boy) was the catamite's female counterpart in Shiraz, Tehran, and Isfahan; and very often, unless ravished, these women and girls retained their virginal hymens throughout life, seeking their pleasure and livelihood in *zeyr-o-zubber*. Many females in the north of India, noted for an impassiveness or frigidity before mentioned, inadvertently came to identify their vagina with the rectum; and in order to procure orgasm in their mates, their husbands were compelled to stimulate the anus with their glans or moistened fingers. Men so erotically conditioned, desiring intercourse per anum with females, were more numerous among the Persians and Chinese than the Hindoos.

Mention of aversa venus is also made in Arab verse:

> She proffered me a tender coynte; quoth I: "I will not futter thee!"
> She drew back, saying: "From the Faith he turns, who's turned by Heaven's decree!
> "And front-wise futtering, in one day, is obsolete persistency!"
> Then swung she round, and shining rump like silvern lump she showeth me;
> I cried: "Well done, O mistress mine! No more am I in pain for thee;

"O thou, of all that Allah oped, showest me
    fairest victory!"

Quoth she—for I to lie with her forbore—"O
    folly-following fool, O fool to core:
"If thou my coynte for mortise to thy tenon
    reject, I'll show thee what shall please thee
    more."[5]

To insure divorce, Persians (as previously noted)
generally abused their wives through unnatural intercourse; but the unfortunate man was one whose spouse
resembled the Turk: indiscriminate and omnivorous in
her sexual appetites.

Sacred prostitution in El-Islam found its place
among holy men: *dervishes, fakeers, welees, peers, mar-
abouts*. A *fakeer* had merely to say: *"Enneh shehweh!"*
(I am lustful) and any woman, were she a True Believer, must yield. When a mendicant-devotee stopped
at a particular house for alms, the master was obliged to
offer his wives and daughters. This was considered highly beneficial, ridding the enclosure and its occupants of
all evil *jinn*. The eldest of naked saints were considered
especially sacred if they suffered from priapism (*azeem,
high in dignity*). For a younger fanatic to display his
bristling secret parts in public was considered damn-
able and gross hypocrisy.
    During the festivals of El-Mohurrum and Er-Ra-
madhan, *fakeers* indulged excessively in hallowed copulation. Virtuous wives surrendered right and left,
maids forfeited their virginity, and prostitutes gave their
favors free in the names of God and His Prophet. In
times of disaster, pestilence, and war, the *fakeer* reigned
supreme, grasping full advantage of enfeebling distrac-
tion. At every graveside and dunghill the traveler
would glare at black-clad women: sobbing, wrenching
out their hair, writhing on the ground, beating their
breasts, and heaping dust on their bleeding heads. And
nearby, like the vultures and pye-dogs (scavengers),
would always be *fakeer* and *dervish*, wild-eyed, naked,

----

[5]*Ibid.*

waiting to console these women, under the shroud of holy fanaticism, with balm of carnal lust.

In the later Sudanese campaigns of the nineteenth century, when Lord Kitchener sought to retake Omdurman and Khartoum from the Dervishes, El-Khalifa Abdullahi, successor to the Mahdi, devised a curious form of sacred prostitution. It was based on the following proverb: "A man without offspring is like a thorntree without fruit."

His emeers in a circle before him, El-Khalifa spoke:

> We weaken. Since the death of our Blessed Messiah, there has ruled degeneration. A vast Army of Infidels, Feringhees and Toorks, is upon us, to devour us. If we succeed in crushing them, we must then be prepared to meet more and more until the fighting-scum of Europe are at length obliterated. Castration or death is too gracious, too inartificial, for any Infidel that falls into our hands. And I have conjured, through a vision, a most artful method of torment: that of self-conversion into eunuchism, driving the Infidel to acknowledge that propagation of his hateful kind is terminated forever. But there is gain in this method, gain that cannot be realized in any other aspect of punishment known to man. For whilst they destroy their own virility, they at the same time increase the strength of the Faithful.

The victims, European captives, young and healthy, only gradually came to notice the experiment through their food and drink. At first, they regarded their heightened sexual desire as normal, as the consequence of forced abstinence. Then the desire wore away until they yearned no more, and sexual relief took second place to survival. Yet now, after many weeks, they sensed a constant itching they had seldom known before, from which they could achieve no relief. It began to dawn on them that everything of which they partook must be drugged. Yet, were they to refuse to eat, horrible disease, swift to grasp the undernourished, must destroy them in a week.

They were ensnared, and the stanch fiber of discipline slowly rotted away. All the weeks of inhibition, painfully achieved, was shattered in hours. Day was unknown from night; in sleep, dream could not be distinguished from reality.

Then women, black, and brown, and olive, and copper, were supplied to them, hour upon hour. Silence and darkness for several paradisaic days. Food and water, pure. Their minds grappled, strained to reason. And then it became obvious: the ghouls, the hyenas, were fattening them for sacrifice. Allowing them to regain strength, strength to face the tempest of ecstatic horror.

Then, the intervals would lessen, from a week to a few days, to a day—scarcely recognized. Driving, meticulously, into the dark chasm. Enfeebling, dazing concentration, engorging with brutal indifference. Molding accurately into beasts that knew no relief from morbid thirst.

Every other day there came the balms, rarely acknowledged, soon hated. In one month there were only thirsting animals, scornful of tranquillity, raging for maniacal intensification. But the ghouls and hyenas were clever; they knew exactly how the mind must be governed, driving to the brink, the sharpest verge of insanity, then sudden release. Ease, waxing into cynical apathy, then desire rekindling into conflagration, undulate horror. Until soon the ghouls and hyenas had need only to watch. No more careful reckoning, fastidious management—not a second miscalculated.

A vibrant climax had been realized. There could only be slow disintegration now. Not violence, rabid terror, but methodic deterioration. For there was no control. It was like eating and drinking, only refinedly intense, systematic, leisurely in destruction.

But they were aware of every moment, rational as they were, now that the crisis was over. They acknowledged; but they were incapable of resistance. The mind had been manipulated, directed with shrilling keenness, brought to a sudden halt and locked into a position that could not be broken.

Each knew how the ghouls laughed at him. Once

he had perhaps felt sorry for the Egyptian Turk, slave as he was to his own self. Now each was to be laughed at as a Toork, an infidel satyr, enslaved by aphrodisia, laughed at as a bestial heathen, gripped by animal lust. So gripped that the fanatic boast, deep in their hearts, ate with rottenness and shame. But neither mind nor flesh were ever free. Only upon the moment of destruction; and then, nothing would matter any more.

When, on September 2, 1898, Kitchener smashed the last grand thrust of El-Islam on the plains outside of Omdurman, the prison doors were flung open to release not bands of impatient prisoners thrilled by long-awaited freedom but an apathetic, morbid lot, scarcely aware of triumph, indifferent to the sensations of joyous liberty.

The Moslem Paradise (El-Genneh), described by one nineteenth-century writer as "an everlasting brothel providing celestial concubines" to each heaven-achieving Moslem male soul was considered the abode of consecrated prostitution by vulgar individuals and the self-seeking priesthood. The bridge (Es-Siraut), spanning hell and leading to Paradise, was sharper than a sword, finer than a hair. Its length was three thousand years' journey: one thousand in descent, one thousand in ascent, and one thousand in level traveling. The Faithful perform their crossing with due ease, but the Infidel falls into one of seven *Gehhennems* (hells) and is there consumed in fiery torture.

The commonest individual, dissolute but orthodox, enjoyed the company of a minimum of eighty thousand beautiful beardless youths and seventy nymphs besides his mundane spouses, if he desired them. If not, they were deemed unfaithful and cast into hell with the rest of the soulless.

God was Compassionate and Merciful; He was all-loving. In the Abode of Eternal Bliss, man enjoyed the fruits of Paradise: boundless aromatic gardens; dazzling pavilions of pearl; chaste, superhumanly beautiful, sloe-eyed *hooreeyehs* (nymphs) formed not of mortal clay but of paradisiac musk, indicative of their divine purity and perfection, bearing voluptuous breasts, swelling with honey sweetness; and fair young lads with plump rosy buttocks, for all those True Believers who should so desire them; and, last but not least, wine and everlasting virility. *Magnifique!*

A vast esoteric literature dealt with physical love. Among the most popular works to be found from Egypt to India, were:

Kitaub-el-Munaukehheh w'el-Mufautehheh fee Esnauf-el-Jimmah w'Aulauteh (Book of Carnal Copulation and the Initiation into the Modes of Coition and its Instrumentation), by Azeez-ed-Deen-el-Meseehee.

Kitaub Rujooeh-es-Sheykh ileh Sebah fee-el Kooweh-el-Bah (Book of Age Rejuvenescence in the Power of Concupiscence), by Ehhmed-bin-Soleymaun.

Kitaub Jaumee-el-Lizzeh (The Compendium of Pleasure), by Ibn Semsemaunee.

Kitaub-el-Eezah fee Ezrar-en-Nikah (Book of Exposition of the Mysteries of Married Fruition), *Kitaub-el-Eezah fee Ilm-en-Nikah* (Book of Exposition in the Science of Coition), *Kitaub Newwauzir-el-Eyk fee-en-Neyk* (Green Splendors of the Copse in Copulation) and *Kitaub-el-Wishah fee Fewwa'id-en-Nikah* (Book of the Zone on Coition-boon), by Jelaul-ed-Deen-es-Seyootee.

Perhaps the most widely read of the *Kutub-el-Bah* (Books of Lust) dealing with *El-Lizzeh-en-Nisseh* (the Pleasures of Women) is a volume composed by a Kabyle Arab of the sixteenth century, Sheykh-en-Nefzawee. Its title is *Roze-el-Autir fee Hezah-el-Khautir* (Scented Garden site for Heart Delight), or, simply, *The Perfumed Garden*.

Wherever displayed, these and many others like them sold tremendously. India, a land of illiteracy, had numerous and sundry books printed in Moslem quarters or shipped out from Cairo, embellished with crude but accurate illustrations of instruction. Those phenomena of the prudish West, *ghesheem* (raw youths, unskilled in the wiles of woman or sodomite) were virtually unknown.

Pornographic literature, delight of the Arabs, was almost unlimited. It delved into every phase of sexual diversion; and its coarseness, shocking to a cultured European, was merely amusing to the simple-minded Oriental. "To the pure in mind, all things are pure," said he. Sex was not an aspect to conceal or scorn; it was baldly discussed in the family circle and in the coffee-shop. The most proper of Arab ladies used such stock terms as "prickle" and "coynte" without any reserve; and, though childish to an extreme in some ways, the average Oriental was thoroughly mature in his attitude toward this aspect of life.

Sex was the most essential and natural part of his existence; therefore, he regarded it nakedly and philosophically, and disdained wearing the grim mask of prudery. Hence, manner of speaking was not indicative of character. The euphemist was carefully observed and avoided; only the outspoken and sincere were to be trusted. How different from the West, where anyone who spoke his mind about sex was considered a lunatic, or a pervert! Consequently the Oriental only added his to his long, wearisome list verifying the madness and hypocrisy of Occidental civilization, and preferred coherent boldness to driveling temerity.

Here is an example of Oriental plain speaking:

> She came up to me and strained me to her breast and kissed me whilst I kissed her, and sucked my upper lip whilst I sucked her lower lip I put my hand to her waist, and pressed it, and we came not to the ground save at the same moment. Then, she undid her petticoat-trousers which slipped down to her ankles, and we fell to clasping and embracing and toying and speaking softly and biting and intertwining of legs and going round about the room, and the corners thereof, till her joints became relaxed for love-delight and she swooned away. I then ruptured the crown of glory, and entered the sanctuary.

Several more examples, vivid though indelicate, are as follows:

She pressed him to her bosom and he pressed her to his bosom, and the twain embraced with closest embrace, rubbing body against body. Letting down her petticoat-trousers, she lay down upon her back; and in an instant that which his father had left him rose in rebellion, and he said: "Go to it, O Father of Rods!" and putting both hands to her flanks, he set the sugar-stick to the mouth of her cleft and thrust on. And finding the carpet after the measure of the dais-floor, he plied the box within its cover until he came to the end of it.

I fell to toying with her, and thrusting and foining at her cleft, her solution of continuity, and she wriggled to and fro, and bucked up and down, after which I tumbled her and we were both in glory.[6]

He at once fell upon her and, with a single push, buried his member completely. Then he set to work like a pestle, and she to shake her croup; and thus they continued until the two ejaculations arrived. Then he got up, wiped his member, and went away.[7]

I was urged by a call of nature, and crouched on my heels to make water. When I had ended, I stood up and wiped the orifice with a pebble. An old bawd, passing by, saw my prickle and all its fine aspect; and, letting down my robe, I was about to wend my way when she stopped me, seizing my hand and kissing it: "O my master! the Lord give thee joyance of thy youth."

Another, found in the *Arabian Nights,* represents what was a common occurrence in actuality, the discussion of two questionable women with regard to the value of man or boy:

How shall I spread-eagle myself under a boy who will emit long before I can go off, and

---

[6]*Ibid.*
[7]Perfumed Garden of the Cheikh Nefzaoui.

forestall me in limpness of penis and clitoris; and leave a man who, when he taketh breath, clippeth close, and when he entereth, goeth leisurely, and, when he hath done, repeateth and, when he pusheth, poketh hard and, as often as he withdraweth, returneth?

The Wiles of Woman was a popular subject of Arab tales and satire, as an astute form of comedy, was as cherished there as anywhere. This extract from Near Eastern folklore follows the general model of Egypto-Arabic humor:

There was, of olden time, a great but dull-witted governor; and he had, among many concubines, a fair and shrewd wife who well-nigh regulated his territory as might a vizier.

One day, this young and astute woman sent her slave girl to the brothel to collect delinquent revenue. The brothel-keeper, whilst counting out the money, displayed his yard to the slave girl. She blushed, and passed to his other side. As she thus turned round, the brothel-keeper displayed his yard on that side also. Thus, the slave girl saw it on that side too. And receiving the tax-money, she hurried back to her mistress and said:

"Yon brothel-keeper, to whom I went, has two yards!"

Intrigued, the governor's wife replied: "Go, and say to yon brothel-keeper: *My mistress wishes thee. Come at night.*"

So the slave girl went, and said this to the brothel-keeper.

As soon as it was dark, the brothel-keeper hurried to the manorhouse and waited by the gate. The slave girl appeared and said to him:

"In a few hours, follow me and have to do with my mistress while she is lying by her husband."

Alarmed, the brothel-keeper said: "Will that not be dangerous?"

The girl replied: "Fear not; my mistress has drugged the governor with hasheesh."

When it was midnight, the slave girl led the brothel-keeper into the manorhouse. The governor's wife lay conveniently, and the brothel-keeper fell to work. She felt that the yard which entered her was but one, and said:

"Ah! my soul, brothel-keeper: at it with both of them."

Whilst she was softly speaking, the effect of hasheesh wore away; and her husband awoke, and uttered: "What means thy saying: *At it with both of them?*" He stretched out his hand to his wife's coynte, and the brothel-keeper's yard came into it.

The brothel-keeper drew himself back, his yard slipped out of the landlord's hand, and he made shift to get away.

The governor started up, growling: "Out on thee, wife! what meant that saying of thine: *At it with both of them?*"

The woman, hesitating not a moment, said: "O husband, I saw in my dream that thou wast fallen into the sea and wast swimming with one hand, and crying out: *Help! I am drowning!* I shouted to thee from the shore: *At it with both of them;* and thou begannest to swim with both thy hands."

Then, grinning sleepily, the landlord said: "Wife, I too know that I was in the sea: from this, that a wet fish came into my hand and then slipped out and escaped. Thou speakest truly."

And he, governor and landlord of all Ted-heer Province, prized his wife more than ever!

The popular Arab belief that woman prefers an additional inch of penis to anything else that this world or Paradise has to offer is again affirmed and analyzed in the tale of "The Man Who Had Three Wishes":

A certain man had longed all his life to look upon the Night of Power; and one night it befell that he gazed at the sky and saw the angels, and Heaven's gates thrown open; and he beheld all things prostrating themselves before their Lord, each in its several stead. So he said to his wife:

"Hark ye, such an one, verily God hath shown me the Night of Power; and it hath been proclaimed to me, from the invisible world, that three prayers will be granted unto me: so I consult thee for counsel as to what shall I ask."

Quoth she: "O man, the perfection of man and his delight is in his prickle; therefore, do thou pray God to greaten thy yard and magnify it."

So he lifted up his hands to Heaven and said: "O God, greaten my yard and magnify it!"

Hardly had he spoken when his tool became as big as a column, and he could neither sit nor stand nor move about nor even stir from his stead; and when he would have carnally known his wife, she fled before him from place to place. So he said to her:

"O accursed woman, what is to be done? This is thy list, by reason of thy lust."

She replied: "No, by God, I did not ask for this length and huge bulk, for which the gate of a street were too strait. Pray Heaven to make it less."

So he raised his eyes to Heaven and said: "O God, rid me of this thing and deliver me therefrom!"

And immediately his prickle disappeared altogether, and he became clean smooth. When his wife saw this, she said: "I have no occasion for thee now thou art become pegless as a eunuch, shaven and shorn." And he answered her, saying:

"All this comes of thine ill-omened counsel and thine imbecile judgment. I had three prayers accepted of God wherewith I might have gotten me my good, both in this world and in the next, and now two wishes are gone in pure waste, by thy lewd will, and there remaineth but one."

Quoth she: "Pray God the Most High to restore thee thy yard as it was."

So he prayed to his Lord, and his prickle was restored to its first estate. Thus, the man lost his three wishes by the ill counsel and lack of wit in the woman.

The moral? Older than Mohammed: "Consult females and do contrariwise!"

In true Boccaccio style, the next, a successive pair, dates back to medieval Iraq:

> The Caliph Haroon-er-Resheed lay one night between two slave-girls, one from El-Medeeneh and the other from Cufa; and the Cufite rubbed his hands, whilst the Medinite rubbed his feet and made his concern stand up.
>
> Quoth the Cufite: "I see thou wouldst keep the whole of the stock-in-trade to thyself. Give me my share of it."
>
> And the other answered: "I have been told that the Prophet said: *Whoso quickeneth the dead, the dead belongeth to him and is his.*"
>
> But the Cufite took her unawares and, pushing her away, seized it all in her own hand and said: "I also have been told that the Prophet declared: *Game belongeth to him who taketh it, not to him who raiseth it.*"

> The Caliph Haroon-er-Resheed once slept with three slave girls: a Meccan, a Medinite, and an Irakite. The El-Medeeneh girl put her hand to his yard and handled it, whereupon it rose; but the Meccan sprang up and drew it to herself. Quoth the Medinite:
>
> "What is this unjust aggression? A tradition was related to me that the Apostle of God— whom God bless and keep!—said: *Whoso enquickeneth a dead land, it is his.*"
>
> And the Meccan answered: "It was related to me that the Apostle of God said: *The quarry is his who catcheth it, not his who starteth it.*"
>
> But the Irakee girl pushed them both away and, taking it to herself, said: "This is mine, till your contention be decided."

Arab verse, equally raw but sincere, often exceeded popular prose; and set to trilled music, it made a still eerie night in the desert come melodiously alive:

> My lover lay the night with me, and gripped me in his arms: while I, with sighs, embraceth him—afaint for ecstasy.
> And hugged him to my breast, and sucked the sweet

wine of his lips, and lauded wrist-thick prickle, as he thrust it into me.

Composed by *sha'irs* (bards) in honor of their favorite mistresses, such verses found their way out of the brothel and into the family circle, where they were chanted by young and old alike:

Merciful God made no fairer sight, than coupled lovers single couch doth hold:
Breast pressing breast and robed in joys all their own with pillowed forearms, cast in finest mold.

Others, from the imaginations of dancing girls and male effeminates, were aimed principally at the gallery:

I have a lover and, when embracing him, He punctureth me with virile limb.

My coynte have I subjected, without shame, To the prickles of more than I can name.

Artistically inclined youths, in experiencing the worldliness of life, often reacted by conjuring suitable verse; and not a few Arabs, cousins of the romanticists of Southern Europe, expressed themselves in rhyme:

O thou who barest leg-calf: better to suggest, for passion-maddened amorist, finer things above!
At its lover doth plump fruit vaunt; slit and slit-one drive me daft with love.

The first three of the following represent the testimonials of two voluptuaries, and the remaining, popular throughout the Moslem world, are from the lips of courtesans:

I—who shiver for fear when I see a mouse, and for very funk I bepiss my clo'!—
I love no foin but the poke in bed, when coynte well knoweth my prickle's prow.

When I drew up her shift from the roof of her slit, I found it as strait as my mind and my money;

So I drove it halfway, and she sighed a loud sigh;
    quoth I: "Why this sigh?"—"For the rest of it,
    honey!"

She cried, while played in her side Desire; and Night
    o'erhung her with blackest blee;
"O Night, shall thy murk bring me ne'er a chum, to
    tumble and futter this coynte of me?"
And she smote that part with her palm, and sighed,
    sore sighs, and, a-weeping, continued she:
"As the toothstick beautifies teeth, e'en so must
    prickle to coynte as a toothstick be;
"O Moslems! is there never a stand to your tools, to
    assist a woman's necessity?"
Thereat rose upstanding, beneath its clothes, my yard,
    as crying: *At thee! at thee!*
And I loosed her trouser-string, startling her; "Who
    art thou?"—and I said, "A reply to thy plea!"
And began to stroke her, with wrist-thick yard: hurt-
    ing hinder cheeks by its potency;
And she cried, as I rose, after courses three: "Suit
    thy gree, the stroke!"—and I: "Suit thy gree!"

By God, rub thy hand upon my coynte: since long,
    long nights for this alone I long;
And whisper tale of love in ear of me: to me, 'tis
    sweeter than the sweetest song!
No other youth upon my breast shall lie: so do it
    often, dear—and do it long.

I kissed him a thousand times, and clipt his waist—
    and spent the night, with cheek to cheek, close
    li'en—
And swooned to the thrill of foin and thrust, as
    prickle were as sword-edge drawn and sheathed
    in radiant line.

I waved to and fro, and he waved to and fro, with a
    motion so pleasant: now fast, and now slow;
And, at last, he sank down on my bosom of snow.[8]

---

[8]Burton, *op. cit.*

3. THE HINDOOS

In India, Annapurna (Goddess of Sacred Prostitution) blessed the temples with an abundance of dedicated women. *Veyshyah sungum-sey poonyum-hey* (to have intercourse with a holy prostitute is a virtue which obliterates all sin) was the chanted advice of Brahminee priests (*poojarees*). In excuse for their hypocrisy and licentiousness, some declared: "For the sake of one's belly, many roles are played!"[9]

The *devadasee* (slave-girl of the gods), whose patron saints were Annapurna and the *upsrahs* (celestial courtesans), held as her symbol Sooee the Parrot: bird of free love, counterpart of Cupid's dove, upon which Kamadeo (the Hindoo Cupid) rode. The temple prostitute, born and bred into sanctified whoredom, was known by many names, among them *moorullee* (bird-girl), *devakunyah* (daughter of the gods) and *devastree* (wife of the gods).

Many regarded it as an act of reverence and great esteem, even holy sacrifice, to give or sell one's daughter into temple harlotry. Such action was considered blessed and certain to win the favors of the gods as well as the approval of the priests. A prince or king, to gain the fidelity of provincial priesthood, often purchased a *ryot*'s (peasant's) daughter and offered her as a temple gift (*dustooree*). This was a way of bribing the priests and assuring that their prayers and preachments served his prosperity as ruler. The *ryot* honored and delighted that His Majesty should choose his child to serve the gods, was pleased to sell his daughter into such service. He could then walk proudly; his daughter was married to the deity. And were he to save his money and pay homage to the gods through intercourse with one of their wives, he might be entertained by his own daughter. This would not be incest since she was in fact no longer his flesh and blood, but something hallowed and spiritual.

---

[9]Abbé J. A. Dubois, *Hindu Manners, Customs and Ceremonies.*

In the interest of increasing the human race, women and maids gladly prostituted themselves in and before the temples; and husbands and fathers readily gave up their wives and daughters to the priests, to have knowledge of the gods and accept their powerful seed. This was of greater prevalence during times of strife, when the fate of the community depended upon its strength in numbers.

The bursting of the Devil's Wind in 1857, Sepoy Rebellion (rebellion of the Sepoys or native troops), was accompanied by symbolic preparatory actions. In promiscuous intercourse designed to appease the angered gods and increase progeny man and woman imagined that they were *deva* and *deyvee,* sacrificially cohabiting in honor of Lord Shiva and Mother Parvuttee. Every prostitute in the cities of Meerut and Delhi had passed at least twice, that fateful week in early May through the Sepoy lines. Throughout the bazaars the women incited the soldiery and riffraf to mutiny, swearing they would not copulate with cowards. The greased cartridge[10] was the pretext, but patriotic womenfolk proved an incisive goad to mass violence ending in a deluge of innocent blood. In every stage of undress, some in *dhotees* and slim breechclouts, others drugged and inebriated, many with naked *bayaderes* (temple dancers) clinging to them with hot thighs and probing fingers, the Sepoys now thought of nothing save that the English must die. Shuddering and squirming in crazed ecstasy, the dancing girls demanded the excised wombs of European *Mem-Sahibehs* (ladies). The moment came, on a Sunday evening, when they gloated as devotees of the Goddess of Death upon scenes of vengeful brutality.

The famed Temple of Juggernaut (a name for Vishnu, Lord of the World) at Pooree, a gigantic brothel, was staffed with no less than a thousand *devadasees.* Their duties as priestesses were to care for

---

[10]One of the causes of the mutiny was the issue of ammunition said to be greased with the fat of cows, and requiring contact with the mouth when loading. This was a violation of a Hindu and Mussulman dietary taboo.

and entertain the god, a lifelike idol. Their performances included dancing, singing, and recitations. Mistresses of *maharuttee* (prurience, hot desire) the *devadasees* of Juggernaut were culturally unexcelled by any other women in India.

The devadasee, slave of Lord Vishnu, toyed with her paramour, exciting, then discouraging him, being coy then bold, easy then difficult, plying him with wine and potions, winking, cooing, pouting and giggling, pinching and clawing, then darting away like a shy sleek gazelle. But soon, as her lover wept with feverish desire, she embraced him lovingly, murmuring and gently touching warm moist lips to his forehead. When he gripped her shoulders, she rent her bodice and clung about his neck and hissed her devotion, her love. She writhed in spasmodic fervor, moaned in demoniac passion and, with hot, moist hands, feverishly sought and grasped his secret parts. Now the provoking fun was over and pleasurable anguish began.

Hindoo courtesans, like those in the Moslem world, were grouped according to physical charm and social caste:

Roopajeebhee or *Raumjunnee* (beautiful tongue-scraper, a ravishing nymph).

Gunikah or *Jaungha-muttaunee* (supercourtesan, lovely churning thighs).

Rajaveyshyah (royal harlot, advisor to the king).

Nuggurnaree (city harlot, the common variety).

Guptaveyshyah (secret harlot, the adulteress).

Ghautveyshyah (harlot of the bathing places, seducer of pilgrims). She might entertain as many as a hundred clients a night. Hence, the allusion to her sudden ascent from rags to riches:

Chuchoondur-key sir-pur chumbeylee-k'teyl:
Jasmine oil on the muskrat's head.

The supercourtesan ("A succubus that mimes the gentle lass, yet loves not what man is but what he has") was in most cases a *lingum-naree* (woman of the celestial penis), with the generative emblem tattooed on her breasts and thighs. She, like her Moslem counterpart, was dedicated to the pleasure of men. Her secretions were likened unto lotus perfume; her thighs were as churning staffs, that convulsed to an ecstatic rhythm; her nickname was *mustee* (she-elephant in heat), for she was rabid in her crisis; and young princes, electrified by her presence, discharged their libation before the altar of Parvuttee.

Symbolic of carnal purity, her favorite beverage was *punch-guvyeh* (a consecrated concoction of the five products of Holy Mother Cow: milk, curds, butter, urine, and dung). A potion called *pawn-sooparee,* which was astringent and inebriating, was adored by the common bona roba. Creating a superficial well-being, called *keyf* by the Arabs, it consisted of areca nut wrapped in a lime-coated betel leaf and soaked in arrack (an Oriental brandy distilled from the coca palm). Its effects often resembled that of an opium pill, and it was a notorious moral weakener and inciter to violent love.

Imsauk (a fabulous potion that lessened hypersensitivity and retarded orgasm), popular throughout Asia, served the art of seminal retention. If the courtesan had no *imsauk* on hand, she counseled her lover to prolong pleasure in their intercourse by avoiding overtension of the muscles and by preoccupying the brain. Care was observed in smoking, in the drinking of sherbet, or chewing of betel nut, as well as the most effective copulative postures. *Imsauk* was especially imperative when embracing frisky catamites, who were vigorous in the techniques of fellatio and masturbation. "In all truth," spake the sage Arab, "circumcision, hardening the delicate glans against spontaneous excitation, natural *imsauk* as it is, cannot approach this blessing from God."

The Hindoo courtesan, goddess of *ruttee* (sexual abuse) and *kaumeh* (ecstasy of love), was greatly skilled in the ancient science of *ausunneh* (coital postures). The medieval Brahmin erotologist, Vutsyayunneh, numbered the *ausunneh* as eighty-four; but Yusodhra, another writer, claimed there are no less than

729! But many of these, needless to say, were impossible save for the contortionist.

Easterners, who are accustomed to squatting, generally assumed such a position in sexual congress. The purpose of *mejlis* (sitting, in Arabic) was to avoid overtension of the muscles, thereby prolonging pleasure and creating a coactive union.

When the woman lay supine and the man sat at squat between her thighs (*yumha'ee,* yawning posture) it proved less tiring for the active man. However, this was only recommended for those males with sizable instruments, since the yawning posture weakened a woman's ability to constrict and also hindered complete masculine penetration.

When both sat at squat (*upavishteh*) the woman, whose limbs gripped the man's waist, became active. A type of courtesan known as *surrotee* (nutcracker) was highly prized for her ability, in this position upon the man's stomach, artfully to squeeze or milk the penis into orgasm with her labial and vaginal muscles. She also assumed this appellation when, beneath the man, she embraced him with her legs and firmly pressed his thighs with her own.

The *surrotee* practiced what in Arabic was familiarly termed *rikib-el-adho* (riding the member). In speaking of this, Sheykh-en-Nefzawee wrote:

> Her pudenda are *choose* (the sucker), for they strive to engulf even the testicles. Once the member is grasped by the sucker, a man can no longer prevent the emission of semen; and the member is tightly held until it is completely drained.

Many other Arab and Hindoo eroticists and physicians in their varied compositions also mentioned the peculiarity:

> The blissful moment soon arrived; for the clinging embrace of her vagina seemed to pump his member as it sucked it, as an infant sucks its mother's breast.

The term *Choose* (sucker), though generally applied to the compressing action of the vaginal walls, was subsequently bestowed upon the absorbing uterus, the function of which, during coition, early Easterners did not understand. It was originally believed that the uterus was a gland of excitation; hence, treatises on the art of love demanded that men have long penes well able to prod and massage the sensitive *ostium externum* (external mouth of the uterus) and *portio vaginalis* (part of the uterus accessible in the vagina). For males with short membra, women with uterine displacements whose uteri had descended into the vaginal passage were much desired. For similar reasons, the astride position that lowers the uterine orifice was also employed. By such methods, climax for the female partner was often achieved in less than one minute.

Purushayut, in which the man lay supine, was not uncommon in Oriental lands, for this position, with woman between man's thighs, assured the greatest amount of pressure that could be brought to bear upon the male genital. Notwithstanding, many Arab writers condemned it by arguing that it hindered impregnation and achieved internal defilement; that the seed only returned into the man's urethra and, with it, much of the woman's impure secretion. Hence, the saying: "Accursed be the man who maketh woman heaven and himself earth!"

Udhiteh (standing) was another favored posture, deemed conducive to ecstatic pressure. The conventional *udhiteh* was that whereby the man raised and held one of the female's knees, then penetrated her. This strenuous position in the woman was thought to hasten her orgasm. Men regarded it for themselves as natural *imsauk.*

Oolud-poolud (topsy-turvy) was also favored, with the female either lying on her stomach or in a stooping position, for its constricting aspect. Coitus a tergo, designed to hinder impregnation, was relished by men seeking merely to stimulate the frenum preputium (*vaug,* bridle) of the penis.

Lying side by side (*paus-paus*), with the man's

legs tightly gripping the female, likewise achieved this desired pressure (*dubbow*).

Mukhmuttunneh (oral churning, fellatio) was a natural and accepted phase of heterosexual copulation in Hindostan. But in Moslem countries it was considered an independent vice known as *reddheh* (to suck). *Lumah* (dark hue of the lips) as an aspect of beauty was, ironically enough, admired by the Arabs; though to the perverse Egyptian it was highly suggestive of mouth coition (*jimmah-bil-fumm*).

Syria infected the entire Mediterranean area with the practice, and the fellators and fellatrices of Rome (sodomites and tribades) became notorious. In Egypt, *er-reddheh* was adopted by eunuchs and catamites and performed in the *hhemmaum,* where they jested of their daily *lukmeh* (mouthful). But when in India a wife or courtesan spoke of *chooskee* (suction) or *mukhmuttunneh,* she meant to convey the fact that, in order to arouse or rearouse her man, fellatio became necessary. As a vice it was almost unknown until the thunderous advent of the Grand Moghuls.

Youthful Arabs often trustingly resorted to *reddheh* so that increased blood be drawn into the part, thereby nourishing it and augmenting its size. Thus, fellatio became part of bath-house ritual.

Europeans, patronizing Hindoo prostitutes for sexual intercourse, were persuaded to try ipsation (mutual masturbation), which they had developed into an erotic art. Some Europeans acknowledged that they, too, came to prefer ipsation to ordinary sexual congress, getting extra pleasure by succeeding in rousing their sexual partners to rapturous orgasm by stimulation of the clitoris. The magnified bliss arises from the peculiarity that male and female achieve an added, new sensitivity and pleasure, unknown in coitus or self-relief, from another's exploration. Oriental bride books have always recommended mutual stimulation in lieu of congress to condition one another, particularly the virgin, and discourage hasty defloration, unnecessary mental pain, and embarrassment. Owing to a strict moral code that so conditioned them, it was thus not unusual for Eastern

men and women to respond to mutual masturbation
alone. Males, attempting immediate union without previous manual excitation on the part of the female, were
often unable to erect their members, or they ejaculated
prematurely. As for love-making with a courtesan, it
was often not till near morning that she, having been
sated by ipsatory gratifications, at last allowed her paramour to slip his organ into her vagina.

The movement in coition known in Arabic as
leklekkeh, in Persian as *awurd-o-burd,* and in Hindostanee as *iddhuroddhur* (to and fro) was, as previously
mentioned, considered a science. In India, the technical
word is *bhaunj* (weaving) and many a harlot spoke of
her favorite paramour as being an "expert basket-
maker." The following two verses, culled from the
Persian, suggest the effects of good weaving:

He thrust and withdrew, thrust and withdrew again:
That I, who lay sighing, to faint was fain.

He plunged and pumped, plunged and pumped again:
That whore, who lay spread-eagled, to faint was fain.

The art of *ghoonj* (passionate wrigglings) on the
part of the female had its counterpart in the skilled motions of the male. The gentleman who sought to ensorcell the most eminent courtesan or vanquish the
most lusty, were he rich or poor, had need to be versed
in such arts. For it required skill to achieve perfect
union. Therefore, apart from *iddhur-oddhur,* special
techniques were employed by men upon the various
classifications of Hindoo women in order to arouse their
passion and hasten them on to pleasurable climax.
Among these were:

Muttun (churning), rotating the head of the
lingam against the *yoni; chode* (blow), striking the
yoni with the *lingam; phooleh* (blossoming), manipulating and pulling the *yoni* bud open like a full-blown
flower; *ling-ruggur* (friction), rubbing the *yoni* with
the *guldhee* (glans penis) in order to moisten it; *dhu-
keyleh* (pushing), applying the *lingam* with force or
thrusting vehemently; *haut-ruggur* (frication), massaging the *yoni* with the hand; *choomah-chaudee* (kissing

and licking), cunnilingus or lip-and-tongue stimulation of the *yoni; chooseh* (sucking), oral excitation of the clitoris (love-twig); *bhidnee-kaumeh* (breast galvanism), kissing, softly pinching, and rubbing the nipples; *singee* (cupping), gently holding and kneading the breasts; and *chootrree* (buttockry), gripping, squeezing, and fist-beating the nates.

Dhukeyloo (pusher) bears another connotation, that of *paramour;* for the "pusher" was the perfect man for enlightened woman, one skilled in carnal copulation.

The female, in turn, that she might quickly augment the strength and thickness of the *lingam* by inducing an abnormal quantity of blood into the part, employed manual pressure, fellatio, and sponges soaked in hot water. Thereafter, the ideal position was that in which mouth lips and pudenda conjoined without discomfort; and the supreme advice, recognized and practiced by the ancients, was always:

> Try, by all means, to make the ejaculation simultaneous; for that is the secret of love.[11]

The technique of physical passion, aside from coital postures and passionate movements, also included the sciences of:

Lingum-yonee (the embrace) which, among others, included *sundhausee, chimdee,* or *surrotee* (pincer or nut-cracker, locking thighs); *bhidnee-dubbow* (breast- or nipple-pressure); *luttah, soot* (tendril, thread, or creeper: in which woman tightly clasps man's waist and neck with her limbs); *vriksh-churrow* (tree-climbing: in which woman mounts to creeper position, and copulation is performed with man standing and woman taking active role); *ood-ghissow, rugrrah* (voracious friction, rubbing: i.e., penis, breasts, clitoris).

Choomah-chaudee (kissing and toying, licking, dalliance) which, among others, included *sootaree, sumpoodeh* (langue-fourree or probing, tongue-sucking kiss: in which teeth seized lips, lips clasped lips, and

[11]Cheikh Nefzaoui, *op. cit.*

tongue sought tongue; also, *maraichinage* or mouth-exploration); *jeebh-juddh* (tongue-tilting); *jeebhee* (tongue-scraper); *hondh-chubbow* (lip-biting, -chewing, or -bleeding); *haut-luggow* (handling; dallying with breasts, genitals, hair).

Nukha-nukhee (mutual clawing, scratching, and tearing) which included distinct markings, such as the tiger-wound (*waughnukh*) on the stomach or the peacock-print (*moredhuppah*) on the breasts.

Deyn-deyn (inarticulate sounds, delirious murmurings) which comprised nasal, guttural, sibilant, and palatal tones: the moan, sigh, coo, hiss, cluck, shrill, and many others. When the bodily hair bristled and the sibilation or ululation came, woman, agitating her thighs, was recognized to have reached her paroxysm.

Paunee-muddhee (hand-stroking) which included slapping the buttocks in coition; tender stroking of hair, back, breasts, stomach, and genitals; and masturbation by gentle caress.

Daunteh-kurmeh (biting) which indicated a succession of multiform markings on breasts, cheeks, stomach, penis, buttocks, thighs, etcetera.

Another branch of erotic knowledge, *kaumeh-ungeh,* dealt with the erotogenic zones. It taught that the most acute were the mouth, anus, and genitals (expressly the glans penis and clitoris).

The frail sisterhood of India were well regarded for their erotic knowledge through which they were thought to render a valuable public service. The crafty *pooja-rees,* masters of propaganda, reaped a fortune by hiring troupes of *bayaderes* out to potentates and wealthy individuals planning weddings, feasts, and other joyous gatherings. But, additionally, no funeral procession was complete without its band of sacred dancing girls.

Prostitutes and nautch girls from the bazaars of Delhi, the vales of Cashmere, the temples and palaces of Madras and Bombay garbed in vivid red, yellow, green, and blue gossamer *sarees* (some even stark naked save for garlands of flowers and gems, bangles and beads) paraded shrieking before the undulate lines of Indian armies, galvanizing the warriors to martial frenzy. For centuries the courtesan was a necessary camp-follower. A king going out to battle would solicit the local temple for a bevy of dancing wenches. Their sinuous grace, their provocative poses, their boundless energy and knowledge of physical love, incited the men more than any other stimulants or incentives.

Venereal disease (*purmeyyo*) was rare until the advent of Western civilization. In British India, after the transfer of rule from the Company to the government, the prudish and backward Army Medical Department was severely to blame for the chronic outbursts of syphilis in the old Bengal Army, for it refused to supply examined and approved strumpets. This had always been the custom since the days of Lord Clive; but the blind and self-righteous Puritans of Victoria's glorious era sought to reform an innately sensual land. The regimental *beebee-khana* (harem) in the eighteenth century used to be an acknowledged portion of the Sepoy lines; but later, with the appearance of armchair martinets and evangelistic Colonel Sahibs, Jack Sepoy had need with the last of his meager coin, to smuggle in disease-ridden sluts from the filthy bazaars. Many, unable to afford anything after sutlers and other governmental thieves had swindled their pay, reverted to homosexuality. This was one of the causes of the bloody Indian Mutiny.

Among Indian castes were those which made their living through procuration and harlotry. Generally of low caste (Pariahs or Soodras), they were wanderers over the land. The most prevalent were the Dhomes of southern India who, by a fraction, exceeded in notoriety their cousins to the north: tribes of itinerant freebooters, professional whores, and sodomists known as Jauts. Others, Goojurs and Meywautees, hill-banditti whose original occupation had been agriculture, were of no better reputation.

Together with the gypsies of the Deccan, there were also sects of Pariah women, adorers of ghastly Kalee, called she-wolves and pye-dogs who hunted men in bands. Like the Bacchantes of Greece, their aim was to spring upon the unwary traveler and sacrifice him to the Dark Mother of Destruction. Torture and sapphic rape were the usual preliminaries to a death involving disembowelment, decapitation, and genital dismemberment. A common method of torment employed by the *singhistreeyun* (tiger-women) was that of slowly and persistently masturbating their victim to the point of senselessness, all the while assailing his ill-fated limb with vellicating oils and hairy pods that engendered irritable constriction and desire.

Nowhere in the world was there anything quite like the Indian *Nautch,* or ballet dance. The most staid nineteenth-century Burra Sahib could attest to that. When viewed in utmost privacy, it was an experience never to be forgotten.

Musicians, upon a cryptic signal, began their sensuous strains. The incense-glutted atmosphere dimmed.

The music ceased. A throbbing, anxious quiet.

In the culmination of straining fantasia, a silken aquagreen purdah drifted effortlessly before the spectators. There sprang out of purple depths a misty troupe of *bayaderes* attired in bejeweled red-and-gold gossamer *sarees.* White cotton shawls glowed in the eerie dimness. Struck by hints of light, aureate arm bangles and beaded anklets, cumbrous pearl earrings and glimmering frontals winked and boiled in white-hot reflection. How striking were they, with their dark expressionless faces accented by glittering eyes and red-tinted lips.

Their movements were of singular grace and precision as they glided forward like the lulling, sinuous waves of the sea. It was monotonous, but it held you. It fastened the yielding eyes of urgent man in mesmeric concentration. Flowing, receding in a continuous pattern of tense bodily movement, with hands, fingers, sweeping wheeling hips, and knees undulating to an unceasingly hypnotic rhythm, these *bayaderes* performed throughout the dinner.

In the dazing, pulsing moments one scarcely saw the dropped garments, but soon the dancers were completely naked—writhing, glistening, plump brown willows, swaying like avid flames in a hot, perfumed, aphrodisiac wind.

An awe-inspiring glide and they swept nearer the spellbound guests, encircling all who sat cross-legged in the center of the room. They thrust out their scented breasts, scarlet-tipped. They twisted ecstatically, effortlessly, to their knees and their buttocks, spreading supple limbs and making suggestive motions with deft, graceful hands and crimson-daubed, parted lips.

In the final moment of the swelling hour, there was an overpowering recessive movement and the voluptuous dream drew back to the misty purplescent borders of the purdah. Abruptly, preceded by a gust of perfume, the astounded guests saw the aquagreen veils flare together.

The music ceased, silence descended. But the vibrance of fantasy and animal passion continued to throb in the atmosphere. Well-nigh ensorcelled, no one spoke.

"The Nautch," commented a grinning, scarlet-bearded Hindee.

As among the Arabs, many yarns were spun round the Indian courtesan, each of them serving to point a moral. A favorite in the north, quite ancient, tells of a great bona roba who was keenly interested in proving the universal hypocrisy of man. In order to do so, she appeared one evening stark naked, except for a circlet of beads around one thigh. In this aspect she advanced to a gathering of Hindoo holy men and mendicant-celibates.

She challenged each of them: "Whoever will break the string of beads encompassing my thigh without seeking satisfaction of his lust, he is a perfect saint."

One by one, all the pretenders to inviolate sanctity, young and old, lean and stout, came before her. But, maddened by her druglike beauty, every holy man save one forgot the terms of her challenge, and on experiencing erection, immediately sought to thrust his member into her vagina or to rub it upon her vulva. At last, it came the turn of the youngest and newest of all, a rawboned, wiry lad, who approached her, gripped her thighs, and demonstrated, simultaneously, his manly strength and absolute self-control by breaking the string of beads with a blow of his stiff organ, and not once directing it to her secret parts.

Having failed in her venture, and fascinated by the youth, she sought in every way to tempt him, but without result. As many times as she would attach a string of beads to her upper thigh, and order him to break it with erect member, so would his *lingam* by religious incantation rise stiff and strong. But the moment she sought to touch it, the holy power died; the *lingam* shrank and remained insensate. Indignant and frustrated, the courtesan left, though somewhat consoled by the realization that *only one* person in all of India, a "pitiably idealistic" young ascetic, had proved incorruptible[12] and had successfully resisted her charms.

Another relates an incident from the colorful and voluptuous life of the medieval eroticist Kokah Pundit, minister-of-state to the eleventh-century court of the Maharajah Bhoje-Purrum. Kokah Pundit, cited as being the most virile man in all of India's history, was said to have carnally known thousands of women and succubi.

The eminent Punditjee, ever searching for the female or spirit capable of surviving his furious assaults, one day heard tell of a secret and forbidden cave in the forests of Malwa.

"There abides in that cave a young priestess," a wizened old *gooroo* told him. "She is what we holy men call *jigger-khweyyah,* a liver-eater. She is capable of snatching away the liver of a man by mere glance and incantations. Glaring into the eyes, she has mesmerized the most unwilling of men. She then obtains their seed, tosses it onto the flames of sacrifice; whereupon the man dies. This has been seen, and not even I can deny it. The ashes of her victims are strewn round her abode. She, as pythoness, possesses an infinite knowledge of all that occurs; for she discerns the future of mankind. You must be wary of Naugee-Dayvee, O my Punditjee. Naugee-Dayvee has been likened to the *pishauchee,* she-demon of the gods."

Kokah smiled, raising his hand. "No she-demon has ever worn me down, O most sublime Gooroojee.

---

[12]David Shea and Anthony Troyer, *The Dabistan.*

Yukshee and *bhootnee:* all of them have wept with fatigue. His Highness can attest to that."

"Ah! but she is even more powerful than the succubi, who come in the night to torment man till there can be no distinction between reality and illusion."

But Kokah only laughed, filled the *gooroo's* begging cup, and demanded to know the course he must take. The old holy man shrugged, shook his head, and reluctantly showed him the way.

In the haze of evening, Kokah Pundit went cautiously through heavy thicket that led into a *nullah,* a sort of gulley, from which rose a fetid steam. The odor of decay was thick and gagging in Kokah's nostrils.

Then the cave yawned before him. It was, at first glance, majestically embellished. An archway of polished *choonum* (shell-lime) glowed primrose in wraithlike dimness, and Kokah could see that each pillar was adorned with the most intricately carved figures. He drew closer, momentarily caught up in the enchantment. Kokah had studied many of his native temples, but rarely had he beheld in any such a display of the indulgences and delights of Paradise. Shiva was smiling as Parvuttee enswathed his waist in the act of coition. Beside them he saw the naked *raukshehs* and *pishauchees,* guardians of Lord Shiva and his lustful spouse, in every conceivable position. Some, being *raukshehs,* were standing with *pishauchees* entwined about their waists, their lips joined in bliss. Others, in perfect symmetry, were touching or fondling one another's secret parts. Kokah saw man and beast locked in ecstasy; willowy goddesses with swelling breasts embracing Hunoomaun the Monkey-God; another image of Mahadeva, the Queen of Serpents, coiled about him, devouring his swollen *lingam.* Then, to finish the panorama and form a cornerstone, there stood in bas-relief a row of naked virgins with spherical bosoms and vulvae delineated in precise detail.

Kokah groped toward the light, an orb of white heat, in a vacuous den of darkness. As further on he sought, carefully placing his feet so that he would not blunder into a pit, Kokah noticed that the light seemed to dim as if it were escaping his grasp.

The vault was hot, ominously still as before thunder. He stopped, nervously unfastened his robe. Sweat rushed from his scalp; it soaked his face, and neck, and chest. He felt it uncomfortably upon his limbs. Kokah wiped his face, and wrapped the skirt of his *puggree* about his neck. He edged forward.

A vibrating brilliance struck his eyes. Kokah lurched back, shielding his face. Heat overwhelmed him, crushing. Flaming images hugged his body, so that he dropped to the ground. Kokah thrashed to grip his senses, and there was daylight. A seductive infinity of luscious verdure, glimmering ponds, billowy groves, swelled before his eyes. Then, there was utter darkness. A voice, as from a conch-shell:

"Useervaudum, ey Maharajee!" (Blessings and welcome, O Great Lord.)

Kokah grappled to gain his feet. He stumbled, clawing the thickness of atmosphere round him.

A vague luminescence pulsed before him, intensifying with the beat of his heart, until it flared rich and yellow. A hand, apart from its arm, quivered in keen silhouette. The middle finger was raised, the thumb and forefinger were squeezed tightly together in the classic sign of *lingam-yoni*.

Kokah pressed his eyes shut, gasping with disbelief; but the hand remained for what seemed many years. Then, the hand dissolved. Brilliance blazed over the vast, drumming cavern and Kokah saw blood, reeking, spilling over a sea of beauty. He was blinded by its sinister glare.

Kokah heard the faint strains of the lutelike *sitar*. The green mists swirled, fumed saffron, then dissolved into the naked glare of sunlight. Kokah emitted a long, sharp cry, starting back on his haunches. He looked upon a bazaar and a face in the bazaar. It was his own face, a laughing face. The face called out to women who sat at their windows above the street, warbling lewd ballads and pouting with henna-stained lips, beckoning with bangled wrists and lithe fingers. Kokah watched himself walking on and on into dimness, into night. And every movement, every sensation, prodded his rigid body. A million voices in his ears, a million images brushing past; his own words and gestures, acknowledged as though he were there and performing as a puppet must perform.

He laughed; and the laugh echoed, wild and sepulchral. And as Kokah Pundit looked into his own eyes, he saw the deep brown waxing into green, blazing, viperous emeralds, which shrilled an evil tint of lust.

The voices dimmed, the images fled; the night fell in eerie rose tints. He entered a strange apartment. Every nerve reacted, every sense gripped what lay before him. A shimmering willow branch rushing toward him seized his body in a hungry embrace. He could feel his every tissue responding to fierce stimuli as his hands clutched soft flesh, as he grasped the foamy shroud, rending it down, to reach firm, pointed breasts, marble-white and demanding.

Kokah shuddered, his mouth gaping. The sleek arms were taut about his neck; sinuous limbs were as creepers, enwreathing his body. A flash of demoniac buoyance took hold of him and the savage ecstasy began to build, pleasurably incisive, as her image moved against him. And her lips sought his own, her tongue his own; and she scarred his back with her nails, and she cried out in rapture, then groaned in a convulsive instant of release.

Kokah felt inebriant pleasure as he sank into unconsciousness. His body was yet her body; and she clung to him fervidly, humming in delirium. But just as he became aware of slowly edging into darkness, a bolt of fire seared his brain. Kokah pitched forward, glared at her; and blood, sickeningly bright, was upon her arms and body, the blood bubbled from his breast. Her hand was upon the dagger, and the dagger was in his heart. But he felt no pain, only loathing. He screamed, clutched her throat and dug with thumbs of pliant steel until she was dead.

He swayed, his eyes sightless. His fingers trembled, touched a floor of nothingness. Kokah seemed to disintegrate; he eased back, plunging into a howling void.

Several hours later, Kokah Pundit groped for his senses, found himself naked and alone. The vague hazy light of early morning allowed him to find his clothing. He seemed weak, taxed in all his muscles, as if he had endured many hours of labor. A shrill blue belabored his reason, having need to shatter it, so that he could not think or move.

Searching the cave from one end to the other, he discovered nothing. And the entire night remained with him as the memory of no other dream ever had. Reality was lost in illusion, but illusion brought before him the frightful truth: *no man is a god, no man has the power of Lord Shiva.*

Kokah Pundit, unable to cope with the supernatural, resumed his search for a woman to equal his strength. Such a one, Kokah promised, he would take as his bride, and settle down in the palace to a normal family life. Otherwise, by the immutable wills of Fate and Lord Shiva, he dedicated himself to the study and impregnation of all womankind.

Learning of the offer of a famous Rajpoot courtesan that she would make any living man fabulously wealthy who carnally satisfied her, Kokah went to investigate. Her rumored boast was that no one had equaled her in physical endurance, and she had yet to encounter man or spirit to match her. Thus, having learned his own lesson, Kokah Pundit eagerly ventured forth to instruct another that *no woman is a goddess, no woman has the power of Mother Parvuttee.*

"Ah, so thou art just another presumptuous one. I wish to see thy coin first; it shall not be long ere I must take it away from thee. No man has ever been that rare that he can leave as wealthy as when he entered."

In stifling dimness, Kokah's naked feet stood upon velvet; and he said nothing.

She glared at him, grinning. "What is thy name?"

Kokah glared back at her, his lips vaguely twisted.

Then she came forward and stroked his cheek. Unbuttoning his damask robe, she pulled it open and smoothed her hand over his chest. "Thou art a strong man," she said, expressionless. She never once took her eyes off him, nor did Kokah cease to gaze at her.

She then embraced him, tightly. He fought desire; he did not want to fall prey. Kokah could feel her unfastening the string of his trousers. Then, as if by instinct, her warm hand sought and gripped with an uncanny deftness. It sent chills rushing through his body.

"You tremble."

He glared at her, his lips unmoving.

"Thou art surely an avatar," she sighed, forcing her lissome body against him. She bit his neck, to hear his voice. Kokah clenched his teeth, did not utter a sound. Her hands and bare thighs were at their work so that it was agony to suppress himself. She again looked into his eyes, and smiled viciously. "Thou wilt not seem vain and cocksure like all the others. Thou wilt drive me to exertion; and then, *ey Hurree!* Surely, ye must slay me."

Kokah grasped her, and she shrilled acceptance. Her arms were tight about his neck; and she cooed, then hissed, her fingernails sharp upon his back.

"When the sky becometh dark," she whispered heatedly, "through the excess of our love, fires are kindled within our bosoms, flaring white-hot in our loins, and sleep is driven from our bed, and often are our bodies afflicted by rabid desire."

Kokah, able and sure, was coarse but ardent with her, like tiger with tigress, and it was what she demanded. Rending her sheer garment, he pressed her to the cushions and marked her shoulder with his teeth. And his fingers streaked, so that she gasped and trembled and dug her nails into his flesh. Then, he whispered to her:

"I am Kokah Pundit, *muntree* to His Highness the Maharajah Bhoje-Purrum of Malwa."

She screamed, spat in his face. "Thou dog! though thou wert His Highness in person, thou hast offended me." She sought to gouge out his eyes, but Kokah grabbed her wrists and held them so that she gasped for mercy. The Rajpootnee glowered at him, sneering: "Why hast thou come to taunt me? *Ey Hurree!* I would walk through fire if I could but bear one of thy children, to know that I wast penetrated by a stallion, that the seed of bulls was in my womb, and that I bred a king in glorious honor of Lord Vishnu. But you laugh at me, you take me by deception. Yet, in truth, no man or spirit has ever cudgeled me into subjection."

Kokah laughed. "Show me your skill."

"I will show you death!" Her hand darted under a pillow. Kokah saw the deadly flare of steel, lurched aside, then fastened both hands upon her arm. She moaned, and the blade fell dully to the floor. Kokah seized the dagger, tossed it across the room.

"Princess," he said.

Her cheeks reddened slightly. Then, as though her eyes and manner were governed by sorcery, she regarded him, intense, magnetic. She pitched forward, clutching him by the shoulders. "I am a lioness; I am a leopard's mate. I am thine for one million years."

He glared hard and earnestly at her, taking her arms firmly but gently. She uttered a weak cry; and he caught her parted mouth to his own, drawing her tenderly upon him on the silken cushions. She clung to him in a sudden fever of awe and spasmodic need. His hands tightened on her thighs.

"Ey Hurree! Hurree! appease me," she sighed.

Kokah lurched to his feet. Dawn was bursting over the copper-green topes (mango groves). Only a few moments before, the eminent and inexhaustible Rajpootnee had fainted under him. Searching into his *puggree,* Kokah laid two hundred rupees next to her body and, slightly dizzy, staggered out of the gagging chamber.

To be sure, his vigorous trial with the spiritual world had rendered him more than capable of defeating the most redoubtable courtesan in all of India.

The erotic literature of the Arabs or even of the Chinese was equaled only by that of the aesthetic Hindoos who, in rank with the French, were eroticists of the first order. Among the most prominent works are:

Kaumeh-Shaustreh (Code of Love) and *Ruttee-Russyeh* (The Secrets of Pleasurable Coition), by Kokah Pundit.

Kaumeh-Sootreh (The Excellence of Love), by
Vutsya-yunneh.

Unungeh-Rungeh (The Nature of Cupid), by Kul-
yaun-mulleh.

4. ANGLO-INDIA

Kipling, repressed by Victorian standards, unfortunately
gave us only the half-truth of Anglo-India and its pleasurable sink of fornication, Simla.

When the first Europeans invaded Hindostan they
were dazzled by a limitless paradise of sensuality. The
steaming, voluptuous clime soon kindled the proverbial-
ly cold, impassive Westerner. "Drink beer, think beer!"
was enlivened by Pariah women and nautch girls who
wrapped their warm pulsing limbs about a man, melting
into his very flesh and soul. Hindoo women, with doe-
like eyes and sculpturesque bosoms, tempted the men to
savor their almost frightening animal receptivity and
ardor. In scented darkness they were naked, hot, and
slippery: lithesome serpents skilled in the amatory arts.
Indeed, there was nothing of the kind in Europe. India
opened a wide and intriguing field of debauchery, and
there need be no concealment.

Officers and civilians of the Honourable East India
Company spent their otherwise lonely nights in the bazaar, in the heated embraces of prostitutes. They, conquerors of the land, boldly entered the temples, tossed
the indignant Brahminee priests a few greasy annas, and
proceeded to sweat and writhe in a slough of rapture
with the snakelike mistresses of the gods.

Soon, as European settlements grew, the *beebee-
khana* (women's quarters) became a veritable institution, an essential part of every bachelor's compound.
One early nineteenth-century Bengalee indigo planter,
when asked by a very proper European journalist to
justify his "notorious" mode of living, replied:

"Well, once ye've tampered with white flesh, ye're
done. But as for the niggers, in all their animal pliability
and fervor, they're just pukka, preliminary exercise

and diversion, y'know. Without 'em—*damnation, man!*
—I might just go stark raving mad in all this perishing
heat and inertia."

The *beebee-khana* survived until the mid-nineteenth century, when European women began to make
their fateful appearance in India. Soldiers no longer
hired a troupe of bazaar prostitutes for the night's entertainment, officers and civilians no longer delighted in
shameless concubinage. The European female came to
reform; the *ayah,* or maid-servant, became her inter-
compound spy and confidante. And the *sirdar*-bearer,
apparently the Burra Sahib's most trustworthy servant,
became, for a few extra rupees per month, the Mem-
Sahibeh's intercantonment informer. Hence, in the coffeeshop, Sepoy officers jested with one another:

"Y'know, Doveton, your bearer has the way of a
cat about the compound and the mouth of an elephant
in the bazaar."

"Dear me! I must cashier the wretch—"

"—or poison your wife, eh?"

It was forever the *gup* (gossip) that Major So-and-
So gambled incessantly with *soucars, bunneahs,* and
dacoits (usurers, sutlers, and thieves); and that he
managed bacchanalian orgies in the *tye-khana* (cellar)
of his bungalow, welcoming any riffraff who could tender a reasonable entrance fee. And Colonel Whatsis-
name, the rotund bald-headed Old Schooler who appeared on parade with the Gospel in one hand and Bengal Army Regulations in the other, was notorious for
keeping strange women, allegedly missionaries' wives
and daughters. And the neighbor of Lieutenant Thus-
and-Such, an old widower, claimed that he owned all
the nautch girls and *devadasees* in the city; and that he
roamed the countryside in the pious guise of a lecherous *dervish,* to discover what the Mussulmans must
think of their devout women.

When the Devil's Wind of 1857 blew over and
Anglo-India was left virtually denuded of Europeans,
the *beebee-khana* made its triumphal comeback. The
Burra Sahibs at Home talked of their "white nigger" relatives and friends who were "going native" out

in India, now that all the ladyfolk were gone and the field was again free for them to "admire the texture of pandy behinds."

Hindoo women, morganatically attached to their white masters, lived and died in the *beebee-khana*. They toiled and procreated, collected their monthly reward for instructing in Hindostanee and other essentials; still, there could never be that perfect bondage. They bore the Sahibs' children, played the passive animal, but never experienced love or complete gratification. The selfish ignorance of the European disdained to recognize this.

Thus, a man had to keep strong in mind and in body. For there were seductive forces tugging at his reason every step of the way, a sensuously deadly gravitation toward oblivion. The supernatural was the East's only effective weapon against Western intrusion. They so perfected it that it even defied and outwitted all reality. There were in India awesome phenomena that no man understood; he merely learned to accept and live with them. An individual with a mind closed to the mystical was the first to go, the prime victim of ungodly Fate. And only the fool probed too deeply in his quest for tolerant understanding; he found himself enmeshed, unable to escape.

For the East was like a feverish woman with whom the unwary Occidental was having sexual congress. She gripped him in blind ecstasy and delirium that built to an intolerable pitch and then, just before the fiery second of release, plunged a knife into his heart. Mother Kalee, Goddess of Sadism, ruled supreme.

And out of this superficial union there evolved what was later to become one of free India's greatest problems: the Eurasian. *Eight annas* (*in the rupee* the standard Hindu coin, which is worth sixteen annas); *half-caste; chee-chee; Christ against Mohammed, Christ against Shiva, and neither gaining any ground.* Yet to the European the Indians were even lower *wogs, niggers,* or *pandies.* The hybrid was far superior for he understood the problem, being of both worlds though he belonged to neither. India did not want him, Eu-

rope would not claim him. Everywhere he turned, he
was left in the lurch. Angrily, never philosophically, he
reviewed his plight in harrowing self-consciousness:

> I'm groveling like a rat. I was engaged to
> an English girl; when she found out I was eight-
> annas, she left the country. I must say: some-
> times, I really fail to understand women. Even
> the outwardly virtuous ones.
>
> Oh, I've seen those. Missionaries' daughters,
> and wives: another man's fingers on their breasts
> and genitals, a native lecher sweating between
> their thighs. I've known of English girls going
> out into the godown with the Pariah sweeper's
> son. I've seen frustrated women roaming the ba-
> zaars, because the Mussulman is a gratifying
> lover.
>
> The Mem-Sahibehs. In Fifty-seven, they
> were tossed naked and mutilated on the dung-
> heaps, into wells and limepits; and not a few
> of them were hissed at by their native para-
> mours, turned butchers. They were called "sluts"
> and "unclean whores," and they had their wombs
> and breasts carved out and burnt.
>
> They're wanton. It's the heat; and it knocks
> a lot out of the European, but only whets the
> appetite of the passionately fascinating Indian.
> The Mem-Sahibehs starve for affection; but the
> heat and duty and financial worries plague the
> Sahib, and he is inconsiderate and psychological-
> ly impotent. He takes a peg of brandy; but when
> he does that, he isn't interested then in going in
> to his wife. He wants to go abroad, for he feels
> he's had his fill of boredom.
>
> It's a sad and loathsome thing.

VI

EUNUCHISM:
Honor in Dishonor

When God made the Sudan, He laughed!

1. BONDAGE

So spake the Arabs of a land they called Blackman's Country. The Sudan was a beast, an abortion; and its capital, El-Khartoum (the Elephant's Trunk) was the fetid nucleus not only of the slave trade but the center of eunuchism, the great den of iniquity. In Khartoum, nearly every man owned a slave (even the poorest Arab, even the scheming castrato, while the rich, despotic Turk owned hordes).

Many died believing that slavery was rooted in the very core of an inexorable land, a thing that must be, like evolution. It was written there in blood and sweat. It was the starving Negro hunting the elephant, the starving Arab hunting the Negro, and the ravenous Turk hunting the Arab to hunt the Negro.[1]

At Dewwausheh (eunuchry), a town in the Messelau-meeyeh District of Darfour, over thirty thousand

---

[1] Richard A. Bermann, *The Mahdi of Allah.*

human beings perished yearly to meet the quota of
three thousand eunuchs. Captured between the ages of
four and ten, Negro boys were personally gelded by
fegeehs (religious lawyers) and herded down to Khartoum for sale. During the notorious reign of Abyssinian
King John, one hundred captured Sudanese soldiers
from Hicks Pasha's Anglo-Egyptian Army were brought
down into Adoweh. There they were subjected to total
mutilation and sent to Khartoum with the message that
if His Highness the Khedive of Egypt wanted eunuchs,
he could have these. Every one of them died.

In the Moslem world, the title *gellaub* (seller of
men) was in its origin synonymous with infamy. It
was first among the three *moherremaut* (forbiddens) of
the Prophet; for Lord Mohammed in his teachings
severely forbade the trading of unsexed individuals.
Many pious but philosophical Arabs were aware of
slavery's long and sinful history and transformation:
that, in spite of El-Koran and in spite of all threats of
hell fire and everlasting perdition, it was a major Moslem profession and provided sustenance for many Children of Allah. In an apathetic world, men had to grub
by any means possible, especially in the barren, brutal
Sudan. And every year, even at the risk of losing
money, vicious *gellaubs* systematically raped many
thousands of defenseless females between the ages of
five and twenty.

In the vibrance of savage African heat and maelstrom, stench and clamor, the Slave Market (Bazaar-el-
Obeyd) in Khartoum was a slough of fluid, steaming
dregs and chaos. Hands, fingers, and arms prodded
like clubs and daggers. Every man jogged and poked,
according to the way of the East, thrusting the limbs,
projecting the nose, waggling the beard, and gabbling
in the most shrill and guttural-sounding of tongues. It
was a bubbling, reeking, hazardous morass; and the
singsong chant, swelled in waves, from every side:

What bid? what bid! Here! here! the finest
of eunuchs, clean of both cullions and yard! The
most beautiful of catamites, with plump blossomy
buttocks; *Ya'llah!* the most luscious of concu-

bines: shapely, full, and ripe! What bid? what
bid!

    Searing, thrumming monotony; slavers tugging at
their garments, touching their beards. Billows of
naked bodies.

    Presently, after suffering raucous importunities and
solicitations along narrow fetid ways, the prospective
buyer lurched into a broad square enclosed by shops
and stalls and brothels and cafés. In the center, by
several steaming, brick-lined fountains and a sprawling
mimosa tree, stood the slave platforms.

    The crowds, like multicolored ants stirred from
their holes, suddenly cascaded into the square. In a
few glutting moments, everyone became distressingly
aware of multitudes, pressing and panting and wheez-
ing, abandoning each enclosure and adjoining street
to ply and jam as close to the platforms as possible.
Someone on the middle dais would howl; a whip would
crack; and then silence. An individual caught his breath,
then a reburst of thunder would swell, engulf a lone
squeal. Another *kourbash* (whip) would streak and
fall, another *gellaub* or Bashi-Bazouk (Turkish soldier)
would boom, and tight silence would again settle over
the waters.

    Then began the restless shoving and blowing one's
nose on one's sleeve or between one's fingers, or coughing a foul breath into other people's faces, or hawking
and spitting, or chewing pungent sweetmeats and allowing tinted saliva to run out of the corners of one's
mouth and down over one's *burnoose,* or emitting such
gargled sounds as to show enjoyment toward that bit
of gluten one was munching, and to make it known
that one's stomach declared *There is one God,* or
sneering and expectorating obscenities at other people
because they are inferior, or kicking and biting and
gnashing one's teeth, or jabbing one's fingers into places
where it is not proper to jab.

    In this throng there stood an occasional woman,
accompanied by her handmaidens or several naked
eunuchs. And amidst all those ill-smelling, ill-mannered
hordes of men these occasional women passed un-

molested. There seemed to be a sacred respect for veiled women, even the most unsavory harlot.

The sea shifted; the soughing waves careened back, then forward. Someone said: "Thou ass-faced dog!" . . . "God be praised!" . . . "In the name of God the Merciful and Compassionate, on with the bidding!" . . . "If God so willeth, that raven-eyed Jewess with the proud nipples!" . . . *"El-gellaub! gellaub!* For God's sake, on with the bidding!" And it converged into a rolling blast of *"Inshallah-Te'auleh: gellaub! gellaub!"* As the waves settled to a tense rumble, another erupted in guttural damnation of all Toorks and Infidels. When it dissolved, a new voice was heard: "That broad-shouldered Shillook there. Yea, the one by the flat-breasted Negress." . . . "Nay, that unbelieving trollop with the swollen belly. Bring twice the sum, as with the wench of a bulbous coynte. Proved more fertile than most of these barren, haggled whores, and with her, that spindle-shanked Hebshee. His copulatory member is laudably thick."

At last the slavers mounted the platforms, followed by several sneering Bashi-Bazouks who flogged naked merchandise as the *gellaubs* strutted along, glistening in fierce sunlight. Taking up their malacca canes, these fair-skinned Turks and a few of them high-bred Arabs commenced the bidding. The poorest merchandise, unhealthy or misshapen slaves, were first driven forward to be traded off to the poorer classes for bolts of cloth, beads, talismans, bric-a-brac, and petty sums.

During this time, all young boys between the ages of four and ten were taken down behind the platforms to meat-cleavers' platforms where razor-wielding *hhekeems* castrated them. The screams of these young victims were drowned in the shuffling of the crowds and the crescendo of heated chaffering, but compassionate individuals could well enough imagine the excruciating, slipshod ordeal. The bodies of many black lads who had succumbed to shock or had bled to death were being hauled away in open, fly-ridden tumbrils, to be dumped into the Nile River.

The Prophet Mohammed condemned the selling

and employment of emasculated men, and yet the followers of Mohammed's religion were placing for sale and offering exorbitant sums for them, the price going up to as high as forty pounds on a successfully gelded youth. In the bidding, a eunuch who retained his penis did not fetch as much as the emasculated one whose parts were all removed, and who was called *sendelee*. But the mortality rate was not as high among the former.

When the more desirable human goods were offered—plump hairless castratos, handsome boys, young maidens, pregnant women, and potent male breeders, the frenzy of bidding diminished. It was now a gentlemanly game and the common folk drew back for eminent *sheykhs* and *beys* and *pashas* and *effendies* to stalk forward in their stately raiments and make their offers.

The first for auction was a Circassian girl about fifteen, a comely, brown-skinned virgin with downcast eyes, and hands folded neatly in front.

"Uncover thy coynte," someone shouted, "that I may savor its aspect."

Her knees trembled violently, and when another called out for her to be soothed the *gellaub* rapped her on the knees with his cane, poked her stomach, and went on with his babbling:

"What am I offered, *yah effendeen,* for this most delicious fruit?"

"Ten dollars!" one crow-beaked old Ja'alee said, emitting a flash of saliva.

"Ten dollars! I'm bid ten! ten! ten!—here, ten—" the *gellaub* said, twirling his malacca. *"Ten!* for this paradisaic houri—" He thrust his cane against the nape of her neck, lifted silky dark tresses. "See, brothers, hair that is worth triple that! Hair that is equaled only by the product of the worm! Hair that is like the thread of corn! That is black like the nymph's, ecstatic to touch, to kiss, to hold in one's mouth! To rend in the fever of love! *Ten—ten—*"

"Fifteen!" said a sallow, frail-looking man, a half-caste Britisher with spectacles, plum-colored *tarboosh,* and immaculate white tunic.

"Fifteen—fifteen! Bid fifteen, by the illustrious Haskill Bey! Fifteen! fifteen, for *lo!"* He tapped her stomach, then slid the cane up under her taut young breasts. "Lo, *effendeen!* as luscious as the melons in the gardens of El-Feyyoom! As delectable as the treats of El-Khargeh and Bahreeyeh! *Hah!* ye squabbling ones, these pomegranates alone are worth the price—"

"Twenty, in the name of God!" rasped a red-eyed, grey-bearded sheykh. "If God willeth, twenty!"

"Twenty? Esteghfirullah! this plump coynte alone is worthy of the price."

"Twenty-five! And be she frigid or barren, the devil take thee, swine—and all the *jinn* and *afreets* devour thee, and the *marids* and *ghuddars* pluck away thy genitals, and Emeen-ed-Deen shall see that thy bones be fed to the ghouls and hyenas! Twenty-five dollars, with the Maria Theresa stamp upon the gold, and beware the tinkling of camel bells!"

"Twenty-five! and all thy slavering, Sheykh Hadjee Emeen-ed-Deen? *Bismillah!"* croaked another patriarch, who flourished a long, polished cudgel. *"Inshallah!* I shall offer thirty for her, and may Shaitan (Satan) seek his victim be I ill in assuming her demoniac passion and productivity!"

"Indeed!" stamped the *gellaub,* fighting against the clamor. "Behold!" He flicked away her folded hands with a sharp manipulation of the cane. "She is as enticing and voluptuous as the *ghooleh* which visits the desert traveler in his dreams, evoking a feverish succession of orgasms unattained save in Paradise. Behold the exquisite folds, the tender mound, the ripe symmetry—"

In another moment she was gone, and they were driving on another—and another. Lissome, statuesque Negresses with henna-tinted nipples, ringlet tresses glossy with camel urine, and pink-dyed pubic hair. Yellow-cast Egyptian *fellaheen* (peasant) women, with sharp pendulous bosoms and protuberant pudenda. Nubian and Hebshee beauties brought from twelve to fifty pounds apiece; one Circassian, a hundred pounds; several Greeks, sixty Austrian dollars; and Jewesses, anywhere from fifty to two hundred *reyauls* (a reyaul was worth about half a dollar in pre-World War I currency exchange).

Dewwaushees (eunuchs) in the prime of life were valued at from thirteen to twenty *mejeedees* (a mejeedee was worth about 90 cents in pre-World War I currency exchange); emasculated youths, under puberty, from fifteen to thirty dollars; and educated slaves, gelded after puberty, from twenty-five to seventy *reyauls*. Some, being the rare *sendelees,* brought almost five hundred pounds.

Those uncastrated slaves purchased to sire new bondsmen were marketed solely on the length and thickness of their virile members. In some cases they were rated according to the number of offspring they were said to have engendered. When the question of manhood arose, customers were granted the right of experimentation. In wealthy households such stud males served as breeders of slaves. But this was not a common practice since castrates fetched such high prices that it did not pay to spare boys to become breeders. Consequently most of the traffic was in boys and slaves and sheykh were in harmony on that score. And, as before mentioned, three out of five Arabs preferred the sexual service of a handsome young beardless lad or a serviceable eunuch to that of any beautiful woman.

From frontier to frontier, slaver, slave, thorn-hedge *zerreebeh,* Bashi-Bazouk, they littered the deserts by thousands, fed ravenously upon the waterholes, defiled the oases, and sated the steaming market places. Black, white, yellow, brown slaves were chaffered over and sold wherever there was someone to purchase; and where there was coin that teeth could not dent, men traded their own families for a greasy shekel that might buy their way into the embrace of a desirable catamite: circumstances so flagrant yet entirely unknown to Western civilization for hundreds of years.

But the real curse of slavery was not in the actual holding of slaves but in the misery caused by the destruction of villages, the severing of family ties, and the cruelties perpetrated in the work of capture. In fact, once a slave came into a decent household he was treated like any other human being, as though he were a part of the master's blood family. Only rarely did one hear of a sadist taking a slave girl's maidenhead, then tying her up over a slow-burning fire till she roasted to death.

> Feed your slaves with food of that which ye eat, and clothe them with such clothing as ye wear, and command them not to do that which they are unable. A man who behaves ill to his slave shall not enter into Paradise.

These are the words of the Prophet Mohammed.

The average slave was granted all the food he could eat, all the proper rest, and enjoyed surreptitious access to the harem. The slave often relished more frequent intercourse with his master's wives than the master himself. In comparative freedom, as prescribed by the Prophet, and with such privileges as his ingenuity could procure, the slave was often contented and loyal and apt to stand beside his master throughout life—even after total freedom was bestowed upon him. For he never had it so good as in bondage.

Thus, the normal slave became the nucleus of all petty intrigue. Women hired him, amongst other duties, to strangle, torture, procure, and copulate; and the larger and more vigorous his sexual parts, the richer he became. Slaves, many of them eunuchs, often rose to high power, becoming generals, ministers, and even rulers. In Turkey, eunuchs commanded the army and advised the Sultan; in Persia, they became Shahs; and in Egypt, the white *memlooks* (Mamelukes) arose and vanquished their venomous masters to rule for five centuries.

2. EMASCULATION

The origin of castration is to be found in the androgynous worship of antiquity. In Egypt, the male organs with their two witnesses of generative force were considered the most sacred portions of the human body and, therefore, worthy of sacrifice. Piles of freshly severed genitals lay beneath the altars in Egyptian temples, where hundreds of virile youths were initiated daily into male prostitution by the emasculated hierarchy. Bagoas, the great eunuch of Egypt, was passionately loved by Alexander the Great, whose distraught childhood and irrational tendencies made him one of the most renowned of bisexuals.

From Egypt, castration and slavery entered the Holy Land, where Moses condemned seizure and disposal of the eunuch (*sereem*).

Castration as a business (*khesseh*) among the Arabs soon became an international syndicate, reaching from North Africa to Malaya. The eunuch (*dewwaushee*), respectfully called *agha* (master), *khadim* (servant), and *khwaudjah* (lord), was generally divided into three distinct classes.

The first and most vicious was *es-sendelee* (cleanshaven, with penis as well as testicles amputated). Vehemently jealous of virility and childishly unreasonable, these corpulent individuals, hairless, slovenly, and with high-pitched voices, were in great demand as guardians of the harem. But, owing to the excessive danger in total mutilation through hemorrhage or infection, the *sendelee* was indeed rare. In manufacturing this class of eunuchs, the patient was secured flat upon the earth, his limbs splayed. Tightly gripping his genitals and pulling hard on them, the *hhekeem* amputated with a single stroke of the razor; the wound was instantly cauterized with boiling ghee, the victim planted in a steaming-fresh dungheap and, were he under puberty, he had some chance of living. For the rest of his days the survivor would pass urine through a hollow reed (*gezzeb*).

The second type of eunuch, less vengeful and a deal more masculine, was *el-ebter* (tailless). Otherwise virile and sexually responsive, he merely lacked the wherewithal to satisfy his desires until the much-welcomed invention of caoutchouc supplied him with a sizable phallus such as he would not have possessed were he complete.

El-ghezee (the stoned) was perhaps the most popular and prevalent of eunuchs. He was a great favorite of the harem, especially if his testicles had been removed after puberty, when his penis had grown nigh its fullest. Since his organ was retained and his erectile powers survived, depraved women descended upon him like *ghoolehs*. He virtually ruled the harem and arrogantly gloried in his eminence, from chief pimp and gobetween to the queen's personal attendant and paramour. One such eunuch, boasting of his esteem, said:

> I am surely a child of the Jinn, slave of Destiny; and I owe allegiance to El-A'awer, spirit of the one-eyed virile member.
>
> In everything God hath created for man there is a use; for He—to Whom be glory!—made the hands to seize, the feet to walk, the eyes to see, the ears to hear, and the penis to increase and multiply—and so on, with all the members of the body, except the two ballocks. There is no use in them. So, one day, a slaver took up his knife and cut mine off; and ever since then, I have futtered and enjoyed thousands of women—and not a one have I sown with child!

Intercourse with a *ghezee* was not only safe, since he could not impregnate, but satisfying to the most avid female. He was as inexhaustible as a bullock, since he experienced no devitalizing emission. Hence females were vastly enamored of him because of the thickness of his organ, his lack of impregnating testicles, and his charming ability to copulate almost indefinitely, realizing one sterile spasm to three of an average woman.

In Persia and India, where the eunuch was termed *khojah* or *hijrrah,* a frequent punishment afforded strangers caught in the harem was to give them over to the male slaves, who generally raped, hacked, and crushed them to pulp. The *seedee* (Zanzibar Negro) was dreaded by Hindoo and Mussulman alike; for gelded he became a dangerous beast roaming the Deccan, employed as mercenary by the Sultaun of Mysore and the Nizaum of Hyderabad.

The usual procedure in making the *ghezee* was through "baptism by fire" (searing or tearing out the testes with a red-hot iron or pincers), simple amputation by razor, bandaging, bruising or beating, and twisting. Another method, a favorite amongst sadistic harem women in torturing a clandestine lover, was by severe and persistent masturbation until the victim was rendered impotent and his erectile powers virtually destroyed. In the zenanas of Moslem India, men were unsexed like the Rajpoots' and Mahrattas' gelded stallions: a humane process by which a cord was secured round the flaccid scrotum and slowly tightened until circulation was hindered and the pouch withered and dropped off. This type of emasculation, known as *phaunsee* (strangulation), was certainly less dangerous and less agonizing.

Castration upon the battlefield was forever imminent in the callous Sudan. Every warrior realized that once he fell, wounded or dead, his precious genitals must yield to brutal hands. An almost masochistic tension and anxiety accompanied this thought.

When a Sudanese warrior gripped another's genitals, spat upon them, and shrilled victory, his orgasm, and that of the victim were spontaneous if the victim were conscious. Upon the second the blade flashed, the conscious victim achieved his incisive apex of morbid pleasure; and he fainted or died with this sacrificial sensation. The semen, gone from both their bodies, insured each against the intervention of evil spirits; for supernatural union and purification had been accomplished through mutual oblation. The only difference was that one died and the other, for the present, lived. Neither deserved greater honor or respect, not even the victor who held high his victim's genitals. But had the victim not ejaculated upon the second of judgment, disrespect was burnt into his soul and ill fortune heaped on the victor who dared chance the sacred amputation.

Thus, dead men were not gelded until all sheykhs and emeers had first driven their spears (*jereeds*) into the bodies, to release a multitude of evil spirits. Preceding death, seminal emission, acting as a bond of purity and sacrifice, cleansed the body. Were the victor not to ejaculate upon the second he applied his blade, his soul and the virile acknowledgment of his victim were defiled unto eternity. Castration exclusive of religious ceremony was, therefore, to the Sudanese Negro, a risky undertaking: one of the supreme trials of manhood.

During the African campaigns in the latter portion of the nineteenth century, when Hicks Pasha's illfated Anglo-Egyptian expedition sought to capture ElObeyd from the Mahdi, scouts and spies taken by the Dervishes were stripped of all their garments and buried alive in murderous ant hills or smothered in rancid ghee, tied to earth, and left to grill in the fat. And not a few of them were castrated or pierced from behind by a red-hot phallus, or staked out, face downward, with a trail of honey leading from the abode of flesh-eating insects to the victim's penis, which was generously smeared.

Begherreh women awaited their chance, by the bidding of renegades, to pluck away the imposing sexual organs of the heathen black soldiers, destroy their pride and confidence and masculinity, and make them deathly afraid. Afraid of the Desert, afraid of the Mahdi. Everywhere the Army of Hicks Pasha turned, wells were found tainted by fresh urine; the remaining food supply was wantonly destroyed by traitors.

Hicks heard all sorts of rumors, many of them unnerving. The camp women, wives and prostitutes, soon died; and, living and dead, milk was forced from their breasts. The traveling catamites, frail as they were, wasted; and soon the Sudanese roasted them, dead and alive, for something to eat. Many of the Turkish soldiers reverted to imbibing their own seminal fluid or that of witless blacks, which often they obtained by violence. But soon man was bone-dry. There was only blood now: blood to take in the night, from a sleeping man too weak and insensible to object. The Army of Hicks Pasha perished, distintegrated by the Desert, disintegrated by the Mahdi.

There was great festivity in El-Obeyd upon the annihilation of all Infidels in Kordofan province. The Mad Messiah, Mohammed Ahmed ibn Seyyid Abdullah, built a pyramid of the skulls of Hicks Pasha's Army. He erected it on the road to El-Obeyd, and in sight of the city. There, vultures darkened the sky. And in a large well close to this there could be viewed the carnal members of ten thousand Egyptians and Turks, symbolic of El-Mahdi's power over the Unbelievers. The largest of these, carefully preserved, hung before Mohammed Ahmed's tent, to remind the Faithful of how the generative strength of the Infidel was summarily shattered. The smallest were spat upon, distributed as trophies; and the women of El-Obeyd, proud of their men, wore Infidel testes upon their garments as if they were decorative tassels.

William Hicks and his entire staff of European officers were beheaded, disemboweled, and castrated, pierced by a thousand ceremonial spears, and brought in fragments before the Mahdi, whose only reaction was a languorous grin.

The incredible incidents at El-Obeyd are among the most detailed recorded examples of religious castration in the East. The frenzied Turk had employed it against the Crusader; for he, like every True Believer, had need to destroy the procreative power of an Infidel before he could gain admittance into Paradise. It became not only an act of piety for the Faithful but of degradation to the victim; following mutilation, the Infidel's head was severed and placed between his thighs: the seat of dishonor.

In India and Afghanistan, religious fanatics (*ghazees*) employed the *waughnukh* or *chungool* (tiger's claw). Concealed in the hand like knuckledusters, the *waughnukh* was a murderous weapon of treachery. Shivajee, the illusive Mountain Rat of the Mahrattas, slew Ufzool Khan, commander-in-chief of the forces of Shah Jehan, with the claw. As the big-bellied general under a flag of truce came forward and formally embraced Shivajee, the latter's tiger's claw caught him hard between the thighs, gouging swift and deep, upward. Without a cry, Ufzool hugged Shivajee in a spasm of insensibility, then relaxed, to slide lifeless to the ground.

Shegg (splitting, laying men open from neck to scrotum) was common in Persia as well as Egypt; and not a few soldiers ere going into battle secured ample cloth round their precious under parts where the knife was first to slash or the insidious hand was first to grip and squeeze. This manner of subduing a man, prevalent among Persian wrestlers, was the favorite method of worming out of a tight spot; for the scrotum was perhaps the most vulnerable part of the Oriental body.

Sacred castration was also carried over into acts of penitence. The masochistic *dervish* and *fakeer,* who also pierced their flesh with bodkins and slashed their bodies with whips and knives, emasculated themselves for ascetic reasons. Tormented by satyriasis, aggravated by abstinence, the martyr felt that Satan had invested his bowels, thrusting nettles into the urethra. Mutilation was more widespread among the *fakeers* of India. In the Sudan, *dervish* and *soofee* were generally more in control of their passions because the vista of fornication with impunity was much greater than in India (where the British government outlawed this religious institution). Transvestite Turks, scornful of their large pendants, deliberately mutilated themselves to become total effeminates; but Bedewwee Arabs, endowed with unimposing genitories, escaped castration when they adopted the platonic effeminacy of ancient Greece.

Harem castration, punishment for infidelity, was frequent in Egypt. The concubine, when embracing her disloyal paramour, usually ripped out his testicles with her fingernails; but another procedure no less terrifying is here described by a youthful unfortunate:

> When it became known to me what they were planning to do, horror fluttered my scrotum. My very ballocks curdled with fear when I realized how trapped I was: that I could not cry out, or escape, because of the eunuchs. By the eyes of the Prophet! I was in such confusion and dread, I piddled in my bag-trousers—and even beskited myself; whereupon, they unfastened the inkle of my drawers. Truly, my spittle was dried up for very uncertitude.
>
> Naked as I was, and with prickle at point, she and her slave-girls pinioned me down. I

begged her to reveal her intent; and finally, after
I was well secured, she said unto me:

"I bear the intention of removing thy precious stones, the honors of thy yard. I must also
apply the blade to thy pizzle, if only to prevent
thee from enjoying the two million orgasms in
Paradise. But there is a slower, more impressive,
means of making thee know of mine anger. Thou
art of no further use to me, nor art thou any
longer fit for my company; I care only for
bachelors and not for married men. Thou hast
sold me for a stinking armful; but, by God, I
will make the whore's heart ache for thee!"

God forbid! a cold fluttering in the cullions
attested to my fear.

She tied a cord round my stones and, giving
it to two of her women, bade them haul at it.
They did so; and I swooned away and was, for
excess of pain, in a world other than this. Then,
she came with a razor of steel and cut off my
member masculine; after which, she seared the
wound with melted cheese and rubbed it with a
powder—and I, the while, unconscious. Now
when I came to myself, the blood had stopped;
so she bade the slave girls unbind me and
made me drink a cup of wine. Then, she said to
me:

"Go, now, to her whom thou hast married
and who begrudged me a single night; for I
needed nought of thee save what I have just cut
off."

And I wept over myself, for that I was become even as a woman: without manly tool
like other men.[2]

An Abyssinian eunuch or *meymoon* (ape) by the
name of Bukheyt relates his experiences in the medieval
Arabian Nights:

Know, O my brothers, that when I was a
little one—some five years old—I was taken
home from my native country by a slave-driver
who sold me to a certain apparitor (court officer).

[2]Burton, *op. cit.*

My purchaser had a daughter, three years old, with whom I was brought up; and they used to make mock of me, letting me play with her and dance for her and sing to her, till I reached the age of twelve and she that of ten. And even then, they did not forbid me seeing her.

One day, I went in to her and found her sitting in an inner room; and she looked as if she had just come out of the bath, which was in the house, for she was scented with essences and reeked of aromatic woods and her face shone like the circle of the moon on the fourteenth night.

She began to sport with me, and I with her. Now I had just reached the age of puberty: so my prickle stood at point, as it were a huge key. Then, she threw me on my back and, mounting astraddle on my breast, fell a-wriggling and a-bucking upon me till she had uncovered my yard. When she saw it standing with head erect, she hent (seized) it in hand and began rubbing it upon the lips of her little slit: outside her petticoat-trousers. Thereat hot lust stirred in me and I threw my arms round her—while she wound hers about my neck and hugged me to her with all her might—till, before I knew what I did, my pizzle split up her trousers and entered her slit and did away with her maidenhead.

When I saw this, I ran off and took refuge with one of my comrades. Presently, her mother came in to her and, seeing her in this case, fainted clean away. However, she managed the matter advisedly and hid it from the girl's father out of good-will to me; nor did they cease to call to me and coax me, till they took me from where I was.

After two months had passed by, her mother married her to a young man—a barber, who used to shave her papa—and portioned and fitted her out of her own monies; whilst the father knew nothing of what had passed. On the night of consummation, they cut the throat of a pigeon-poult and sprinkled the blood on her shift. After a while, they seized me unawares and gelded me; and, when they brought her to her bridegroom, they made me her Agha—her eunuch—to walk before her wheresoever she went, whether to the bath or to her father's house. I abode with her a long time, enjoying her beauty and loveliness by way of kissing and clipping and coupling with her, till she died—and her husband and mother and father died also—when they seized me for the Royal Treasury as being the property of an intestate; and I found my way hither, where I became your comrade.

This, then, O my brethren, is the cause of my cullions being cut off; and peace be with you!

Miscegenation was extensive in the East, particularly in degenerate Egypt where avid young females, neglected in the harem, fell prey to the black slaves and their impressive natural parts. Innocent and naïve, the pubescent harem girl found the eunuch an awe-inspiring creature, huge, muscular, glossy-black, with austere countenance and a fascinatingly tremendous *shurraubeh* (tassel) resembling in symmetry a powerful bull-whip (*kourbash*).

The eunuchry of Egypt became so bold that every new virgin slave girl purchased and brought into the harem was deflowered before she even entered the master's bed; and with this flagrant prevalence of rape and great disrespect shown the master of the house, something rigorous had to be done. In Sudanese harems, following defloration by the master, women, walking short and daintily, with tiny bells attached to their feet and wrists, were protected from lustful eunuchs by a thick, twelve-inch bamboo staff thrust a third of the way into the vagina and strapped about the waist and thighs, with a woven straw shield in front to cover the vulva. Hence tinkling bells and a somewhat painful waddle became indicative of chastity. Every wise Egyptian, adopting Sudanese practice, locked away his new addition to the women's apartment until he had personally deflowered her, then set her loose well protected by this genital fortification.

But in retaliation eunuchs, scornful of those wom-

en who refused to unstrap their devices behind a hall-
way curtain and submit to penetration in a standing
position, spilt the whites of eggs on the bed sheets;
whereupon the master suspected adultery or fornication, virile men smuggled into the seraglio, and had
each new concubine summarily beheaded.

VII

SEXUAL PERVERSION:
Matter of Taste

There is no accounting for taste!

1. SODOMY

The *Mashallah* (it is the will of Allah) of the Moslems, excusing or shrugging away all acts as the immutable decree of God or as a matter of inexorable Fate (*kismet*), is the *Dustoor hey* (it is the custom) of the Hindoos. Worldly Arabs merely uttered *"Mashallah!"* as a matter of habit; but others, less free of mind, solemnly believed that everything they did was pre-ordained and, if the action occurred, it must be sanctioned by God or it would not have been thus.

"I am a man-stealer," said the crafty Persian, "but that is justified. The Prophet has not warned me in sleep against such actions; therefore, my conscience is clear."

Another, quite innocent, would say: "Man's destiny is written in the sutures of his skull, but none can understand the meaning thereof. There is no fighting against Fate, nor hath any man ever fled from that which is written on his forehead; for surely, by the immutable will of God, there is but a feeble breath between the womb and the grave."

In other terms: "We lack understanding of what, in the Light of Truth, is good or evil. Therefore, as long as ye may, eat and drink and be merry! Thus was it written on our foreheads; no being can escape that which is written on his forehead. What is written on the forehead must be fulfilled, and it is not in our power to avoid it."[1]

The Brahmin, in excusing away all sin and worldliness, simply lifted his arms and chanted:

N'rhohum! n'munmeyhum! n'hum!

> I exist not in anything;
> Nothing exists in me;
> I, myself, exist not.[2]

The philosopher (*punditjee*), more elegant, would teach his flock:

> It is written: We may descend into hell, establish our dwelling in the abode of Brahma or in the paradise of Indra, throw ourselves into the depths of the sea, ascend to the summit of the highest mountain, take up our habitation in the howling desert or in the town where fortune reigns, take refuge with the King of Death, bury ourselves in the bowels of the earth, brave the dangers of battle, sojourn in the midst of venomous reptiles, or take up our abode on the moon; yet our destiny will none the less be accomplished. All that will happen to us will be such as it is not in our power to avoid. Destiny is enscrolled on man's forehead by the very hand of Almighty Brahm![3]

Finding a fatalistic and philosophic justification for free will and strong sensual inclinations, the Orien-

---

[1]Dubois, *Hindu Manners, Customs and Ceremonies*, op. cit.
[2]*Ibid.*
[3]*Ibid.*

tal, prodded by climate, spicy foods, and custom, plunged headlong into the sea of diverse sexual pleasure.

In geographically locating the vast area of sexual perversion, Sir Richard Burton referred to the Sotadic Zone:

> . . . bounded westwards by the northern shores of the Mediterranean (N. Lat. 43°) and by the southern (N. Lat. 30°). Thus, the depth would be 780 to 800 miles: including meridional France, the Iberian Peninsula, Italy and Greece, with the coast-regions of Africa from Morocco to Egypt.
>
> Running eastward, the Sotadic Zone narrows: embracing Asia Minor, Mesopotamia and Chaldea, Afghanistan, Sindh, the Ponjaub, and Cashmere.
>
> In Indo-China, the belt begins to broaden: enfolding China, Japan, and Turkestan.
>
> It then embraces the South Sea Islands and the New World: where, at the time of its discovery, sotadic love was, with some exceptions, an established racial institution.
>
> Within the Sotadic Zone, the vice is popular and endemic, held, at the worst, to be a mere peccadillo, whilst the races to the north and south of the limits here defined practice it only sporadically amid the opprobrium of their fellows who, as a rule, are physically incapable of performing the operation and look upon it with the liveliest disgust.
>
> Outside the Sotadic Zone, *le vice* is sporadic, not endemic; yet the physical and moral effect of great cities, where puberty, they say, is induced earlier than in country sites, has been the same in most lands, causing modesty to decay and pederasty to flourish.

Writing in 1886, Burton added:

> In the present age, extensive intercourse with Europeans has produced not a reformation, but a certain reticence amongst the upper classes. They are as vicious as ever, but they do not

care for displaying their vices to the eyes of mocking strangers.

The same might well be said for today, when the Occidentalized East, abandoning realism and sincerity, has refined debauchery to a clandestine art. What was once voluptuous custom may now be regarded as hidden vice.

Burton's analysis held sodomy to be geographic and climatic, not racial; but the following statement illuminates an extensive and partially false generalization:

> Within the Sotadic Zone, there is a blending of the masculine and feminine temperaments: a crasis (fusion) which elsewhere occurs only sporadically.

By the keen influence of climate and foods and lethargic, necessitarian environment, coupled with physical hyperesthesia and innate hysterical tendencies, nearly all Eastern races were naturally masochistic and morbidly sensual. Hence, technically, Oriental perversion may be said to have been in true essence geographic and climatic. Physical and material complexes soon offered justification; hence, from the dawn of mankind, sexual divergence was formalized into social and religious custom.

The origin of ritualistic sodomy finds its place in early androgynous worship. It, like female prostitution, was considered venerable and holy, instituted in the temples and consecrated by priests and priestesses. The pyramid, a penis-cunnus symbol, and the Sphinx, hermaphroditic deity, were shrouded in sacred mystery, as were the inscrutable powers of orgasm and procreation, and symbolic of the conjoined wisdom and fecundity of man and woman.

Much later, because of rapidly increased population, sodomy became sanctioned and encouraged outside of temple and ritual. The Persian Code, including one of the most ancient of Malthusian laws seeking population control, fostered sodomy in social and theological practice. Thus, Persians became one of the first of endemically and customarily inverted peoples.

As seen in the Old Testament, Moses forbade sodomy to the already infected Israelites, but not for entirely moral reasons. Its Malthusian aspect worried him considerably; the tribes, in order to survive, had to be strong in numbers, therefore sodomy was forbidden. For the same reason he also outlawed celibacy, onanism, bestiality, and other popular forms of sexual deviation. Therefore, any sexual act not leading to propagation, any sexual act through which the tribe could not augment its strength, was damned as iniquitous. Formerly hallowed, it came to bear the stigma of unnatural and sinful love.

But Moses, much as he strove, failed. There was the incandescent Moloch whose altars were huge ovens where children were burned as sacrifices, and where fanatical male worshipers, who had no children to offer, danced before the fiery mouth of the oven and rhythmically masturbated so that their seed passed into the flames as compensation. In later life even the wise and righteous Solomon took to this worship, wearied of all other manners and excesses.

In the temples, male and female prostitutes, *kedeyshim* (consecrated ones), lay for hire. The *kedeysh* (sodomite) and *kedeysheh* (prostitute) were young men and women dedicated to the androgynous gods. Night and day, the temples were deluged with lustful and pious adorers; and the youthful *kedeyshim* were so engaged that their organs of generation, hour upon hour, were unceasingly congested and abused till, at length, exhausted of their erectile powers, they sank into decay.

Sodomy in its religious aspect was held to be pure and fraternal. In contrast to the young male body, the young woman's body with its menstrual and hymeneal blood was thought to be the cause of disease and death. Where the worship held, a virgin was tied down upon a stone altar, limbs widely splayed, and then was ritually and mechanically bled by the priests who thrust a golden phallus large enough to rend every fragment of virginal tissue into her vagina. Following that defloration she served as prostitute.

Catamites were similarly available in religious prostitution, though generally scorned as passive curs; hence, the Biblical allusion to the "price of a dog."

The Syrians, generators of sterile pleasure and refined in vice, spread deviations throughout the Mediterranean area. This gave rise to all forms of mouth and genital diseases. Writing in the latter half of the nineteenth century, Burton noted that "Syria has not forgotten her old praxis. At Damascus, I found some noteworthy cases amongst the religious of the great Amewwee Mosque" (one of the four Wonders of the Moslem World).

Strange as it may seem, sexual inversion was most endemic amid circumcised peoples of the East. Though rife among the uncircumcised Chinese, it was comparatively rare amongst Hindoos, the second greatest race of unmutilated Orientals. The cruel manner of Arab circumcision certainly discouraged masturbation as well as every other form of sexual pleasure for some time following the operation, in which all integumental flesh was torn from the penial shaft. Later, the youth's gratification lay solely in friction of the glans which, large to begin with, through activity and massage attained remarkable size. The average Arab glans, though the penis be diminutive, was generally large, a distinct peculiarity of hot, moist climates which swelled the flesh and, among Negroes, caused the entire organ to lose its elasticity and suspend smoothly. The pudendal size of Arab girls in such climes was also remarkable and augmented by habitual ipsation, labia and clitoris being enlarged by masturbation, though the unstimulated breasts generally remained undeveloped until marriage. After marriage, with the orgasms of self-relief replaced by those in sexual congress, over-all development occurred.

The Moslem youth circumcised by scarification (*es-selkh*) was little concerned about the size of his privy member in relation to the needs of women, and naturally turned to sodomy. The anal canal, a far narrower channel than the vagina served well for his purpose. When with a woman, he merely stimulated the labia, clitoris, and vaginal orifice (where, normally, most female excitation occurs), while his frenum preputium (*ligaum,* bridle) received similar rubbing. To gratify a woman whose erogenous nerves extended over a large area, the Arab, to achieve any pleasure himself, must incite the urethra and the insensible penial shaft by application of potions. So, more or less, male circumcision, intended among other things to harden the delicate glans against excitement and pollutions, actually made that portion the *sine qua non* of pleasure.

Psychological inversion was rare in the pure Arab; environmental factors alone determined his sexual outlets. Only when his blood became infused with that of other Moslems did psychological inclinations toward sodomy make its definite appearance. For despite the marked homosexual tendencies of many heterosexual individuals at one period of life or another, history reveals that an apparent strain of bisexuality or total inversion affected the average Oriental to a greater degree than the Westerner.

The Turk and the Persian were atavistically tempered to voluntary and involuntary homosexuality, but not the free Arab of the desert. Young love in the East was not so free or fornication so flagrant as in Europe. Prostitution was a profession, not a perversity of character. When a young man desired a maiden, he had need to purchase and wed her. Otherwise, he must frequent the house of ill fame. But for the average youth professional harlots were dear, and apt to scorn even the lad able to pay, because of his quick performance of the deed of kind. Thus the untainted Arab fell prey to the wily old pederast or to the charms of his own comrade. At the least, mutual masturbation became more enjoyable than the solitary self-relief; at the most, sodomy was an awesome adventure.

An enigma that many early travelers could never understand about some of the Eastern races, an enigma which, along with the lack of medical knowledge, led to the dubious belief in congenital inversion, was their apparently innate propensity to homosexual (or, as it was then termed, "hermaphroditic") behavior. But, as

in the case of pure-bred Arab boys, the germ of inversion was not inherent. It was the result of fatalistic custom set off by a normally sensuous and responsive
constitution. The sexes being much restricted from one
another, emotional relations with one of the same sex
were therefore highly encouraged.

The Egyptian Turk or *fellah,* inadequately or brutally circumcised, was generally *mowaulid* (of mixed
breeds). Proof of this lay in genital comparison. The
pure bred Arab, with a stature approaching that of the
average northern European, was fortunate to possess a
penis measuring from three to five inches in erection;
whereas the Egyptian, in Burton's opinion a "white-
washed nigger," possessed one that measured six inches
or more in a flaccid state. Were someone to place a
Bedewwee Arab next to an Egyptian *fellah,* the difference must have been conspicuous. Hence an Egyptian
can never be called an Arab; and sang the Arab:

> The prickle of the pure, in quiescence, retracts;
> The prickle of the vile, unwrinkled, protracts.

From the very cradle, Egyptian *fellaheen* (peas-
ants) were prompted to enjoy every variety of sexual
gratification. In youth, they engaged in excessive genital
manipulation and sodomy, then proceeded to forms of
bestiality (to be discussed later). Not a few of them
eventually destroyed their manhood and became strict,
neurotic pederasts. Satyriasis and nymphomania were
common among them, erection and nocturnal and other
emissions through reflex action were overcommon.

"Thrust thy finger into the fundament of a Toork
(Egyptian)," said the Arabs, "and he will pollute his
raiments. Brush past him from the fore, and his carnal
implement stab thee ere ye can run away." Another
very old saying discloses that "the Toork would much
rather defecate than have intercourse with a woman,
for the inestimable pleasure derived thereby."

One logical and little-known reason why the
average Turk wore bag-trousers (*shirwaul*) and the
Egyptian a *tobe* (gown) was that they could not bear

the perpetual chafing of tight European dress. The voluminous white pantaloons of the fierce but effeminate Bashi-Bazouk (Turkish soldier) were so designed as to conceal partially or wholly erections that were surprisingly common, even on the parade ground. For these lewd berserkers could not keep their itchy hands to themselves. As European officers[4] attested, there was just no bridling their lust. At first it appeared humorous—then disgusting—then utterly depressing.

The Egyptian *hhemmaum* was a veritable sink of iniquity. There Turks and *fellaheen* formed what was called *essilsileh* (chain, or circle) and thus engaged in ceremonial round-robin sodomy: an impressive sight in the estimations of Southern European artists, who delighted in painting the scene for wealthy Crairene debauchees. Often, as in classical Paris, were shifting ranks of Egyptians to be seen outside the *hhemmaums* at night, fumbling and chaffering with their podices (buttocks) laid bare. This proceeding in Arab *facetiae* (pornography) became known as *Whitewashing the Turkish Bath* (beyyedh-el-hhemmaum). In viewing this, the philosophical Arab merely growled: "The Toork is insulted if, in the least, ye do not tickle his hinder parts."

European officials, curious but often unsuccessful in their investigations, wondered greatly at the galaxy of fops—*beys* and *pashas*—cluttering the streets of Upper Egypt, assuming airs, and thriving in veritable luxury. What kept them, despotic as they were, in esteem? The Arab, above all, well knew that the only material thing that held a "bestial Toork" in prestige was the size of his phallus or his insatiable capacity for sotadic love.

The Turk ruled the Arab, for there thrived in him savage ambition. The Arab possessed subtle genius, but the Turk had keen emotional drive.[5] Public declarations were placarded as to physical measurements; and

---

[4]Among them Burton, Gordon Pasha, and Colonel James Neill.

[5]This pattern of temperament has certainly not changed, as witnessed by the current Middle Eastern crisis.

the overawed subjects were therefore obliged to submit to the Turk's power. For the Arabs, like the Hindoos, held an uncanny, perhaps instinctive, reverence for the phallus. It was the cogenerator of human existence: a vigorous, fecundate symbol of power. Certain Eastern women even adorned their garments with phallic tassels, to show how many men they had slept with. And just as with the hallowed *dervish* or venerable *soofee,* in some areas it was considered virtuous for a young wench to be penetrated by an eminent Turk. The same honor and dignity were thus bestowed upon any new addition to the Turkish harem of a wealthy *bey* or *pasha* and, upon the eve of consummation, crowds gathered outside the residency to drive away evil *jinn* and cheer the couple on to fruitful orgasms.

Barren women and aspiring virgins habitually clamored round Zubeyr Pasha, the slim, mustachioed Great Slaver of the Sudan. However, before impotence overtook him he had to give many of them over to his dissipated, twenty-year-old son, Suleyman. Before being executed by the famous Gordon Pasha, Suleyman was described by this Eminent Victorian as being "a spoiled child," glutted with wine and drugs and eaten away by venereal disease.

Hence the Turk, highly sophisticated, countered fatalistic sagacity with precipitate ambition; and, since the annihilation of the Mamelukes, Egypt was governed by "Toorks."

The *fellah,* rawboned, wiry, semi-Negroid, was in Arab opinion a distinct "lover of the middle finger." The epithet *el-fa'eel* (sodomite) could be safely affixed to a goodly deal of male Egyptian names, and *el-fa'eeleh* (she-sodomite, lesbian) to very many females. In sodomy, bestiality, and fornication the *fellaheen* equalled the proverbial Spartans; but, according to reliable General Gordon who had to put up with them during the fateful siege of Khartoum, "a more contemptible soldier than the Egyptian never existed. Cowardly, lying, effeminate brutes. Continual oppression has made them of such material that you could find no sound principle to work on. *I hate them!* There! A

two-penny-halfpenny nation, for whom it is not worth
while to stay a day in these countries."[6] This in 1875
was Gordon's first impression. Ten years later he was
yet not inclined to change that impression: "As far
as my experience goes, there are not more contemptible troops—officers and men—than the Egyptians, so
beware of them; and, with scarcely an exception, all
Turks and Circassians in Egyptian employ are emasculated." Gordon compared the Egyptians to the Abyssinians: "a furtive, pole-cat race."

Though Gordon never mentioned it, he well
enough knew that sodomy had been the prime cause of
more than one mutiny in the pitiable Egyptian *fellaheen*
contingent. And bearing no respect for discipline, the
fellah bore none for his own hybrid ruler:

> Mohammed Tewfik Pasha Khedive is not
> only a fool, but a tool besides. Europe fondles
> and manipulates him like a puppet. He is *el-
> mefool*, a hateful passive; and his yawning
> fundament has endured the uncircumcised
> prickles of sundry Unbelievers.

So read a typical circular distributed throughout
Egypt during the chaotic revolt for independence in
1882. Someone, as usual, had to be the scapegoat. It
may as well have been unpopular Tewfik, scarcely the
fiery man his father was, whom Gordon Pasha described as "really quite astounding; he was not profuse
at all. In fact, to this day, he has paid me not one single
compliment."[7]

To early travelers, no one appeared more natural
and admirable than the pure uncivilized Negro. Civilization alone bred in him corruption and treachery.
Then, like the Egyptian *fellah,* he became a domiciled
barbarian. In the unadulterated state the Sudanese
Negro, before the devastating storm of El-Islam, was a
brave and kindly and simple-minded human being dedicated to nature, his own people, and exhibiting a high

---

[6]Lord Godfrey Elton, *General Gordon.*
[7]*Ibid.*

degree of tolerance and compassion. Even his manner of walking aroused the admiration of the fascinated foreigner. It was distinctive in its natural grace. Long and slim, with polished black sculpturesque bodies, the Sudanese Negroes appeared as giant, sable cranes stalking in the brush. Lithe, proud, and handsome, they even stood like cranes, with one foot perched on the opposite knee. And the Sudanese Negro was virile as a bull, yet timid as a dove. Then, in swept brutalizing civilization.

The witless Negro, taken unawares and deluded by false traditions, became sorely depraved. Naïve, he fell an easy prey to the wiles of alien men who lusted after the statuesque body. Guided by the worldly Turk, the Sudanese native abandoned his free and unassuming mode of life and plunged headlong into the fetid slough of Western degradation. Sold into slavery, he came to learn and practice every vice known to mankind. When freed, he introduced these habits among his people. In the army, with a shortage of Negresses, he adopted sodomy. The Turk, insanely jealous of the Negro's strength and masculinity, sought gleefully to seduce him into decay. And the blacks, like inquisitive children, fell victim. Many a lonely Negress wrought terrible vengeance upon a Turk because her paramour was so diverted.

The Turks, an apathetic race of traditional bisexuals, had an unsavory reputation throughout Europe and Asia. They were made the subjects of well-nigh limitless pornography of which these verses were among the most popular:

> Ne'er trust Turks with an ass: for they
> > Once roasted ass-pizzle, the rabble
> > > rout;
> And, when sight they guest, to their dams they
> > say:
> > > "Piss quick on the guest fire, and put it
> > > out!"

The Toork will poison his own mother, rape his own daughter, for gain.

If you find a snake, don't kill it; but if you find a
Turk, that is another matter.

Avoid the Turk; for either he eats you out of
love or, in his rage, tears you to pieces.

Ogres, satyrs, and anus-bruisers, the lot of them.
The Toork is a dog. There are no two ways
about it. He worships the devil.

The phrase *Imsik-lisaunek* which, in Arabic,
means *Hold thy tongue!* could never without jibes and
embarrassment be used in Turkey, where it clearly
meant *Hold thy coynte and prickle! Imsik,* in vulgar
Turkish, was *penis-cunnus;* and many a witless Arab
wayfarer indignantly recorded how he was thus
laughed to scorn. Those who were more adept in retort
used a parody of the famous bard Hafiz, in making their
grinning reply:

> Uggur aun budma'ash Toorkee hah!
> b'duhauneh aurud auzar-e-maurah:

> If that blackguard—ah! the Turk—would deign
> to take my tool in mouth (rather than
> *heart in hand*).

When desirous of soliciting a man, the *moghlim*
(sodomist) of Constantinople (Istanbul) inserted his
thumb between index and middle fingers, indicative of
fellatio. British troops en route to the Crimea were rather startled at Turkish morals; but the more sophisticated
French were only amused, especially at the *imsik* farce
which, in fact, also bore overtones of denoting fellatio:
Turkish delight.

The Russians too, at the battles of Kars (Crimea)
and Plevna (Russo-Turkish War) got an unpleasant
taste of the Bashi-Bazouk, whose procedure on killing
a man was to take full sexual advantage of the anal
spasms. With horror the Russians beheld that familiar
flagrancy on a Turkish battlefield, the "bestial Toorks,"
their pantaloons down, working heatedly upon the
freshly slain. When hesitantly asked about this "horrible

desecration of human beings" by a certain war corres-
pondent, the indifferent Turk characteristically replied:
"It is, to be sure, effendi, a most devilish matter of expert timing."

A stock appellation granted the Turk was *Lootee*
(pillaging he-whore) or *el-Lyte* (of Lot's tribe). In
Turkey, a band of fanatics known as Lewwautee were
professional sodomists; and their favorite motto ran
thus:

> The penis, smooth and round, was made with
>   anus best to match it;
> Had it been made for vulva's sake, it had been
>   formed like a hatchet!

El-Ginkeyn (transvestists) known among Europeans as *ginks* or *jinks,* were notorious throughout
Egypt. They comprised Turks, Jews, Greeks, and Armenians. They were young men in the effeminate flower
of that kind of youth, and they dressed and minced like
flirtatious girls. Aside from being skillful sodomites
the *ginks* were adept at pickpocketing. In the seething
maelstrom of crowds, they would slit a man's trousers
with razor-sharp tiny blades and then, with vocational
deftness, tenderly grip his genitals. They derived pleasure by deflowering pert young virgins in much the
same fashion, slitting the backs of their gowns, streak-
ing between their thighs, and puncturing their sacred
hymens with slender fingers and sharp nails. Others,
carefully rending the rear of corpulent men's garments, summarily rubbed their sensitive penes in the
nates (*deez*), achieving orgasmic relief in but a few
seconds and escaping into the throngs before the defiled victim could react.

The *khelboose* or *mesgherreh* (buffoon, pimp), a
psychopathic type of *gink,* attached an enormous wood-
en phallus to his body and, raging about the streets of
Cairo, assailed men, women, and children from behind, much to the delight of those who were not caught
unawares.

The transvestite *el-gink* usually dressed as a woman, wore long pomaded hair, a blossom behind each

ear, a cleanly shaven face, scrupulously depilated pubes and anus, kohl smeared about his eyes, his lips, fingers, and toes painted with henna, and his flesh daubed with attar-of-roses. In every manner of motion and speech and passions he behaved as a female. Not a few, having undergone total dismemberment, thus becoming *el-me-fooleyn* (passives), appeared in "muslin of evening dew." They unconsciously indentified the male anus (*teen,* fig) with the feminine vagina, and their usual mode of applause or opprobrium was: *Zeggeh zubbek fee isteh!* (Thrust thy penis up my fundament).

Firmly believing that the sexual organs and anus were created by the devil, therefore in propitiation and defiance to be ill used, the *ginks* were extremists in anal eroticism. "When thou art happy," said they, "thrust thy finger into thine anus, even as the reveling *jinn* do."

Being for the most part devil-worshipers, *el-Gink-eyn* sought to emulate the homosexual spirits in every way. In Arab tales, the sign of applause was to insert the index finger between the buttocks, as witness the following two passages:

> At this the accursed was hugely pleased, and
> thrust his finger up his fundament.
> He doffed all that was on him of clothes; then he
> kissed the earth and danced, and he thrust
> his finger up his fundament.[8]

Others, when elated, were accustomed to seizing the private parts or tearing their garments, in the ecstatic self-punishment so agreeable to the masochistic disposition of most Orientals.

The popular nickname given *el-gink* was *ghun-seh* (flexible, flaccid) from the root *ghens* (bending downward), the snakelike mouth of a waterskin. Along with *moghenness, ghunseh* referred to a hermaphrodite, a eunuch, or a passive sodomist, owing to the fact that, through continual sexual use of the anus to which erotic sensibility was transposed, he no longer felt excitation nor experienced erection in the generative organ.

---

[8]Burton, *op. cit.*

Hence, as before mentioned, many *ginks* had themselves castrated in order that they might nearer resemble the female.

Excluding the unlettered Negro, perhaps the most virtuous Mohammedans of northern Africa were the Bedewween. All round them, black and Toork and Arab were tainted with pederasty. The Berbers, the Moors (*Meghribees* who infected Spain), were vicious groups of notorious sodomites surrounding the desert man. But, considerably free of perversion, the Bedewwee remained stanch. And, incongruous as it may seem, he was the only Moslem who scorned trousers. So the Arab saying:

> "The virtuous run naked; the more clothes, the more evil—the more you've got to hide and are ashamed of. What shame has the Toork? He makes his living by keeping it hidden, keeping others in suspense. One has to pay a Toork to see what he keeps hidden below the waist."

Yet the Bedewween plodded along quite naked, with but *keffeeyeh* and thin cloak protecting head and shoulders, as pure and simple as the early Greeks, before *paederastia* staled beauty and demanded mechanical infibulation. The reason for Bedewween virtue lay primarily in the fact that their women were independent and accorded an equality unknown in other Oriental societies. There were established tribes of professional strumpets and sodomists among all Arabs save the Bedewwee, who kept to himself and the Desert, scorning tainted civilization. On every side of him Turkish and Arab males, restricted from the company of females until marriage at puberty or even far beyond, inordinately masturbated in mutuality. Girls, taken under the guidance of *sheykhehs* and castratos, were instructed in the technique of habitual ipsation. Daily manipulation, a customary ritual in Egyptian harems and alleyways, was rare in both sexes of the Bedewween, who enjoyed platonic heterosexual freedom.

Sodomy (*lewwaudeh, ighlaum*) is not as severely condemned in the Koran as in the Old Testament; for, unlike Moses, the Prophet regarded it philosophically, since only an inconsiderably few Arabs were *totally* homosexual. The majority had normal relations with women, thereby strengthening the tribes while, at the same time or later in life, they sought adventure and diversion midst their own sex. The important question, free of fabricated moralities, was always:

"Art thou ceremonially pure and, therefore, fit for handling by a great man like myself?"

The possible impurity of the act was scarcely acknowledged; precleanliness and postablution answered for that; and Mohammed, when mentioning sodomy, merely chose the terms of Moses without realizing their fullest intent:

> "Do ye approach unto the males among mankind, and leave your wives which your Lord hath created for you? Surely, ye are people who transgress. Do ye approach lustfully unto men, leaving the women? Ye are surely an ignorant people."

Notwithstanding, as Western culture began to make its rude appearance and a completely diverse code of ethics was thrust upon him, the Arab became more and more self-conscious of his sexual habits. The playful dancing boy was seen no more in the raucous coffeeshop; the ogling *gink* no longer wriggled his haunches in the bazaar; prostitutes ceased to gaze and beckon openly from their windows.

"Sodomy abroad, fornication at home!" laughed the Arab, in alluding to convenience and discretion. As the Hindoo would say: "Whole Brahmin in the village street, half a Brahmin when seen from afar, and an Untouchable when utterly out of sight."[9]

When the Aryan said: "Beware of a black Brahmin or a fair Pariah!" the Moslem was apt to advise: "If thy neighbor hath performed the Hadj, trust him not; and if he hath done it twice, hasten thee to remove thine abode from his vicinity."

Impiety as well as sanctity was ever attached to

[9]Dubois, *op. cit.*

the obligatory Pilgrimage (*el-Hhejj*) to Mecca (*El-Mekkeh,* Mother of Cities). Here, among the vast assemblage of men from all parts of the East, innocence and simplicity were soon abandoned; one acquired cynical sophistication. Thus, the honorary title of *hhaujee* (pilgrim) also bore its disrespectful side, though not nearly as notorious as *mojauwir* (one who lives at Mecca). "He pilgrimaged and, for his villainy, lives at Mecca" was a popular saying among jealous or virtuous Arabs: meaning that he could find no other place evil enough for his taste. This in due sequence gave rise to the stock phrase *Sher fee el-Hherremeyn* (wickedness in the two Holy Places, Mecca and El-Medeeneh), which obviously intimated the flagrant prevalence of sodomy even during circumbulation of the sacred Caaba, which was ritualistically performed in the nude by all Persians and many tribes from Arabia.

Nearly all Mohammedan schismatic sects, among them the Druzes, Assassins, Janissaries, and the Hindee Thugs, indulged in varieties of homosexuality; and similar practices occurred among the celibate hierarchy (Sheykh-el-Islaum and the *olemmah*) of the Moslem Church. One sect in particular, the Barmecides of Baghdad, was frequently associated with perversion by medieval Arabs. In the characteristic punning style of the Turks, an adherent of the Abbasides, a rival cult, translated Barmecide (*Bermekkee*) as follows: *ber* (up) and *mekkee* (to suck), thereby allying the Barmecides with a distinct tribe of fellators and claiming that Ja'afer-bin-Yahyeh-bin-Khaulid-el-Bermekkee—Wezeer-el-Haroon-er Resheed, founder of the sect, was a *rauddheh-ez-zubb* (pintle-sucker) of the first order: Born without anus and suckled on the blood of pigs and snakes.

The mendicant-devotee or mystic, *derweesh, soofee, mejzoob,* was allowed to make water while walking along the road, without even retiring to the side; and every man or youth he signaled was obliged to go behind a bush with him, expose his buttocks, and suffer holy penetration. The respectful way of greeting a *soofee* in many areas was by kissing him, first upon the mouth, then, lifting his shaggy robe, upon the navel, the penis and scrotum, and the podex. This physical manner of devout salutation was also employed in the secret initiation of every proselyte who was made to endure the enervating caresses of the entire company and, in turn, prove his boundless virility by retaining stiff erection throughout over a dozen climaxes in the revered nates of his brethren. Were a proselyte to go limp before all were justly honored by his intromission, he was kicked and spat upon and summarily evicted from the venerable fraternity.

In Moslem practice, active (*fa'eel*) was indicated by the sign of the middle finger (*ishaureh-ed-dewweel*) and passive (*mefool*) by squeezing the fist, thumb, and index finger, the whole representing the anus.

In the coffeehouse, fast youths raked love through popular wordplay:

 a. *Heneeyen!* (may it do thee good).

 b. God pleasure (*copulate with*) thee!

 a. Thou drinkest for ten! (*I am the cock and thou art the hen*).

 b. Pray, equal—if y'dare! (*I am the stallion and thou art the mare*) and so forth, until euphemy was exhausted (*I am the thick one and thou art the thin; I am a mouthful whilst thou art a pin*); horseplay was indulged, bag-trousers fell, and two besotted Arabs attacked one another incontinently.

Moslem philosophy bred in Syria and Turkey, thence transported to Southern Europe, regarded the question of "to be or not to be" in the following verse:

> Neither male nor female, I;
>   It is to know which one, I sigh;
> To choose between them, I am loath;
> But, after all, what difference?
>   Surely, there is no offense,
> But greater pleasure, in choosing both![10]

---

[10]Paul Lacroix, *History of Prostitution.*

Taking the matter up from here, Arab physiologists found benefits in sodomy; and one, a serious *hakeem* in Persia, was proud and pleased to report:

> The use of clysters (Enemas) is almost unknown amongst Moslems, since the penis serves well enough to massage and stir the rectum.

Thus in Persia it was not uncommon for a lecherous physician to order his constipated patient to bend over and then insert either his own fleshly one or an artificial phallus smeared with olive oil. They also, similarly, found rationalizations for fellatio, under the spurious labels of rejuvenating and strengthening virile power, though thereby they took bread out of the mouths of professional boys. A *hakeem* with a particularly lusty membrum virile was ever the favorite physician of the coffeeshop clique, who seemed chronic sufferers of constipation.

A perceptive Hindoo traveler analyzing the Persians wrote his terse opinion of El-Islam:

> In religious duties, these men show their hind-parts to heaven; the warm breeze titillates the anus.
> In civil duties, these men show their hind-parts to horse-leeches; the warm syringe titillates the anus.
> In personal duties, these men show their hind-parts to each other; the warm finger titillates the anus.
> So it is that man's buttocks are a matter of strict adoration among all true Mussulmans.

Though our sagacious Hindoo had learned that certain Arabs deified the anus (*Umm-es-Sooweyd*, Mother of Darkness) he was not aware that the majority regarded it as the refuge of evil *jinn*. Hence, familiar and effective modes of punishment, exterminating all bodily evil, were to thrust the barrel of a pistol or musket into the rectum and discharge it, or slowly insert a red-hot iron phallus.

Sen'ah, the capital of El-Yemen, was the center of Arab sodomy. "I should have knocked him into El-

Yemen" was the usual comment made about someone who, hatefully passive, suddenly turned active (thus insulting his partner). For in El-Yemen all passives were total castrates to certify against insolent counterassaults.

Aleppo, nucleus of Syrian perversion, always possessed an evil reputation. Its streets were literally glutted with *shellebees* (dandies; queans) and a stock saying was:

Hellebee-Shellebee:
The Aleppine is a fellow fine.

Mosul in Iraq was another noteworthy seat of debauchery (home of the Mandaean devil worshipers). Here, upon the site of ancient Babylon, thrived androgynous adoration represented by a bearded goddess with swelling breasts and phallus erectus. In the ritual of pubescent initiation into manhood, each lad inserted his organ into the vulvar-symbolic mouth of a Baal-like golden image. Girls, in turn, were made to sit upon the aureate projection of a squatting Priapuslike idol, thereby sacrificing their hymeneal membranes.

The French conquest of Algeria in the early nineteenth century saw the rampant infection of L'Armee Français with sexual inversion as well as all manner of venereal diseases. The Imperial troops brought the unique Arab variations of sodomy triumphantly back to France, while in North Africa the Foreign Legion and Zouaves instructed the Arabs in European perversity.

In Coptic ritual, a blending of paganism and Christianity, male fornication played an extensive role symbolized by two male partridges alternately copulating. As amid certain Tibetan sects, each worshiper during the ceremony sacrificially entered the priest (*geseese*), thereby purifying his system and casting out the evil seed of lust to be cleansed and consecrated in the priest's body. To facilitate this rite and, at the same time, to preserve shrouded sanctity, every *geseese* had a small slit in the rear of his religious robe (*libausrohbauneeyeh*); and it was his wont to lean over as each worshiper passed the altar.

The Armenians, like the downtrodden Jews, would prostitute their bodies for survival; but they were not as a whole bisexually inclined, rather disliking the practice. But man must eat; thus, some Armenians too became *ginks*. And guilty-minded Turks, forever seeking a scapegoat, delighted in proclaiming that sodomy originated in the highlands of Armenia.

In Japanese teahouses and the red-light Yoshiwara districts, male *courtesans* lay for hire; and many secret societies in both China and Japan dedicated themselves to homosexual functions. The Samurai, a martial caste of sadomasochistic inverts, were the most famous in Japan where, as in ancient Greece, it became a matter of chivalry to love a strong and handsome comrade in place of an unclean woman. These youths, like the Assassins of Persia and certain Tongs of China, devoted their lives to vengeful hysteria and, in shame or defeat, sought pleasurable glory in *hara-kiri*. Violence and pain were their *sine qua non* of orgasm, and they ranked high on the immense list of Oriental flagellants and suicide cultists.

The Bashi-Bazouk, a bastard Turkish military breed notorious for ruthlessness and brutality, in disposition resembled the Mejnoon Dervish of Egypt or the Nehung-Akalee Sikh of the Punjaub. All of these might run berserk sexually and rage about stark naked, murdering and abusing people in the cause of holy fanaticism. They were given up to wild orgies.

The atheistic or shamanistic Turanians, Cossacks and Bulgars (whence the word *bugger*), Huns, Tartars, Mongols, Kurds, Turkomans, Yakuts, many of them nomadic brigands and savage warriors, were dubbed *hurfooshees* (scoundrels) by civilized Asia because of their flagrant sodomy. Dry, cold highland climate did little to improve their morals. Inversion, incited by seemingly insatiable lusts, was traditional amid these hybrid groups. Vicious but childlike in emotions, one sex was as useful as another to them. The women were pack mules and she-studs, male children were ganymedes, and the men were killers and rapists. Excessive riding, causing frication of the genitals, was conjoined to frenzied masturbation. Moreover, the high altitudes induced a peculiar effeminacy amongst them. As their potency languished they turned to boys. Their sorcerous mode of worship, embracing diabolism and fetishistic masochism, further encouraged sodomy in its rawest and most neurotic forms. Tranquillizing self-relief, taught and practiced from mere infancy, was attended by formidable erections and chronic erotomania. Hence, the raging Turanian became the scourge and dread of all Central Asia.

The Sikhs, Rajpoots, Mahrattas, and Pathans (*Pudhauns*) adopted a rigid homosexual camaraderie in order to maintain martial strength and unity. The Honourable East India Company blushingly acknowledged that this made the Sikhs and Mahrattas tough nuts to crack. Homosexual fraternity fostered this unity. These men were of varied and unorthodox temperaments: atheistic, unitarian, humanistic, cynical, but universally fanatic. They for the most part practiced female infanticide; their women were few, often unattractive, through burdensome and unceasing labor, carried on while their menfolk indulged in the pleasures of war, sport, and sensual excess. Thus these tribes were in nature closely related to the Spartans and other warlike Greeks: strong, virile, fraternal men of dauntless but depraved disposition.

In Delhi, early May of 1857, the old drug-sodden titular King was preaching Holy War. In Constantinople, the Sultan of Turkey delivered a *firmaun* (manifesto) to the peoples of India. *Jehaud,* Holy War in Cabul, Cashmere; Holy War over the face of Moslem Hindostan. It was a mounting fever. On the Eve of Power and Destiny (Leyleh-el-Kedr), the climax of the month-long Ramadhanic devotions, all True Believers formed a pact of inviolate brotherhood, sealed by homosexual affection. This was indeed significant. It portended the unity of Indian Moslems, who were ordinarily distrustful and independent of one another. In this way, too, Greece had become united against Persia.

The Ghilzyes, Dooranee Afghans, and hill frontiersmen of northern India presented unique examples of sensitive fellowship (a union through tribe after tribe

against cousins who shared like manners but desired
their land and wealth). The Pathan (Afridi, Shinwari)
was subtle, brutally ironic. He boasted of being Beni-
Israeli (of the sons of Israel) but hated the Jews, term-
ing them *sughs* (curs), *yehoodees* (yids), and emasculated mules (*naumurd-o-uster*).

An Afridi lad at twelve was regarded as a man.
He must have no further dealings with his mother. He
was directly taken into rigorous instruction by his sire
and made a veritable master of guerrilla warfare, hunting, torture, and deceit. Then he was ceremonially in-
augurated into the brotherhood of warriors; his foreskin
was severed and his eyes kohl'd. Scorning women as unclean and only fit for breeding, he sought love among
his brethren; and comradeship knit by such love made
the Afridi the most formidable adversary on earth. It
was because of him that the British government was
compelled to manufacture the ghastly dumdum bullet,
guaranteed to stop the most indomitable fanatic.

The sexual disposition of the hillman sprang primarily from his environment, his rugged and cynical
life. Sir Robert Warburton, Warden of the Khyber Pass
and one of the few Europeans appreciably to understand the hillman, wrote:

> The Afridi lad, from his earliest childhood,
> is taught by the circumstances of his existence
> and life to distrust all mankind; and very often
> his near relations, heirs to his small plot of land
> by right of inheritance, are his deadliest enemies.
> Distrust of all mankind, and readiness to strike
> the first blow for the safety of his own life, have
> therefore become the maxims of the Afridi.

Hence, brotherhood was imperative to survival;
the motivations of Afridi character are quite obvious
and show the normal responses of a life of peril.

The Afridi woman (*ghazeeyeh,* she-wolf), sup-
pressed and customarily given over to an unrewarded
life of toil, was no better disposed than her spouse.
Driven to almost instinctive vengeance against the male
sex, she was most adept at torturing with thorn and
jagged stone and developed an unquenchable passion

for slashing the uncircumcised penis. Centuries of endured brutality rendered her masochistic or virtually insensible to pain; centuries of bondage imbued her with sadistic needs for orgiastic freedom. She followed her man into battle and, thirsting for relief, seldom did a fallen enemy escape her vengeful nails and, injured or dead, be later borne away uncastrated.

Though sodomy and masturbation were practiced as a matter of tradition by Afridi males, the female, singularly tempered, apparently ignored all sapphic love and found gratification in vapid connubial intercourse or delicious, man-hating cruelty.

The Afghan of the walled city and the Pathan of the Eternal Hills were of vastly diverse breeds. A Platonic homosexuality imposed realism on the latter's sexual practices, but the former was unprincipled in his vice. *Suleymaunee-huraumee* (the Afghan is a villainous man) was a stock phrase in India. Hindoo mothers warned their naughty offspring that, if they did not behave, the wildmen from the Hills would descend to gobble them up. The Frontier, the Hills, the Khyber Pass: these became awesomely legendary, ill-omened, indicative of ungodly terror and admonition.

The notoriety of the Afghan, particularly among Indian peoples, gave rise to the famous expression:

> Uggurchey kuht-e-murdoom uz-een seh gee-
> ree:
> Ufghaun, Buloochee, w'budma'ash-e-Kushmee-
> ree!

> Though of men there be famine, yet shun these
> three:
> Afghan, Beloochee, rascally Cashmeree.

The sodomists of Cabul, notably the Moghwar Kuzzilbash (Guebres), were never clandestine in their practices; only such religious sects as the Aly-Ilahee were secret in their debauches and held them in utter darkness. When the Turko-Persian Kuzzilbashees gathered to drink and to get drunk as quickly and elegantly as possible, they did so in the brightest light and garbed in the gaudiest of robes: yellow, green, and red. Then, according to one eminent native of Kurrachee, "they stripped naked, mauled, mounted, spat, and urinated upon one another to facilitate carnal entry, practising all the unseemly acts of love."

Cabul and its inhabitants always brought unsavory expressions into the minds of Hindostanees:

> Kudr-e-kuss Ufghaunee,
> Kudr-e-sooraukh Kaubulee:

> The merit of coynte the Afghan knows;
> The merit of hole the Cabulee chose.

Another version, more general and used in various instances throughout India, was:

> The worth of slit the Hindoo knows;
> The worth of hole the Moslem chose.

An Arab traveler, speaking of Cabul and the Afghan, wrote the following:

> It is the wont of the rakish Cabulees, when greeted with the *Selaum-aleykum*, to reply in deep sibilant tones: "May the devil rub thy buttocks, yah Huzoor!"
> In the Street of Sodomy (Bazaar-e-Ighlaum), men plunge deep and come up with nought but dung. It is a pandemonium of perversely ecstatic groans and curses, squeals and driveling: a disgusting whine of depraved life. There, the True Believer, *sooraukh-maulish,* anus-rubber as he is, has his head turned towards Mecca and his hinder parts among ruins. But know, thou, that there are no fans in hell.

In the Grand Sudder Bazaar at Cabul, vibrant thunder pulsed. A keen moment of lull, a quiver, a monotonous hum—then a blast of undulating shrillness engulfing the lone squeal, deluging the market place with awe-striking clamor. Gobble, rasp, howl; cloying fumes of spices, then dregs, then human and bestial odor.

The Arab was greatly astounded. Hands and

heads and feet were terrifying, nudging, prodding, fingering. Female breasts rubbed his body, masculine fingers searched, and large-rumped youths clawed. In one dark passage he blundered against a young Ghilzye and a scarlet-veiled woman. They were nearly hidden in the corner of a wall, their thighs pressing; and our traveler could see by the way the Ghilzye clutched her that beneath her garments they were united.

At first glance, the Mussulmans of Cabul seemed for the most part to do little more than sit cross-legged in the coffeeshops and leer at one another, occasionally jesting, laughing, attempting playfully to seize one another between the thighs. They were all of them elegantly dressed, but the perceptive newcomer knew this to be a deception. He recalled an old proverb: "The wealthier the man, the poorer his garb; thus are thieves and slanderers misled."

The thoroughfares were narrow, writhing; and our curious traveler fought to make way through choppy seas. He was jabbed and bruised, with people's fingers in every conceivable place. He soon became aware of particular groups of young libertines who, skillful in manipulation, frequented the bazaars to derive pleasure out of handling the secret parts of men. Much to his surprise, at least four openly solicited him with the *ungoosht-e-ishaurut* (sign of the middle finger). In India they were styled *zunkhas* (effeminates) with "plaited tresses and swaying hips, florid gestures and painted lips," as the popular chant affirmed. All the while, he had need to recall just what someone had told him in Persia: "The Cabulee is like a dog; give him that which he barks for, and pass on unmolested." Some followed after him with the avidness of bloodhounds, trying their best to overtake him; but the denseness of multitudes aided in his escape.

Darting into another street, he was met with a shrieking storm. A *dervish,* stark naked and afflicted with holy madness, led a bellowing parade of disrobed fanatics, *wulees* and *wuleeyehs, seyyids* and *seyyidehs,* young men and women, a few children and dogs. They were linked into a frightening chain. He sought refuge in an open shop as they rushed past. The *dervish,* wild-eyed and drugged, assumed the character of Priapus; and his very glance, his touch, induced many to cast off their garments and follow. Within a few clamorous seconds they had left the street and were then invading brothels, the harems of rich merchants, and several houses containing opium-eaters and male prostitutes.

A tremendous, resonant concussion. The earth tremored; he glanced skyward, saw ugly gray-and-blue burnished cloud columns. Luminous crackling fingers gouged the dimness. It began to rain; and a torrent of slush—dregs, saliva, refuse, swept the streets, boiling down to the Cabul River, exuding a horrible reek. Our traveler sank against the wall, dry-mouthed and breathless. A bit hesitant at first, he questioned a frail white-bearded man.

"Bazaar-e-Ighlaum, yah Khodawund," was the grinning reply, denoting the Rialto of Sodomy.

He peered about him, saw only a bright haze, and acknowledged the stench of kerosene. A *degcheh* of sandalwood simmered acridly sweet a few yards away.

Slaves were in line, naked and bathed in scented oils, and scrupulous examinations were being made of them: the shape of their hands and feet, the condition of mouth and nose and ears and teeth. Then, he saw them bending over so that the cackling customers could scrutinize their podices.

He shrank within himself.

The old man grinned, lips taut against yellow ivory. "If the turban complains of a slight wind, what must be the state of the inner drawers, yah Khoda-wund?"

Fingers clasped together, a man in saffron robe lurched forward. He was extremely fat and red-be-whiskered, with an immense nose and thick trembling lips. *"Selaum-aleykum, yah Huzrut—yah Huzrut—"* he bleated, inclining hurriedly. Our traveler and the old man returned his salute. The fat gentleman rubbed his hands together. "Ah, *Bismillah!* welcome to the Street of Delights. The Market of Debauch is ever open. Here our thoughts are in Paradise, our bodies in dirt. My name, pray God, is Mukhlook the Man-eater. Hire a slave; he will show thee his hinder parts."

"My deepest regrets, yah Khwaudjeh," the Arab said, in Syrian accent, touching his breast and bowing.

The fat gentleman scowled, shrugging deeply. "*In-shallah!* Appearance was not proof enough of the recognition of bullmen; the Huzrut demanded to have seed in the palm of his hand." The fat slaver swung round, shook his fist. "*Bismillah!*"

"You misunderstand," our traveler said, clutching the man's arm.

The slaver arched his wiry red brows. "Praise be to Almighty God! of what hast thou need, yah Huzrut? I, Mukhlook Khan, am called a man-eater because I thrive off the bloody coin of slavery; but I am far above most men, for there is little that escapes my perception. I would hazard that thou art nought but a pernicious inquisitor."

Our traveler felt uneasy under this suspicion. "You perceive that the rain has stopped, *yah Khwaudjeh?*" he blurted.

The fat gentleman leered, grinning.

Our traveler made haste to depart, and many a barbed laugh followed him.

The Persian (Ajemee), connoisseur of profanity, heresy, and sodomy was among contemptuous Arabs known as "the prickle and anus of Ali," owing to his separation, as the Sheeah sect, from the majority of Mohammedans known as the Sunnee. The Sheeah are companions of Ali, nephew of Mohammed, who was slain in a dispute over the succession to the leadership of the Moslems. There are few Sheeah outside of Iran.

The Persians (Sheeahs: recognizing Ali, Lion of God, as true successor to the Prophet) were firm haters of the Caliph Omar, a Sunnee, who defeated Ali in the contest for the leadership. Omar made a brutal raid into Persia in the mid-seventh-century. Hence the Persians have composed facetiae in damnation of Omar:

> This tale never ends, like the entrails of Omar.
> This road is as long as the pizzle of Omar.
> This blackguard is like Omar, born without

anus and suckled on blood, an hermaphrodite with no urinary orifice and a eunuch with no ballocks.

Persian buffoons delighted in producing puppet shows and live pantomimes satirizing the life of Omar. One scene portrayed the Caliph marching about with an artificial phallus longer than himself, and giving his officers cause to complain of its abuse. Another showed him mounting an osbtinate donkey backward and prodding it on by thrusting his fingers into its fundament. Another hilarious scene involved a eunuch ascending a ladder so that Omar could penetrate him with his enormous limb.

The agnostic, striking a mean, simply declared in mimicking irony: "All long men are fools save onanist Omar, and all short men are knaves save anusing Ali."

"I am a Persian; but, *Wullahee!* I am not lying."

So mistrusted were Persians throughout the East that one who traveled in Persia understood that he was risking his life. At the inns (*serai*) between Shiraz and Isfahan, wayfarers, led to believe that their saddlery was to be stored, were stripped, robbed, and raped by freebooters; consequently the saying: *Zeen-o-zeenposhe bundee unduroon!* (tie within saddle and saddlecloth). Many an early European traveler and missionary, unfamiliar with Ajemee customs, suffered sexual molestation and like abuse by government officials and others, from whom they expected courtesies or services.

One mortified missionary, staked down and pierced by a green-bearded governor in the province of Yezd, noted for devil-worshiping sodomists, demanded the rogue's name, that he might report him to the Shah.

"Name? Call me anything. Call me the devil. I have thirty wives and sixty children. Of course, my cousins have taken a few away. One of them just abducted a young son whilst he was hunting, and sent him back blinded and castrated. But my moment of Divine Vengeance shall come for that anus-bruising dog. As *waulee* of this *wilauyut*, I must attend all ceremonies of wedlock. I make fair coin by instructing youths in the art of love, and I deflower virgins so that it is much easier on the marriage-bed for the shy ones. I am also a man-stealer and a he-whore. I must offer you several of my wives, as you are my honored guest, if that is in your desires." He belched, comfortably. "The devil is kindly."

(It is interesting to note his use of the personal "you" in place of "thou," indicative of homosexual familiarity in the East. Among men and boys the personal pronoun was common; the impersonal, plus the masculine and neuter genders, were used only in conversation with females.)

The green-bewhiskered *waulee* added:

> *Yehoodees* make fine concubines, once the icy barrier is melted. I stopped a caravan of Jews bound for Afghanistan, penetrating all forty of their females in one night. The men protested that such action was an outrage, but I said the outrage was justified in that all of their offspring would be Mohammedans.

Our Arab traveler en route between Isfahan and Shiraz, two rival cities in debauchery, mentioned:

> . . . a group of scoundrels who lie in waiting at a serai and ravish other men during the night.
> "If a wayfarer refuses admittance," say they, "we employ a sharpened tent-peg to change his mind."
> Soon, God so willing, in the flames of Tophet the devil shall perform this very act upon these scurrilous men and, on a still night, one must even hear their bellowing as though it were but a mile hence.

Persian erotologists in accounting for widespread sodomy sought its origin in parental austerity. Barbarous circumcision, leaving the penis like a skinned eel, discouraged masturbation; and to meddle with father's concubines was to invite severe punishment or even death. Hence the puerile practice of *ulish-tukish* (turn by turn) or, in Arabic, *meroof-mejhool* (active-passive) became universal:

> Then eat of these, and drink of those: old wines
>   that bring thee jollity;
> And have each other, turn by turn: shampooing
>   these, thy tools, y'see!

Compressing his nates, one lad would admit the glans (*gudood,* acorn) of another, then vice versa, and no discomfort was afforded the penial shaft, tender and sensitive following cruel scarification. *Ulish-tukish* also applies to mutual fellatio.

Sodomy, regarded philosophically by Mohammed, was in modern Persian laws granted its ancient prerogative. In the *Daudistaun-e-Daunish,* a mild denunciation pleased the Zoroastrian voluptuary:

> He who is wasting seed makes a practice of
> causing the death of progeny. When the custom
> is completely continuous, which produces an evil
> stoppage of the progress of the race, the crea-
> tures have become annihilated; and, certainly,
> such action—from which, when it is universally
> proceeding, the depopulation of the world must
> arise, has become and furthered the greatest wish
> of Uhremaun (the evil principle).

> In the Lore of Love, he was wondrous wise—
>   and wide awake, with all-seeing eyes;
> Its rough and its smooth he had tried, and tries
>   —and hugged buck and doe in the self-
>   same guise—
>   And with greybeard and beardless alike,
>   he plies.

And so, in the hedonist spirit of Omar Khayyam, lived the indifferent Persian.

In accordance with the sacred *Code of Menu,* sodomy was not a serious offense, though rare with the Hindoos:

> A twice-born man, who commits an unnat-
> ural act with a male, shall bathe and be purified
> in his clothes.

Yet the average Hindoo was generally open-minded toward *gaundh-ruttee* (anal coition) because of Lord Shiva, the celestial embodiment of worldly vice, who was said to have copulated with the *raukshehs,* Vishnu, and others of the gods. Shiva was also solemnly masturbated by Agnee the Fire-Lord who, bearing his precious semen across the Ganges, accidentally dropped it and witnessed the miraculous birth of Kartikeh (or Koomareh) the misogynist war god.

Vishnu, in his effeminate phase as god of self-love, had his counterpart in Shiva under the androgynous (*lingam-yoni*) image of Urdhunaree or Urdhuneeshwurreh. Vishnu in his bisexual representation caused his navel (*nauvhee*) to become associated with the female pudendum; and in effigies of Shiva the right side of the body was masculine and the left feminine. Such representation, springing from early belief in the unity of sex (*lingam-yoni,* penis-cunnus) justified hermaphroditic worship and homosexual traditions.

These, however, soon faded with the powerful advent of exclusively maternal or paternal adoration; and androgynous ceremonies became restricted to small or obscure tribes, worshipers of Bhooteyseh (Shiva), Lord of Demonkind. He, in Osirislike sculpture, was seen clutching phallus erectus, glans exposed by retracted prepuce, and thus swearing by his divine power. Castration amongst the priesthood was enjoined and the wombs of priestesses were mutilated with iron rod. Though not a religious duty, celibate holy men, living together in *mutts* (hovels) often indulged in hallowed sodomy. Led by a *sunt-gooroo* or *gosa'een* they, like the Tibetan *lamas,* sought fresh ascetics, teaching them to substitute mutual stimulation in lieu of women.

Throughout Hindoo India, the active sodomite was popularly termed *gaundh-mara* (anus-beater) or *gaundhoo* (anuser). There was no particular name granted the passive homosexual, save that he was an outcast (*mleytcheh*).

A Brahmin found by another in the act of sodomy forfeited eternal bliss unless he made atonement by suicide. This was especially urgent when the act occurred between a twice-born soul and one of lower

caste, and when the latter took the active role. When
sodomy was practiced within the caste, its impurity
might be cleansed away in simple ablution. Sodomy
meant loss of caste unless carried on in a strictly
spiritual and prescribed manner. It was considered a
defilement for the Brahmin when a low-caste man
touched his body.

Having been tainted below the waist, the dis-
honored Brahmin desired to be suspended by his feet
so that his soul would not pass out his anus, a foul
route, into the purgatory of eternal reincarnation in the
basest forms of life. By rending stomach and genitals,
the sinful Brahmin allowed evil spirits to escape above,
from his loins. If the Brahmin did not commit suicide,
his partner was privileged to call him an anus-beater in
public; and this proved a delight to untouchables, thus
enabled to avenge their unceasing humiliation by the
upper castes.

After the blood-bath in Delhi, May, 1857, the
Burra Mahajun (Great Banker), Mungnee-Raum, was
found hanging stark naked by the feet from the rafters
of his house. Mungnee Raum's entrails were dangling
from great slashes in his stomach and pubic region. A
steel-clawed *waughnukh* lay on the floor below him. A
note, found on the secretaire, read:

> He that is born to be Hanged, shall never
> be Drowned.
> A Brahmin in Honor, ere He dies, takes the
> Tail of Mother Cow in His hands: that She may
> guide him into Eternal Bliss. But a Brahmin in
> Disgrace knows no such Ecstasy and expectation
> in Death. The Way ahead is Dark, ambiguous.
> He succumbs in unholy Misery, damned, de-
> graded, without Name, without Face.

Mungnee-Raum, like every other usurer and
moneylender in Hindostan, had two alternatives: a
base death by suicide (*khud-kushee*) or a baser death
at the hands of vengeful debtors. The Burra Mahajun,
being a sodomist, had reason to choose the former.
Were his soul (*praun*) diverted from the anal path,

misery in life would then be compensated by glory in
re-embodiment.

Wajid Ali Shah, Runjeet Singh, Tippoo Sultaun,
and Suraj-ud-Dowlah were all known Indian sodomites,
in company with many of the European officers they
embraced as advisors.

Wajid Ali Shah, King of Oudh and beau ideal of
Oriental voluptuaries, was described by Sir William
Sleeman as:

> . . . frivolous and sensual in the extreme.
> His time and attention are devoted entirely to
> the pursuits of personal gratification; he asso-
> ciates with none but those who can contribute
> to such gratification—namely women, singers,
> and eunuchs. Dressed in female attire, Wajid
> Ali Shah enters into rivalry with nautch girls or
> trifles in his garden with swarms of beautiful
> women dressed in transparent gauze, with wings
> fastened to their shoulders, in imitation of the
> Houris of the Mohammedan paradise.

Suraj-ud-Dowlah, a dissipated tyrant of nineteen
whom Lord Clive defeated at Plassey, was the favorite
of *dervishes* and *fakeers*. He relished what were familiarly called *poggly-nautches* (lunatic-ballets) which
were more or less transvestite orgies wherein effeminates were attended by painted and begowned catamites, enjoying what was likened to a classical French
fancy dress ball.

The frail, one-eyed, pock-marked, white-bearded
Lion of Lahore, Runjeet Singh, was greatly enamored of
the posterior of the Maharajah Gholuab Singh of Cashmere and Jummoo. What travelers and officials often
mistook for dancing girls in quaint Don Giovanni guise,
who encompassed and fondled the old Lion, were in
reality an elite troupe of catamites.

Tippoo Sahib, the demented Tiger of Mysore, took
pains to capture the children of Europeans. Then, when
he felt the urge, he ordered them out of the dungeons
and into his private chamber. There, he defecated upon
them, lashed them, hung them over slow-burning fires,
and, having drugged them to insensibility, murdered

each by decapitation after a single session. Sometimes he would employ a brace of Abyssinian slaves (*hubshees*) who, taking each child by the head and legs, would twist and mash them into pulp and toss their remains out of the palace windows. These same Abyssinians were said to be able to crush a man in their embrace and they were no less feared than the Sultaun's man-eating tigers.

Following summary circumcision of all Infidel captives, the Tiger came personally to know each of them carnally. He would even make them handle his private part and bring it to their lips. As rare testimony shows, more than once did he set enormous black vulgarians upon them who, stark naked, held them down and unmercifully abused their bodies. In emulation of the Turk, Tippoo Sahib sought and tried every method of gratification known to man. Women had long ago sated the Tiger; and he tired of men and boys as well. One evening, he showed his prisoners a trick he had learned from a traveler who had been to China. Taking a large goose, he loosened his rose-embroidered *jamdanee* and said: "Ye must one day try this; it is wondrously singular. God willing. I will penetrate the goose and, upon approaching my ejaculation, I will wrench off its neck: thereby relishing the ecstatic convulsions experienced in the anus." He was also wont to display his ability with sows and goats, making no effort to conceal his raptures.

"But surely," commented one cynical British officer, "His Lewdness has something of justice in his bones." For everything Tippoo did, there was apparently justification in his own mind. Witness the time he caught one of his French wives and a black slave, whom he had not granted permission to enter the harem, in each other's embrace. It seemed that the only way Tippoo could gratify his six hundred women and keep them from sapphic diversions was through artificial phalli or agreeing to a certain number of chosen courtiers and bondsmen entering the harem. As custom willed, he had the delinquent black's lips, tongue, nose, and genitals removed, to prevent his ever being loved again, then, waiting with all due patience until the damsel was in her last month of pregnancy, he ordered her to be ripped open and the unborn child impaled on a lance.

Another story is related about a woman who complained that a starving wretch had forcefully taken milk from her breasts, which her twin infants were living upon. Brought before the Sultaun, the thief denied this and upbraided the woman severely. But she insisted, breaking into hysteria, and so His Highness passed down Solomonic judgment: "The man's stomach shall be ripped open and, if no milk is discovered, the woman shall be executed." Milk was found; the unfortunate thief perished in the operation; and the woman reveled—in Tippoo's embrace. Indeed, the Tiger of Mysore shone brightly as a great and just ruler as well as an artful lecher.

Tippoo Sahib in his spare time was also an interpreter of dreams. Every night he looked forward to a prophetic vision, appetizingly sensuous, which he might contemplate over during the morning hookah-hour. One of them, written in the Sultaun's diary, is as follows:

> By His grace, I had a dream.
> Methought a young man of beautiful countenance, a stranger, came and sat down; and methought I jested with him, in the manner that a person playfully talks with a woman. At the same time, I said in my heart: "It is not my custom to enter into playful discourse with anyone." In the instant the youth rose and, walking a few paces, returned, he loosened his hair from beneath his turban and, opening the fastening of his robe, displayed his bosom; and I saw it was a woman. I immediately called and seated her, and said unto her: "Whereas I before looked upon you as a woman, and jested with you, it now appears that you are a woman—in the dress of a man. My conjecture has well succeeded." In the midst of this discourse the morning dawned, and I awoke.
> Please God, these English hounds have put on the clothing of men but, in fact, are in character of women.

Thus, it was not uncommon for the Hindostanee to call the European *gaundhoo* nor the European to call the Hindostanee a *bugger*.

2. PEDERASTY

> Stay not thy gaze upon the beardless, for in them
> is a momentary eye-glance at the nymphs of
> Paradise.

The Prophet Mohammed, glory-hunter and humanitarian, was far from naïve. He steered the Arab tribesmen from the ancient path of idolatry, leading them into pure and simple monotheism, but he could not steer the inherent complexity of emotions and wonted sexual inclinations. Religious belief was superficial, but passion and taste were not; conviction changed with years and rulers and environment, but human nature remained virtually unaltered. Thus, like any man of sagacity, tact, and discretion, Mohammed retained in his judgment upon sex a surprisingly fatalistic attitude. In order to wield power, he had to impose tolerable unity and discipline yet preserve vital social custom, to avoid indiscretions that might cause his downfall.

Mohammed thereby won over a stanch and free-thinking people. His mesmeric fanaticism, tempered by national pride and common sense, made this innovator one of the greatest and most curious of earth-shaking human beings. And that mesmeric fanaticism, proclaiming the ideals men long held in their hearts, roared as wildfire throughout the East.

Ishk-ozree or *uflautoonee* (excusable, platonic love) was deeply felt amongst the idealistic Arabs. Once virtuous, as in venerable Greece, it soon became debased into vice. Natural affection for the pert, comely, girlish youth declined into licentious desire and uninhibited debauchery.

When the tempestuous storm of El-Islam had blown its last proselytizing blasts across Asia and men settled down to apply the practical tenets of Lord Mohammed, justification for pederasty was sought in the

Koran. Besides sloe-eyed *hooreeyehs,* the Prophet promised beautiful young boys to wait upon all True Believers in Paradise. Subsequently, this tradition paved the way for mundane adoration and emulation of the glories of Eternal Bliss:

> And when one blast shall sound the trumpet, and the earth shall be moved from its place, and the mountains also—and shall be dashed in pieces at one stroke—on that day, the inevitable Hour of Judgment shall suddenly come. And for the pious is prepared a place of bliss: gardens planted with trees, and vineyards, and damsels with swelling breasts—of equal age with themselves—and a full cup. Therein shall receive them beautiful damsels, refraining their eyes from beholding any besides their spouses, whom no man shall have debowered before their destined spouses, neither any *jinn.* Verily, we have created the damsels of Paradise by a peculiar creation; and we have made them virgins beloved by their husbands, of equal age with them and deflowered by neither man nor spirit. And youths, which shall continue forever in their bloom, shall go round to attend them with goblets brimming of wine.

The Brahmins did famously with their temple brothels, but vast income was soon reaped by houses of male prostitution in the Moslem *casbahs;* the fathers of desirable youths became wealthy overnight. After boy-prostitution had become firmly established as a lucrative and recognized custom, shrewd Mohammedans inverted Koranic meaning and boasted to the sensual Hindoos that their scriptures allowed no more profit through sexual liberty than did El-Koran. Sacred dogmas soon became complexly corrupted. Mohammed, were he aware of this, must have turned over in his grave. The virtuous *wuldaun* or *ghilmaun* of Paradise (beautiful beardless youths) were interpreted as salacious catamites; the Abode of Eternal Bliss was, for the vulgar and ignorant mind, converted into a slough of dissipation of which Rizwaun, the Moslem St. Peter, was sacred whoremaster.

A beardless and handsome youth (*emred*) was scarcely safe in the streets of Cairo. Whenever he passed the coffeeshop, men glared heatedly, grinned, and gesticulated for him to come over and sit down. Were he by caution to pass them by, they invariably shrilled in all mournfulness: "Heaven deprive us not of thee!" or, coarsely ironic: *"Behhefzillah!"* (God preserve thee *for another day*).

The American street corner with its collection of scrutinizers of passing girls finds its historical counterpart in the open Mohammedan *gehweh* (coffeehouse), where men utterly ignored the passing doe-eyed lass. Women were abundant and cheap, but the provocative, rump-wriggling lad was a treasure; and men puffed and snorted, devouring with glaring eyes any tender willow-branch of a lad who quivered by.

> Seest not the bazaar, with its fruit in rows?
> These men are for figs, and for sycamore those!

The Oriental market place with its congregations of oglers certainly presented a bizarre scene to the uninformed newcomer.

> Quoth they—and I had trained my taste thereto, nor cared for other fruits whereby they swore—
> "Why lovest so the Fig?"—whereto, quoth I:
> "Some men love Fig and, others, Sycamore."

This philosophic expression of taste, common throughout Asia, was of various forms, all wryly euphemistic. "He loves to eat both figs and pomegranates," signified bisexuality (the *fig* metaphorically indicating *anus,* and the *pomegranate,* often *sycamore, vulva*). There was apparently no shame in such disclosure; in fact, to be capable of equally handling both sexes was the substance of great pride and denoted inexhaustible virility. Only the few self-conscious or a lecherous holy man chanced to reveal:

> Indeed, my heart loves all the lovely boys as girls
> —nor am I slow to such delight;

But, though I sight them every night and morn,
    I'm neither of Lot's folk nor wencher-wight.

Others, boasting of their virtue and strength of will
against diabolic temptation, made themselves unpopular as hypocrites by reciting:

My prickle is big; and the catamite said: "Thrust
    boldly in vitals, with lionlike stroke!"
Then, I: " 'Tis a sin!" and he: "No sin to me!"
    So I had him at once, with a counterfeit
    poke.

But the average full-blooded Moslem, cross-legged
and swinging his sherbet cup in the market-place, proclaimed loud and clear:

None wotteth best joyance but generous youth,
    when the pretty ones deign with me com-
    pany keep;
Heaven bless them! how sweetly my night with
    them sped; a wonderful harvest of pleasure
    I reap;
Let us drink our good liquor, both watered and
    pure, and agree to swive all who dare slum-
    ber and sleep.

To this, the average full-blooded Moslem wench
would more than likely reply: *"Ehhsen-el-medaurehh-
lil-kereem shebaub-el-Gehennem!"* (the best of places
for generous youth is Gehenna).

Womankind: what, as a whole, must they have
thought? Many, characteristically acknowledging bald
custom, thought little of it or were amused, but rarely
jealous or scornful. Little is recorded as to feminine reaction toward pederasty; but one crude yet earnest
poem, composed by a learned matriarch (*sheykheh*),
may be said to have answered for the more intelligent
of Arab women:

Men's turning unto bums of boys is bumptious;
    whoso loveth noble women show their own
    noblesse.

How many goodly wights have slept the night,
     enjoying buttocks of boys, and woke at
     morn in foulest mess—
Their garments stained by safflower, which is yel-
     low merde—their shame proclaiming,
     showing color of, distress?
Who can deny the charge, when so bewrayed
     are they, that e'en by daylight shows the
     dung upon their dress?
What contrast wi' the man, who slept a glad-
     some night by houri-maid: for glance, a
     mere enchantress?
He rises off her, borrowing wholesome bonny
     scent: that fills the house with whiffs of
     perfumed goodliness.
No boy deserved place by side of her to hold—
     nor canst e'en aloes-wood with that which
     fills a pool of cess![11]

But feminine opinion in regard to the diversions of
men was irrelevant. In lands where a wife might be sent
packing with only the utterance of three peremptory
words as sufficient divorce proceedings, woman was apt
discreetly to adopt the fatalistic indifference of her
spouse even when, angry at her for a miscarriage or
periodic indisposition, he chanted:

Fair to the sight, a well-shaped wight!
Slim waist and boyish wits delight wencher as
     well as sodomite!
I clipt his form and wax'd drunk with his
     scent,
     Fair branch to whom Zephyr gave nutri-
     ment!
The least of him is the being free from monthly
     courses and pregnancy!

The neurotic temperament of Moslem, particularly
Egyptian youths, assisted by a generally morbid dis-
tribution of sensory tissue, made them highly apt for
such a profession as pederasty (*ishk-el-oolaud,* love of
boys). And the voracious Son of Islam, lusting for
novelty, fashioned the ganymede into an almost indis-

[11]Burton, *op. cit.*

pensable manner of entertainment. As dancing boys they obsessed nearly every Eastern potentate, and they were found writhing in nearly every bazaar. And, next to the female prostitute, the catamite or ganymede (*welled, meloot*) reaped the fortunes and celebration of princes.

> The weals of this world are the catamite's meed;
> Would that I were of the sodomite breed!

Entering male prostitution in Egypt was quite elementary; one had only to be attractive. The methods of rising to fame were manifold. Boys of the gypsy tribes were born into pederasty; others, seized by slavers, were sold into it. And not a few, dazzled by the allure of riches and esteem, broke in of their own free will. Poverty accounted for a goodly deal of it, and shame and discomfort often were its conditions. But the zealous male prostitute truly enjoyed his mode of existence.

In order to attract attention, one determined lad boldly interrupted a gathering of men in a large Cairene establishment. Assisted by his older brother, manager and chief mountebank, the youth demanded a coin from each. More amused than insulted, for the presumptuous lad tickled their curiosity, they obliged; and brother mountebank heartily collected. Letting down his bag-trousers, sitting upon a stool and closing his eyes, by apparent conjuration and sheer force of imagination the youth effected almost immediate erection and orgasm, to the amazement of all. But a second later the grinning lad showed each of them a tiny hole in the stool, allowing a titillating finger to touch his anus. Having thus fallen for the deception, each man laughed to tears; the youth was brought into their confidence and clique, and their money flowed into the pockets of his brother who, of course, handled the procuring and management.

A boy prostitute was often called *nedeem* (cup-companion). Sharing the company of mature men, he was generally between fifteen and twenty-five years of age; hence, the saying: "A boy of twice ten is fit for a

King!" Having enjoyed more experience, he was termed *gulleh* (wide-mouthed jug, alluding to his abused podex) whereas a novice was affectionately called *dorek* (the narrow). *El-gulleh* frequently dressed in feminine attire, as witness this line of verse referring to the acceptance of wine:

> From hand of yarded lad, begarbed like coynted
> > lass:
> > wencher and tribe of Lot alike enamoring.

This was also inverted to form "from hand of coynted lass, begarbed like yarded lad" (alluding to she-catamites).

The most gainful position, next to serving royalty, was attending in the bath (*hhemmaum*).

> Luck to the Rubber, whose deft hands o'erfly a
> > frame much enamored of a plump little
> > troll;
> He shows the thaumaturgy of his craft, by induc-
> > ing the traveler to futter his hole.

Uncouth as it may seem to Western ears, this couplet summed the matter up well. The *mokeyyis* (rubber or shampooer) was a guileful tempter taking a weak, inexperienced and dissolute wayfarer high above full price while in the *meslekh* (stripping room) another rifled the traveler's clothes.

When entering the *hhemmaum,* the operator of the bath collected the entrant's fee and directed him to the stripping room where the *leewaunjee* (a beardless youth who attends the bather when undressing) came forward, demanded a substantial gratuity and, whilst peeling off the traveler's garments, made lascivious movements. The fleecing did not end yet; for, preceding the bath, the traveler reclined naked on a mattress, sipped coffee or drew on the waterpipe, and said: "*Yah mokeyyis! t'auleh keyyisneh* (Attendant! come, rub me down). Thereupon, a nude boy, generally well-proportioned, scurried in and commenced to knead, pound, kick, massage, and fondle the wayfarer. In the languor following a hot cleansing, the *mokeyyis*'s fingers seemed charmed, evoking a voluptuous sensation, and the more expert job he did, especially in retarding orgasm, the greater his reward. Some, less skillful, stroked the muscles in such a precipitous manner that erection and emission were involuntary and almost simultaneous. Such unskilled individuals received only half to a quarter of the sum usually granted for massage that included artful prolongation of pleasure.

Following shampoo, the plump and comely *mokeyyis* customarily sold his body to the bather for an hour (his specialty being fellatio); whereupon the bather relished another dip in a cooling tank, got dressed, and left.

> A wretched Turk is my heart's desire:
> Beardless boys set his bowels afire.

Turkey furnished Georgia with catamites, while Circassia sent concubines into Turkey. The Turks, notorious race of pederasts, were regarded everywhere in the same dingy light by unsympathetic travelers:

> They partake of wine until they cannot distinguish between masculine and feminine, and use the rumps of boys as they would the coyntes of women.

Ranking with Alexander, Caesar, and Bonaparte, the eminent and glorious Saladin (Sellah-ed-Deen), Sultan of Egypt and Syria, was like Rome's greatest emperor "the husband of all women and the wife of all men," a habitual pederast. Arab historians of the twelfth century cited him as being wise, noble, and courageous, coping with the invading Crusaders with martial prudence but, when it came to fair beardless youths, more salacious than a he-goat. They attributed this to early impotence.

Mosul and El-Yemen, before mentioned, were always locales of unsavory reputation as the nuclei of Middle Eastern homosexuality. A man of propriety and respect dared never to boast that he was from Mosul, lest he face a sarcastic retort:

> The foulest and filthiest of a catamite race,
> whose youth is a scapegrace and whose old age
> hath wits as the wits of an ass.

As for El-Yemen:

> There, the noblest make womanly use of
> beardless boys; and the meanest of them fre-
> quent eunuchs; and the lowest amongst them
> train baboons to futter; and others are weavers
> of strumpet's sheaths.

In China at the age of four, boys were sold and trained into pederasty, a thriving and honorable profession sanctified by Tcheou-Wang, God of Sodomy, and in Japan, where male prostitution was also a consecrated practice, Buddhist monks kept ganymedes and regulated boy brothels for the use of worshipers.

Strange as it may seem, vocational pederasty never tainted Hindooism; none of the sacred texts enjoined or even mentioned it simply because androgynous adoration, sanctifying sodomy, had died an inglorious death in the mists of antiquity. Hence pederasty amid the Aryans in India was oftentimes regarded with amusement or jeered in local abuse:

> Mayaunjee tee-tee!
> *Butcheh-k'gaundh meyn ungulee-k'heel*
> Schoolmaster, *hum!*
> Who fumbled and fingered the little boy's bum!

Though rare in Hindostan, pederasty was rampant among the peoples of the Punjaub, the Deccan, and Sindh: Sikhs, Hindoo Mussulmans, and Afghans. In Kurrachee, famed for its *poggly-nautches* and bordels of youths and eunuchs, epidemic pederasty (*lowndhey-bauzee,* boy-sport) far outnumbered houses of female prostitution. Dancing boys, painted, scented with saffron water, and bedecked in the finest raiment, paraded through the streets, heatedly soliciting; while in open stalls and palatial residencies naked lads and castratos, perfumed and polished with mustard oil, stood for sale. These boys, choice, delicate, with large rosy buttocks, were affectionately styled *mucknas*

(Hind. *mukhnah*), tuskless baby elephants, because
of their rudimentary genitals (unshorn by the cruel
razor). *Mukhnah* (tailless, hairless, flea-prick) also became a vicious term of jealous reproach since these fastidious youths brought double the price of eunuchs and
beardless castratos, simply because their unmutilated
scrotums served as bridles to direct movement.[12]

> Wullud sureen shuftauloo-maunind duryah,
>   Ufsose! mun n'shinnah:
> There's a boy across the river with a podex like
>   a peach; but, alas! I cannot swim.

This is the first stanza of a ballad entitled *Zukhmee-
Dil* (Wounded Heart), popular with the Afridi Nation.
It was sung by lone hillman and campfire troubadour
from one end of the Indus to the other; and *Zukhmee-
Dil* became the favorite marching air of the Khyber
Rifles at Fort Jumrood. ·

Zun-e-suffuree (traveling wives) were the essential part of any camel caravan or other company of
travelers passing through the forbidding Khyber and
into the fertile Punjaub. But these so-called "wives,"
not only the ideals of Afghan traders but of Pathan
troops going forth to battle on the Frontier, were in
fact catamites. Hidden from strangers and the evil eye
in camel panniers (*kejawahs*), these youths, ranging in
age from five to twenty years, were scented, depilated,
rouged, hennaed, and adorned with long silken pomaded hair and kohl-rimmed provocative eyes. In a
word, no one could have distinguished them from wom-
en or girls unless they stripped them of their costly
gowns.

When an Afghan's wife died, she was soon forgotten and her body moldered in the ravine where it
was usually thrown. But when an Afghan lost his catamite his heart was never the same. He mourned the loss
like that of a loyal camel or a hardy steed, and burial
rites were indeed extravagant and impressive. Woman
was only an unattractive drudge, a means of propagat-

---

[12]Burton's evidence.

ing the race; but *"ah! the delight in whimsical and flir-*
tatious youth, smooth and comely."

These *zun-e-suffuree,* the pride of slavers, were
well received in Peshawar, where merchants and noblemen paid several hundred to many thousands of
golden *ushruffees* to bruise the nates of a beardless lad.

> There was once a boy or, rather, a youth of ex-
> ceeding beauty; and he had very many lov-
> ers.

This was the tone of venerable Hafiz and Saadi,
poets laureate of Persia.

> In passion our Sheykh was an Ajemee, with a
> Catamite ever in company;
> In the Love of Woman, a Platonist he, but, in
> either, versed to the full degree,
> And stallion to him was the same as a filly.

From antiquity the Persian was a connoisseur of
any sort of amorous glances, but he preferred the love
of boys to that of girls. Charming but sinister Sheykh-
en-Nezr, Governor of Bushire, was wont to entertain
midshipmen of the Bombay Marines, plying them with
Shirazee wine till they were insensate. On awaking, the
young Englishmen complained of how the wine caused
a strange vellication and soreness between their buttocks. Nezr, also a clever wit, loved to entertain his
European guests with the *adumee-tope* (man-cannon).
A Negro slave was dragged in and held on all fours,
while peppercorns were thrust into his anus. A sheet of
parchment served as target; cayenne was applied to the
nostrils, the Negro sneezed, and tiny grapeshot erupted
full blast. Bets were often placed, and every strike was
accounted for.

The Magians (*Mujoosee*) were the first Parsic
pederasts. They, fire-worshiping sorcerers, danced
frenziedly in the nude round the flames at midnight,
wailing eerie incantations and fornicating among themselves and with boys doomed to evil sacrifice.

With the advent of immaculate Parseeism, pederasty rose from the depths of witchcraft and acquired platonism:

> Ul-wujood suzaur bosah khoob?
> Buloogghut b'now-e-pushm khoob!
> What best deserves bussing?
> A bobadilla with a young bush!

The last line, altered to *Subyeh b'kuss-e-now-e-pushm khoob,* referred to a girl with tender vulva and downy pubes.

In Shiraz, an eminent *mujtahid* (spiritual director of the Sheeah sect) was suddenly approached by one of his colleagues. "There is a question I would fain address to thine Eminence," he said, hesitant and pensive, "but I lack the daring to do so."

"Ask, and fear not!"

"Then it is this, O Mujtahid! Figure thee in a garden of roses and hyacinths, with the evening breeze waving the cypress heads, a fair youth of twenty sitting by thy side, and the assurance of perfect privacy. What, prithee, would be the result?"

The theologian grinned, then scowled and, wringing his fists and beating his ears, hastened away. "Almighty God defend me from such temptation!"

When an Isfahanee youth mocked the great Saadi by comparing his bald glossy dome to the bottom of a brass vase, the sagacious bard turned the vase upside-down and retaliated by comparing its wide mouth to the youth's well-abused anus.

Persia, analogous to ancient Greece, knew both philosophic and vicious pederasty. Its pleasures were. glorified by both poets and priests. Its popularity ascended from a matter of flagrant custom to that of holy idolatry. Houses of feminine ill fame were entirely unknown but bagnios of boys (*butcha-khanas*) were an established institution. All early travelers were shocked and surprised and, be they Arab, a trifle humored to discover this peculiarity.

In the *butcha-khana,* each troupe of dancing boys was bathed, dieted and depilated, to present the desired smooth appearance. Instruction was given them in the arts and sciences of entertainment and coquetry, with careful consideration shown to the posterior. A science in itself was the ability deftly to control the anal sphincter. A lad so skilled in this spasmodic performance, like the woman able to milk the penis with her pubic muscles, commanded double to triple the price of others, provided he retained his bridlelike genitories.

The prevalence of boy brothels in Persia diminished, however, when astute fathers began setting their sons up in business and selling their daughters into the whoredom of concubinage. As in the decadence of Greece and Rome, youths from six to twenty solicited and procured a substantial and independent living; and *zunkhas* (bands of itinerant professional effeminates) were often seen swaying along the roads, arm in arm, and singing in clear, ardent tones:

> I am enamoured of a fawn, with languishing
> black eyes;
>> The willow-branches envy him when he
>> walketh and sighs.
> The moisture of his mouth is like melted con-
> fection,
>> And his teeth are as pearls in exquisite con-
>> nection.
> His countenance surpasseth the glorious full
> moon,
>> And, ravished by his beauty, I disdain not to
>> swoon.

One traveler to Cabul, a physician from Delhi, described his experiences while attending a private dinner in the home of a wealthy and respectable merchant:

> I regarded Afghan delicacies, cockroaches fried in ghee, bullock's testicles in date-wine sauce, and I knew that surely I must belch for more reasons than being ordinarily courteous. The fruit and the sherbet seemed harmless enough, though they may have been infused with some maddening drug. I chanced looking at the host; and the host, partaking heartily, grinned.

I recalled his words: "When a Cabulee presents thee with viands, it is not a common courtesy to offer him some first; ye do so to test its purity from poison." Notwithstanding, I possessed the strangest feeling that all Afghans took daily of poison to achieve immunity; for everyone appeared out to poison another, and hospitality was merely a shroud for gain.

An eerie resonance swelled from above, the sinuous, undulate twang of lute and lyre, and throughout the meal I noticed the feeling, a light-headed sensation, as of a spell gradually overcoming me. Rain cannoned dully outside; there were dim abysmal strains, inebriate scent, uncanny light.

I watched, glassy-eyed, as a pubescent lad ambled forward with a huge silver tray. He was strongly Greek (Yoonaunee) in appearance: with blue eyes, yellow locks, and muscular white frame. The host said nothing but regarded him proudly, occasionally glimpsing at myself. The lad was very civil; he stood before me and salaamed. Then, quite unashamedly and as if by habit, he drew up his robe to display his nakedness: at which, by inviolate custom, I was obliged to lift my hands in praise. Then, once again bowing, the youth departed with a clearly suggestive glint in his eyes.

"He is a Caffre, from Cafiristan," the host, a wizened Cabulee, said. "No less than a descendant of the Great Alexander (Iskunder-Dilkhan); I paid enormously for him, and he is progressing well."

"In what respect, yah Huzoor?" I chanced, hesitatingly.

The host inclined, touching his fingers to his breast. "Indeed, yah Khawind, in helping me to retire from the trading profession at a very early age. In another month, I shall take him before the Ameer of Afghanistan, insane for rare handsome white youths, and, in the month thereafter, thine host must be appointed chief pander to the Court of Cabul."

He laughed, and I laughed, but he was! And soon thereafter, the fair lads of Cafiristan were much prized in Cabul; and every one captured was treated with utmost kindness and sold at fabulous sums.

By this it is clearly shown that while the Southern Europeans greatly cherished skillful Oriental prostitutes, the Orientals greatly cherished rosy-cheeked European catamites. White lads were as lily blossoms to them; and in Egypt and Turkey, where *memlooks* (fair Circassian slaves) and Janissaries (Greco-Christian militia) reigned supreme, white flesh was valued far above rubies.

3. SAPPHISM

In the harem, wrote a prominent Arab erotologist,

> . . . thou wilt come across all manner of women; but in choosing one, there are several things to be remembered.
> Display thy sagacity by accepting one not only firm of breasts and slim of waist and heavy of hips, but with praiseworthy hinder cheeks. As with the more endowed of Moslems, Negroes in particular adore posterior prominence and wide hips in women: especially if their natural parts are large, in due proportion.
> The Hebshee female is most laudable. Strong interior muscles insure greater intensity of carnal pleasure. But above all else, ye must be wary and sagacious enough not to dare choose a *sehheekeh*.
> *Es-sehheekeh*'s greatest delight lies in rubbing clitoris against clitoris, handling the yarded eunuchs and having them play the futtering baboon. She is scornful of virile men. Her satanic joy demands arousing a man till his prickle stands at fullest point, then bidding a eunuch slice the member off. Others, in the foreplay, beat the testicles, twist and crush them, or rend them out with razor-sharp fingernails. Some are so treacherous and demoniacal that they will tear away the swollen yard, or its large proud head, with their teeth. Such women are to be detected by their coarse semblance and a protruding clitoris.

Egyptian harems were veritable hotbeds of *musahhekeh* tribadism, (art of rubbing). It is known that many Turko-Egyptian women, being uncircumcised and retaining the clitorial glans, were avid nymphomaniacs. As in the hybrid male, sexual neurosis was chiefly innate, rarely voluntarily acquired, though intensified by will power, an hysterical temperament augmented by climatic and physical sensuality, neglect and inactivity, rich foods and overdeveloped, hyperactive organs.

Isolated in enormous seraglios, females were generally given over to fanatic sapphism (*sehhaukeh*) employing the ancient substitutes for the appeasing phallus, the tongue, candle, banana, and artificial penis. The Egyptian, pederast and sodomite as he was, scornfully called them *sehheekehs* (rubbers, fricatrices). Hence, the uncircumcised woman was categorically of two distinct temperaments: sapphic or heterosexual-hypersensitive, with shades of each affecting both.

Apart from *sehhaukeh,* various crude and euphemistic titles were granted female inversion, among them, *mejhool-el-izarbund* (laxity of the trouser-string) and *lisaun-fee-gubb* (tongue-in-bush, cunnilingus.) Most Arabs were of the opinion that women corrupt women more than men do; thus the prudent Arab was always more jealous of his sweetheart's lady friends than any suspected male admirers. And he had every right to be, for sapphism was just as rampant among certain classes of women as sodomy among *all* classes of men. Bred by ennui and atavistic sensuality and fostered by depraved matrons in the seraglio, it became the favorite method of prepubescent gratification in girls. But, of course, mutual and solitary clitoral and labial masturbation were common throughout.

The *mowerriseh* (she-pimp) and the *bellauneh* (female bath attendant) became mistresses of perversion in society; while in the restricted harem, *esh-sheykheh-el-bezzreh* (one who teaches the art of rubbing clitoris against clitoris) taught every girl in the sapphic sciences. To solace her in long hours of desire for the male, nearly every concubine had her own private companion whom she styled *merseeneh* or *ree-*

hauneh (myrtle) and with whom she practiced all the sapphic pleasures. Murder by poison or strangulation became prevalent not only on account of the master's favoritism but because of rabid lesbian rivalry and infidelity, as one girl enticed or stole another's companion.

Umm-et-Tertoor (Mother of Hoods) was a tribade of the grossest order, a woman with overdeveloped projecting clitoris (*bezzer*) often exceeding two inches. These women were obviously capable of sapphic venery among themselves or with eunuchs, which they sought avidly, anointing their partners with aphrodisiac saffron so that, in the atmosphere and disposition of sensuous hysteria, they would swoon straight away.

In India and Persia the fricatrice was called *burra zumbooreh* (large clitoris-woman) or pythoness (*naugee*) with erectile powers known as *beybauk* (bold). In the aromatic gardens of the Red Fort at Delhi, the Fort of Akbar in Lahore, and the Kaiserbagh Palace .t Lucknow, zenana women with highly developed organs like those in China and Japan practiced sapphic venery in hammocks. Those who were declitorised, called *tubzeerehs,* as well as those unmutilated but primarily heterosexual in nature, consorted with eunuchs or utilized artificial priapi (*m'yaujung*). Stimulation of the labia or even the vaginal walls (*muttun,* churning) was permitted the circumcised female and was performed by well-endowed eunuchs or with wooden stalks. But emasculated slaves who retained the hyperesthetic glans penes were reserved for the uncircumcised, who experienced utmost pleasure in external massage. This and rapid convulsive orgasms indicated their highly sexed and neurotic temperament, bordering on total inversion. Therefore, lesbian passion in women was in nearly all cases acquired to supplant heterosexual needs.

4. BESTIALITY

Talmudists declared that, before the creation of Eve, Adam copulated with any number of beasts. This form of perversion, nearly as endemic in man without woman or woman without man as masturbation, was like sodomy or sapphism regarded philosophically or with grim humor by the early tribes. Only when unnatural vice threatened the existence and strength of the sons of Israel did Moses create an unheard-of-moral code and preach vehemently:

Whosoever lieth with a beast shall surely be put to death.

Bestiality (*hheywauneeyeh*) among the Egyptians was spread by the omnivorous Mamelukes, who were fanatic inverts of active and passive disposition.

"The Pilgrimage to Mecca is not perfected save by copulation with the camel!" was a popular expression in El-Islam, preluding the worldly binge after pious abstinence. The Arab, adopting his virtues and vices primarily from the Hebrew, held bestiality at its worst as a mere peccadillo; and no mention of it is made in the Koran. Originally, it led to the death by lapidation (stoning) of both man and animal; but with the increased influence of Syrian, Parsaic, and Chinese debauchery, bestial perversion lost both its original sanctity and its later wickedness, and presently became, like everything else, a matter of taste.

In such hot, moist and sensuous lands as the Indus and Nile Valleys, the ape's apparently natural propensity for man was quickly acknowledged. She-monkeys tempted villagers and travelers by intimating the desire to fondle and by displaying their secret parts; and, curious as to the animal's reaction and receptiveness, man yielded and found it as pleasing as, if not better than, any catamite.

As history underhandedly relates, the Turk and his mare were always well attached, "but for many reasons," say the Arabs. "A dungheap, the Toork: he —God forbid!—has managed to defile every domestic beast save the reverent camel." The camel, arrogant and independent as it is, had fanatical pride. A French officer on Napoleon's staff reported that he saw an Egyptian youth attempting sexually to mount a she-dromedary in El-Feyyoom, a veritable sink of debauchery; but the camel, stout of limb, kicked him into the air—"and ruined him," the amused *soldat* added. Not even an Arab could get away with it, and the Arab was the camel's brother. For the animal acquired a nasty reputation in severely injuring or killing drivers and other unwary individuals for less treatment than that.

In the Nile villages and a few populated oases, all manner of bestiality prevailed. The young shepherd (*ra'ee*), isolated as he was, abused his animals by a diversity of bestial practices. One, extensive in the pastoral East and frequently performed openly, was to offer his penis to a suckling goat. When the animal could not be aroused to this mode of bestial fellatio, the youth would smear honey or melted candy upon his genital as an inducement. This (*reddheh*) was considered highly refined, preferred to simple intromission with the animal.

Others along the sacred Nile rolled sleeping she-crocodiles over upon their backs, when they were quite helpless, and then had their will of them. But, however this form of *hheywauneeyeh* appears, there was undoubtedly deep religious significance in this; for Egyptians, both virtuous and depraved, had worshiped the crocodile (*et-timsahh*) for many centuries. Congress with one, so hallowed legend proclaimed, secured everlasting prosperity and rebirth of power for aging and exhausted men.

Neglected or pathologic women, especially in Abyssinia and the Sudan, smuggled dog-faced apes (*girds*) into the harem. These were lusty brutes, known to kill men and rape women in many parts of the country; and an old Egyptian saying declared: "Nothing poketh and stroketh, nor lusteth after a female, more strenuously than the baboon." Trained, the cynocephalus, drilling vigorously, endured much longer than the hardiest eunuch. The only shortcoming was that the penis of the baboon proved more stiff and sturdy than long and thick, and concubines demanded ample girth for proper response. Yet those who could achieve venereal paroxysm by friction of the vaginal orifice and external genitalia were greatly enamored of monkeys. Thus the Arab, student of medicine, definitely held that nymphomania was due to black and yellow worms in the vagina: black being bred by the strokings of a Negro, and yellow by the strokings of a domiciled baboon. Many such women having animal contacts were considered saints and *hooreeyehs* (nymphs of heaven).

Scarcely any mention at all is made of male bestiality, but Egypto-Arab tales are stuffed with descriptions of clandestine female activities. This was perhaps due to general but superficial misogyny. Several writers, portraying the death of a lady, delighted in making her last words those of eternal gratitude and devotion to the dog-faced baboon who took her virginity and caused her to swoon by excess of pleasure never forgotten and never equaled since. Other facetiae tell of women who, following connection and ecstatic swoon, awoke to find their beloved pet dead and a compassionate or contemptuous man standing over it. "Are men so few?" he would shout; but she, bursting into hysterical tears and throwing herself upon the animal's body, preferred death to life without pleasure:

"God curse thee for what thou hast done! No man on earth thrusteth and foineth so featly as the cynocephalus; and now, thou hast destroyed him, there is no further consolation in my existence."

The compassionate individual generally took her to wife but, being unable to gratify her as had the baboon, had resort to rid her body of worms. This was done by applying a steaming bowl of herbs between the thighs, until the lumbrici fled her vulva and perished. But the contemptuous man, unsympathetic, either despatched her forthwith or sadistically looked on as she plunged a dagger into her own lamenting heart.

The following scene, written by an Egyptian whose errant wife led him many a chase, took place in a bear's cave on the outskirts of Cairo, to which he had trailed her:

As soon as she was heated with wine, she put off her petticoat-trousers and lay down on her back; whereupon, the bear rose and came up to her, and mounted and stroked her, and she gave him the best of what belongeth to the sons of Adam till he had made an end, when he sat down and rested. Presently, he sprang upon her and futtered her again and, when he ended, again sat down to rest; and he ceased not so doing till he had futtered her ten times, and they both descended into fainting-fit and lay without motion.[18]

Incidents, like these, horrifying to the occasional European who heard of them but would not believe that such things occurred, were eagerly heard, and the tellers of such tales were greatly applauded by the coffeehouse clique, which could not seem to get enough of these stories. And the denouement was over when, the husband or bachelor secretly observing:

"She set on wine and drank and gave the ape to drink; and he stroked her nigh half a score times without drawing till she swooned away, when he spread over her a silken coverlet and returned to his place." And the inevitable climax when the compassionate bachelor "spoke her fair for a while, and pledged myself to stand in the ape's stead in the matter of much poking, till her trouble subsided and I took her to wife. But when I came to perform my promise, I proved a failure and I fell short in this matter and could not endure such hard labor; so I complained of my case and mentioned her exorbitant requirements to a certain old woman, who engaged to manage the affair and said to me: 'Needs must thou bring me a cooking-pot full of virgin vinegar and a pound of the herb-pellitory called wound-wort.' So I brought her what she sought; and she laid the pellitory in the pot, with the vinegar, and set it on the fire till it was thoroughly boiled. Then, she bade me futter the girl; and I futtered her till she fainted away, when the old woman took her up, and she unconscious, and set her parts to the mouth of the cooking pot. The steam of the pot entered

---

[18]Burton, *op. cit.*

her slit, and there fell from it somewhat which I examined; and behold! it was two small worms, one black and the other yellow."[14]

As in ancient Egypt, the Hindoo, especially fanatic *saddhoos* and *gooroos,* generally practiced some form of bestiality with sacred cattle and monkeys. They recommended the same to lay worshipers, and the priests collected handsomely for arranging the matter. They invariably warned an ignorant man that, unless he offered to have carnal knowledge of the Mother of the Gods, he would be destined to everlasting hell fire; and, were he a faithful Hindoo, he wasted in worry until he had violated his nature by obliging. Considered an act of piety, venery with sacred beasts was thought to free the body of sin and remedy all ills.

In worshiping and tendering sacrifice to Hunoomaun the Monkey-God (avatar of Vishnu, and symbol of martial power and virility), bestiality assumed an essential role throughout Veyshnuvee adoration. The priests kept a huge, white-bearded ape, known as Lungoornaut (Lord Baboon), in the temple for religious rites; and smaller varieties, each one holy and inviolate, ran loose by the thousands.

During the clandestine ceremony, Hunoomaun-Poojah, the Chosen One, a virgin priestess or *devadasee,* gave Lord Lungoor to drink of *soma.* Then, she wailed hallowed *muntrums,* writhed blissfully, and beckoned with serpentine desire. Rending her garments, the ape embraced and attacked her carnally until she, screaming in shock of ecstasy and through repeated orgasms, became senseless with exhaustion; whereupon Lord Lungoor, thoroughly trained, draped her body with the cloth-of-gold stained by hymeneal blood and retired to his throne of honor above the sacrificial altar. Then, to the beating of drums and the blare of conchshells, spread-eagled maidens of libation were assailed by *lungoors.* Attached to their necks were leashes whereby the prodding priesthood directed them.

---

[14] Burton, *op. cit.*

Women, to insure fertility or the birth of a strong healthy child, denied their husbands and, for a period of time prescribed by the hierarchy, gave themselves over to sacred monkeys. No one thought evil of it, for Hunoomaun and Vishnu were believed to be embodied in all simiae. Religious paintings and sculpture depicted celestial courtesans and goddesses in the embrace of Hunoomaun, half-human, half-simian, and even man, god and mortal, was shown honoring the holy beast by intromission and the libation of his seed. In reality, Hindoo priests and worshipers not only had connection with animals but sprayed images of Guneysheh (Plutus, the elephant-god) and Nundee (venerable bull of Shiva) with their seminal fluid.

VIII

HYGIENE:
Ritualistic Compulsion

O True Believers: when you prepare to pray, wash your faces, and your hands unto the elbows, and rub your hands and your feet unto the ankles; and if ye be unclean by having lain with a woman, wash yourselves all over. A perfect ablution driveth away Satan.[1]

1. SACRED ABLUTION

The pungent squalor of the East has impressed or depressed nearly every traveler; but this condition, the result of fatalistic indifference and privation, was but superficial.

In the pure hot sand ·and sharp dry atmosphere of the Sahara, man performed his ablutions with coarse sand granules while, in moist, civilized Europe, people scarcely used water and covered up the odors of their unwashed bodies with perfume, disdaining even to wash their faces. Strange as it may seem, primitive man

---

[1]El-Koran.

was generally the perfection of cleanliness; the customary negligence of many civilized people, with their superstitious aversion to water, was unknown or hateful to many primitive races. In the Orient it was only among the poor, in congested cities and villages occupied by untouchables, that men wore loincloths until they rotted from their bodies. But underneath the dingy rags there more than often breathed an immaculate body. Clothes, to people who knew not pomp and vanity, were but inconsiderable means of concealing nakedness. When cast off, they left the human flesh free and pure, a body ceremoniously prepared for the glories of death and rebirth. But in the West clothes were often proud fancy flesh; for the true flesh was foul.

Throughout the Moslem world, *wudhoo* or *tewweddhee* (religious ablution) was imperative before prayer as authorized in the Koran. *Teyyemmum* (washing with sand, in absence of water) was common practice in the desert. Complete ceremonial ablution was also essential, commanded by the Prophet in a *hhedeese* (tradition), following seminal emission in venery and sodomy, or at the sight of a beautiful woman or beardless youth, or in masturbation or fellatio, or in nocturnal pollution.

Certain Hindoos, apart from total cleansing, rinsed the mouth four times following urination, eight times following evacuation, twelve following ingestion, and sixteen following coition. During these ritual cleansings, the individual concentrated on their significance as a sacred purification and cogitated on appropriate verses. Brahmins and other holy men in the fields or bazaars gathered hallowed cow urine (*moot*) in their brass *lotahs* or, catching and sipping it in cupped hands, smeared it over face and limbs. Thus imbibed, the water of Mother Cow was believed to cure all ills and obliterate bodily sin, unintentional or deliberate. Directly after a Brahmin committed worldly acts he sipped of *moot* or purified himself by drinking other liquids consecrated to the gods. Cow dung (*upuleypun*) was also considered a sacred, purifying, and healing substance. It was daubed fresh and moist

over the countenances and in the mouths of penitent
holy men; otherwise, fashioned and dried into chips or
cakes (*uplah*), it was used as fuel, wall plaster, and
flooring, or in the making of idols. Ashes of cow dung
(*bhuboot*) was a favorite powder of *saddhoos* and
other religious mendicants who would roll in it, spray
their hair, and rub it on their foreheads. Urine baths
were also used for external purification.

Nurgow-peyshaub (ox urine), mixed with water,
was considered especially divine by the Parsees. It and
zubble-o-paukee (holy merde) or *surgeen* (also *chir-
keen,* cow dung) were smeared in the hair and about
the eyes, in the course of their *t'harut* (purity) ablutions.

2. The Calls of Nature

Irteyaud may be translated as urinal. It is an Arabic
word meaning, in full context, "seeking a place, soft
and sloping, so that the urine spray will not defile the
dress." In the absence of such a location, the Arab was
obliged to stir the earth before him ere making water
(*seyyer-moyeh*); for one drop of urine, if detected,
was sufficient to foul the body. The stock saying, *Lah
gemmel-enteh* (don't be a camel), bore a double entendre: *don't be cantankerous and vindictive* or *don't
be as an animal who, when relieving itself, whisks its
tail and sprays the excrement all about.*

Customs in urinating and defecating were ritual-
ized throughout the East. In the scriptures of Zoroaster
the posture for urinating was prescribed:

> It is improper, while in an erect posture, to
> make water; it is therefore necessary to stoop or
> sit down, and force it to some distance, repeat-
> ing the Avesta mentally.

The rules observed by the twice-born souls of India when answering the call of nature are as follows:

> A Brahmin is not to perform the offices of
> nature in running water, nor in a cowshed, nor

in ashes, nor before another Brahmin, nor a cow, nor in sight of the great luminary. When he retires to any place for this purpose he is not, in that state of nudity, to look toward the stars; neither is he to go out naked in rain. He is not to cast saliva, blood, or semen into water.

He will stoop down as low as possible. It would be a great offense to relieve oneself standing upright or only half-stooping; it would be a still greater offense to do so sitting on the branch of a tree or upon a wall.

While in this posture, he should take particular care to avoid the great offense of looking at the sun or the moon, the stars, fire, a Brahmin, a temple, an image, or one of the sacred trees.

He will keep perfect silence.

He must chew nothing, have nothing in his mouth, and hold nothing on his head.

He must do what he has to do as quickly as possible, and rise immediately.

After rising, he will commit a great offense if he looks behind his heels.

He will wash his feet and hands on the very spot with the water contained in the brass vessel which he has brought; then, taking the vessel in his right hand and holding his private parts in his left, he will go to the stream to purify himself of the great defilement which he has contracted.

Taking a handful of earth in his left hand, he will pour water on it and rub it well on the dirty part of his body. He will repeat the operation, using only half the amount of earth, and so on, three times more, the amount of earth being lessened each time.

After cleansing himself thus, he will wash each of his hands five times with earth and water: beginning with the left hand.

He will wash his private parts once with water and potter's earth mixed.

The same performance for his two feet, repeated five times for each foot: beginning, under the penalty of eternal damnation, with the right foot.

After that, he will wash his face and rinse

his mouth out eight times. When he is doing this last act, he must take very great care to spit out the water on his left side; for, if by carelessness or otherwise he unfortunately spits it out on the other side, he will assuredly go to hell.

He will think three times on Vishnu, and will swallow a little water three times in doing so.[2]

In the State of Mysore, women habitually attended their husbands, male children, relatives, and sweethearts at the call of nature, cleansing their privy members when they were through. The individual merely said: *"Meyn choonah hoon jowl"* (I am going to leak) and one of the females of the house was obliged to attend him. When instituted in Egypt, with the formula *"Biddeh eseyyer moyeh!"* (I want to make water), it led to all manner of rape and incest and was finally outlawed by decree.

Among both Hindoos and Moslems, human urine, like saliva, was used for deliberate defilement; thus, Orientals often watered upon the dead bodies of their enemies. And the *karooreh* (water doctor, one who examines urine and semen) was very frequently employed, especially by Tippoo Sultaun, as a sorcerer to conjure seminal and urinary ills, impotence, or even death in one's adversary. For the liver (*kibdeh*) was considered the core of manliness, in fact, the very soul, and snatching away the liver by incantation was a prominent portion of Arab voodooism (*sehhr*).

Following urination and preparatory to ablution, the scrupulous Mohammedan daubed the orifice of his instrument upon a stone or some other dry surface. Some Moslems, facetiously inclined, powdered the corners of walls with fine pepper, ground nettles, or some other irritating substance, where Sons of the Prophet were wont to stop and rub the meatus urinarius after stale or copulation.

In Egypt, *el-musterahh* (water closet), *el-keneef* or *beyt-el-ghellah* (privy, chapel of ease) was the fa-

---

[2]Dubois, *op. cit.*

vorite haunting-place of *jinn*. Before entering, one had need to ask permission in the name of God the Compassionate and Merciful (*"Destoor! destoor! Bismillahee-er-Rehmaun-er-Reheem! destoor!"*) lest evil befall him, the *jinn* destroying his manhood or plucking away his genitals.

Anyone audacious and impious enough to offer the *jinn* disrespect was termed *El-Orreh* (the Dung) or *Ez-Zebaul* (dung-drawer). He was "foul water upon disks of dung" (*fahish-moyeh aleh me'mool-ez-zebbel*) and it was not uncommon for him to be addressed thus: *"Yah gherreh!"* (O skite and skite-son; thou art skite); "O thou abuser of the salt, thou eatest skite!" or even "O son of a dungheap! O ye dung of mankind: feeder on ass-turds! imbiber of ass-water! may thy mouth be filled with dregs, thy nose and ears with cur's urine, and may thy grave be defiled by *ghouls* and *afreets* and evil *jinn!*" In reverse feeling, "I would eat thy merde!" indicated affection: just as the complimentary counterpart of "Fizzling fool! savorer of thine own farts!" was "I would savor thine own farts!"

In defecation, the observance of *istinjah* (washing the fundament after stool) meant applying water or sand with the fingers. Nothing appeared more filthy to the Oriental than European toilet paper; hence in Persia the Infidel Feringhee (Western Christian) was scornfully called *kaughuz-khauneh* (paper closet).

For a hot-weather laxative (*jullaub*), the Arabs ordinarily ate unripened dates (*bellehh*); the Hindoos were accustomed to green mangoes (*aum*), with the flavor of turpentine, or chewing astringent betel-nut (*sooparee*). The rarity of constipation (*kubzeyut, inkibauz*) among leisurely Easterners, particularly Hindoos and Chinese, who believed in and practiced dawn and evening evacuation, is said to have contributed to their mildness, fatalistic indolence, and marked effeminacy. The Arabs, though as fastidious as Brahmins, were for the most part of nervous and hysterical temperament; whereas the Brahmin had an apathetic temperament.

The Persian ate to get fat, drank to get drunk and, as previously observed, did so with the greatest ceremony and candor. In certain circles the preliminary decorum and salutations ("Open thy spittle and partake of food and drink!" and "God requite thee abundantly!") were added to or replaced by homosexual horseplay (*budmustee*) and such phrases as *"Us-summaleykum!"* (poison to thee) instead of *selaum aleykum* (peace to thee), "Art thou demon-mad and *jinn*-struck? Thou hast been eating *brinjauls!*" and so forth, as mentioned in the chapter on sodomy. *Budmustee* (sodomy as a means of stimulating evacuation) following the meal substituted for the use of cathartics was disliked by Orientals as being unclean. When in the beginning a feeding Persian philosophically remarked: "A cup of wine is drunk, then have I drunk it. What is it to anyone?" he also thought of his postfiesta inebrious excuse for sodomite debauchery: "A flesh-clyster (enema) is employed, then have I employed it. What is it to anyone?"

The stock Persian remedy for inebriation was to hang one by the heels and stuff his mouth with feces, which was effective in procuring emesis (vomiting).

3. DEPILATION

In a warm and humid clime where bacteria thrived, the process of depilation (*hhellegeh*) was almost essential to bodily sanitation and purity. Nearly every Moslem and Hindoo woman shaved her veil of nature, using a depilatory in the *hhemmaum* on perspiring skin. Such action not only insured cleanliness and beauty but also facilitated congress. "Then," quoth the facetious Arab, "there is no need to slash through entanglement to seek pleasure; every ripe aspect of lip and cleft is smooth, measurable, and naked to the examining touch."

Mohammedans therefore regarded any male or female as being ceremoniously impure who did not shave the pubes (*she'r*). The Koran in allusion tells us that Solomon (Suleymaun) would not copulate with Bil-

kese, Queen of Sheba, until she had thoroughly removed her body-pile. Legend has it that the Queen's
silken pubic veil extended to her knees; hence, Solomon's trick:

> It was said unto her, Enter the palace. And
> when she saw it, she imagined it to be a great
> water; and she discovered her legs, by lifting up
> her robe to pass through it. Whereupon Solomon
> said unto her: Verily, this is a palace evenly
> floored with glass.

In the Sudan, courtesans were held in esteem if
their pubic hair so extended to their knees; for the veil
of nature (*mendeeleh-ed-debeeyeh*) recognized this
condition as indicative of female sexual capacity as were
the beards of men that of masculine potency.

The habit of extracting all bodily hair soon spread
to Europeans residing in the East, particularly Anglo-
Indians; and any individual not thus cleansed was
looked upon with suspicion. The first impulse raged that
he was an Infidel (*Kaufir*) and the second cried that he
concealed something therein, jewels or perfidious com-
muniques, a frequent practice among spies, in lieu of
hollow reeds and secret pockets. In a word, the unshav-
en individual was not to be trusted; he was held as
worldly and deceitful as one who had made the Pilgrimage. Hence, a popular method of torture was to
fire or tear out the hair; and *es-selkh*, the rite of scarification, thus cleansed a circumcised lad throughout,
leaving the ashen scars of manhood and purity.

Resmeh and *nooreh* were commonly used as depila-
tories in Egypt. The latter, also known as *dewweh-
nooreh* (lustre medicine), was compounded of quick-
lime (*sofeydee*) and orpiment (*zerneegh*), and mixed
with water to form a paste. It loosened and removed
hair with considerable ease in about two or three min-
utes, then was washed off. *Resmeh* was primarily a
simple substance: boiled honey and turpentine or gum.
Another variety was known as *teghfeef* (alleviation) or
Lobaun-Shaumee (Syrian incense), a compress of fir-
gum. Other types, strongly compounded, badly seared
the flesh, eating away at the genitals like syphilis, and

eventually entering the bloodstream to poison and consume the entire body.

In Egypt, a peculiar system of extracting pubic hair by application of bat's blood was employed in the harem; and a concubine so depilated was called *wedwaudeeyeh*, or bat-woman. When his Highness discovered fresh semen in the bed sheets, m'lady's excuse was that her depilatory attracted bats and must have aroused an aphrodisiac reaction in those creatures.

Plucking and shaving by razor were also practiced, usually after depilation which, in most cases, destroyed only excess hair. The compound that damaged root-follicle also damaged flesh, and many an unwitting individual ruined his sex by careless application.

Following depilation, fast youths, principally sodomists, daubed ambergris beneath their testicles and between the nates; while young women generally utilized a burnishing oil upon the mons veneris and vulva.

4. FLATULENCE

If generous youth be blessed with luck and
    wealth, displeasures fly his path and perils
    fleet;
His enviers pimp for him and, parasite-wise, e'en
    without tryst his mistress hastens to meet;
When loud he farts, they say: "How well he
    sings!"—and, when he fizzles, cry they: "Oh,
    how sweet!"[3]

Mohammed said: "If a man sneeze or eructate (belch), and say *Elhhemd-o-lillah!* (God be praised), he averts seventy diseases of which the least is leprosy."

Breaking wind (*zirt*, fart), like belching (*itkerreh*), was considered by Arab and Hindoo as an act of purification; for it sought to drive all evil spirits from the body. *Zirteh,* a loud discharge was highly civil and proper in the company of others; but insidious *fesweh* (fizzle, creeper), with stench, was regarded as an insult. Many an Arab died because of it, especially when

_____
[3]Burton, *op. cit.*

vented in the presence of royalty. Such an individual was termed Fezwaun (Fizzler) whereas his counterpart, a man of purity and esteem, was venerably entitled Eboo-ez-Zirteh (Father of Farts). Simo-jeh-el-Hewweh (Breaker of Wind) was the appellation granted an Egyptian bean-eater who could break wind in tune, a favorite accomplishment of *fellaheen* boys.

Deyyer (to let fly a loud flatus) became a popular word in Arab tales, and nothing aroused more laughter than this: "He let fly two great farts, one of which blew up the dust from the earth's face and the other steamed up to the gates of Heaven." Among the Bedewween, one of the most familiar and popular tales of the *Arabian Nights,* is "How Eboo-Hessen Brake Wind." It recounts the humorously lamentable story of a young man who, upon his wedding night, "let fly a fart, great and terrible" that shamed him into abandoning his bride and a house full of startled guests. Thereafter *zirt,* for its sanitary and respectful nature, acquired such attention that records were kept indicating the first time a person of distinction was heard to break wind. Thus, in conversation with a stranger, it was not uncommon for an Arab proudly to say: "I was born on the very night that Eboo-Hessen farted!"

Goze (flatus, eructation, belch) was practiced by Indian *yogees* in their feats of concentration, in ridding the flesh of all evil and achieving annihilation of hurtful consciousness through union with the Supreme Being (Nirvana). Belching and forcing wind from the buttocks, in rapid sequence, the *yogee* chanted: "Glory to those keen ebullitions which escape above and below!"[4]

Taking full advantage of appropriate lulls in conversation during meals, every respectable Persian spat into a receptacle by his side. He emitted grotesque shapes of vapor from his mouth, drawing noisily on the gurgling hubble-bubble. When he sensed an itchiness between his thighs, he unhesitatingly sought for and scratched it. And, displaying strict Eastern etiquette to

[4]Dubois, *op. cit.*

his companions, he allowed his throat and stomach to erupt a series of appreciative eructations as he masticated and swallowed morsels of food and sipped beverages from his own personal tray, muttering with inclinations to his friends: "It is my stomach, and it says that *there is but one God; may He be eulogized!*" The belch, long and resonant, was always followed by the excusing low: "The belly declares, *There is one God!*" or, simply: "There is one God!"

Saliva (Hindoo *took,* Arab *bizaug*) was, like urine or semen, considered grossly unclean by Moslem and Hindoo except in the case of holy men. When, in reverent announcement, a *saddhoo* said: "I must expectorate!" his disciples intoned. *"Hur-hur Mahadeva!"* and clamored round to catch the hallowed ejection in their hands. For the Moslem, spitting (*teff*) involved scorn, defilement, and dishonor; a Brahmin rarely spat at all, a Mohammedan only in anger. To do so otherwise, in merely clearing the throat, was extremely indecorous.

When sneezing (*cheenk*), a Hindoo generally drew up his body and exclaimed: *"Bum-bum Mahadeva!"* (Glory to Lord Shiva). He thereupon blew his nose on his left fingers (the right hand was regarded as clean and could not be used for such purposes). Then he wiped off the mucus (*reynd*) upon a clean surface. In his firm opinion, nothing was more abominable than a handkerchief which, after defilement, was tucked away in one's clothing for further use. The very thought made him sick. He, shocked to horror and scorn, felt the same way about tooth brushes made from the bristles of dead animals and continually fouled by saliva; the usual mode of scrubbing was with a green twig.

Yawning and coughing demanded snapping the fingers on either side of the head to repel evil spirits from entering and defiling the body; and this belief justified Mohammed's saying that sneezing, yawning, and coughing were compounded to shorten men's lives. He knew very little or nothing about heart disease, but he possessed a great deal of common sense. Evil *jinn* were personifications of harmful influences.

A distinct set of rules governing human conduct
and securing the prolongation of life was composed by
Sudanese Arab:

> God so willing, eat only with thy right
> hand; but when thou seekest to touch thy secret
> implement, or poke thy fingers into hinder places,
> employ thy left.
>
> Ye must squat to make water, asking permis-
> sion of God and the Jinn, and make certain
> to utilize thy left hand for all uncleanliness. Only
> a woman stands to make water, and a jackass
> performs such as it walks. Be sure to loosen
> the earth before thee, so that there is no be-
> fouling spray. Ye must then daub thine imple-
> ment upon a clean stone, evoking God's blessing.
>
> In defecation, ye must cleanse thine hinder
> part with wet clay: being certain not to defile
> thy clothes.
>
> When breaking wind, either above or be-
> low, ye should curse the devil and praise God.
>
> In purifying thy teeth, a fresh twig is em-
> ployed with moist salt.
>
> Never whistle, for it is the speech of evil
> Jinn.
>
> When smiling, press thy lips tightly against
> thy teeth. When laughing, cackle like a hyena
> and vibrate: clapping thy hands and thighs.
>
> Whenever sneezing, coughing, spitting or
> sighing, ye must ask permission of God; and
> never leave thy mouth open for long, lest harm-
> ful Jinn enter thy body.

Another stated:

> Thou needst only remember a few impor-
> tant things. Forever stroke thy beard; constantly
> interject Bismillah or Inshallah, formulas as in-
> stinctive as speech; hawk, and spit; curse the
> devil, praise God; and always gesticulate. Even
> if ye do nothing else, no one will think of dis-
> turbing thee. The wisest man says little to
> nought; he is honored and respected for listening,
> murmuring a few formulas, and going his way.
> Others will notice, and step aside for him. He

will never have fear of darkness, nor of men
who reckon the mind in one penetrative glance.

Public health and prosperity also demanded that a
man not sit with his feet toward Mecca, which was an
outrage; and it was also indecorous and disrespectful
for a Mohammedan to show the soles of his feet, or re-
cline with legs outstretched, just as it was insulting for a
newcomer to retain his footwear or bare his hands.

And, in conclusion, general etiquette warned the
staid Oriental: "Don't guffaw; leave giggling and grinning to monkeys and Christians."

Conclusion

The question of European morality lies not in the judgment of any Western individual; it lies in Oriental history. Innocent prostitution, once sanctified, became tainted when its original motivations were supplanted by self-interest. The organs of generation, adored for their mysterious fecundate power, were later debased by attitudes founded on materialism and hypocrisy.

Human nature, inconstant and diverse, is not to be generalized. The saint is not to say to the devil: "I am blessed, thou art evil." For somewhere and at some time the saint is evil and the devil blessed. The judgment of blessedness and iniquity lies solely with those whose philosophy exalts one or the other.

The Occidental is ordinarily shocked by Eastern morals: but he is shocked mainly by its sincerity and candor, unknowingly ashamed of his own concealment and falseness. Before the advent of Western culture, the Oriental never degraded human nature by passing judgment upon its whims; self was free, insincerity hateful. The candid sinner was far more noble than the lecherous saint. The outer gravity of civilization, with its superficial codes and hidden vices, did not affect the Easterner. To condemn, in his philosophy, was to tempt. Condemnation was idolatry, the individual assuming the role of deity and omnipotent judge above all others.

Burton writes:

> Moslems who do their best to countermine
> the ascetic idea inherent in Christianity are not
> ashamed of the sensual appetite. Crude and in-
> delicate, with infantile plainness—even gross
> and, at times, "nasty" in their terrible frank-
> ness—they cannot be accused of corrupting sug-
> gestiveness or subtle insinuation. Theirs is a
> coarseness of language, not of idea; they are in-
> decent, not depraved; and the pure and perfect
> naturalness of their nudity seems almost to puri-
> fy it, showing that the matter is rather of man-
> ners than of morals. Such throughout the East
> is the language of every man, woman and
> child: from prince to peasant, from matron to
> prostitute.

> Amongst savages and barbarians, the com-
> paratively unrestrained intercourse between men
> and women relieves the brain through the body;
> the mind and memory have scant reason, physi-
> cal or mental, to dwell fondly upon visions ama-
> tory and venereal: to live in a "rustle of (imagi-
> nary) copulation." On the other hand, the utterly
> artificial life of civilization, which debauches
> even the monkeys in the zoo, and which expands
> the period proper for the reproductory process
> from the vernal season into the whole twelve-
> month, leaves to the many, whose lot is celibacy,
> no bodily want save one and that in a host of
> cases either unattainable or procurable only by
> difficulty and danger. Hence the prodigious
> amount of mental excitement and material im-
> purity which is found wherever civilization ex-
> tends—in maid, matron and widow—save and
> except those solely who allay it by some counter-
> agent: religion, pride, or physical frigidity.

> And a paper like the (modern) *Pall Mall
> Gazette*,* which deliberately pimps and panders

---

*A London publication of Burton's time, similar to some current
magazines published in the United States known as "The Gutter
Gazette," it was edited by the renoun William T. Stead, a respectable
Methodist "devoted to Christian chivalry" who in gruesome detail
denounced London as the world's center of sodomy and child-
prostitution, and who landed three months in jail "for abduction and
indecent assault" in his attempt to prove it. Hence, "to *Pall Mall
Gazette* a man" was to slander him in sensationalism.

to this latent sense and state of aphrodisiac excitement, is as much the more infamous than the loose book as hypocrisy is more hateful than vice and prevarication is more ignoble than a lie. And when such vile system is professionally practiced under the disguise and in the holy names of Religion and Morality, the effect is loathsome as that spectacle sometimes seen in the East of a wrinkled old eunuch garbed in woman's nautch-dress ogling with painted eyes and waving and wriggling like a young *bayadere*.

There is nothing new about the sexual relations of mankind, only their technical explanation. Homosexuality, a matter of taste and custom, was more open in the East; the East was quite familiar with its sundry aspects. The East, lacking explanation, could only reply: "Who can account for taste?" But, regardless of this lack of understanding, the East did not condemn or pass universal judgment; this was also their position in regard to other nondestructive sexual expression. *Tolerance* was the word.

The expression of tolerance is a fundamental requisite in any human relationship. It is especially important when one studies cultures that developed from sources and conditions different from our own. If tolerance is used as a scientific device to withhold premature judgment, rather than as an attribute of God and nobleman, it is still an essential factor in permitting more of what is being studied to emerge into view. Then, if judgment is still required, that judgment would be based upon the awareness of more actual data and fact.

Bibliography

ABDEL-REMUSAT. *Nouveaux Melanges Asiatiques.* 2 vols., Paris, 1829.

ABUL FAZL ALLAMI. *Ain-i-Akbari.* 3 vols., Calcutta: Asiatic Society of Bengal, 1873.

ABULGHAZI. *Histoire des Mogols et des Tatares.* 2 vols., St. Petersbourg, 1871.

ACOSTA, JOSEPH DE. *Natural and Moral History of the Indies.* London: Hakluyt Society, 1604.

Age Rejuvenescence in the Power of Concupiscence. Aden, 1898.

ALBIRUNI. *Chronology of Ancient Nations.* Paris: Oriental Translation Fund, 1879.

ALI, MRS. MEER HASSAN. *Observations on the Mussulmauns of India.* 2 vols., London, 1832.

ALLARDYCE, A. *The City of Sunshine.* 3 vols., Edinburgh, 1877.

ALLEN, BERNARD M. *Gordon and the Sudan.* London: Macmillan, 1931.

AMICIS, EDMONDO DE. *Morocco.* London: Cassell, 1882.

ANANGA RANGA. London: Kama Shastra Society, 1885.

Angria Tulagee. London, 1756.

ASHBEE, H. S. *Index Librorum Prohibitorum.* London, 1877.

————. *Centuria Librorum Absconditorum.* London, 1879.

————. *Catena Librorum Tacendorum.* London, 1885.

ATKINSON, GEORGE FRANCKLIN. *Curry & Rice.* London: Day, *circa* 1860.

BACON, T. *First Impressions of Hindustan*. 2 vols., London, 1837.

BADEN-POWELL, SIR ROBERT. *Memories of India*. Philadelphia: McKay, circa 1930.

BAILLIE, N. B. E. *Digest of Moohummudan Law*. 2 vols., London, 1865–69.

BALFOUR, DR. E. *Cyclopaedia of India*. London, 1885.

BALL, CHARLES. *The History of the Indian Mutiny*. 2 vols., London: London Printing and Publishing, circa 1860.

BALL, J. D. *Things Chinese*. London, 1900.

BARTH, A. *Les Religions de l'Inde*. Paris, 1879.

BEALE, REV. SAMUEL. *Travels of Fah-hian and Sung-yun*. London, 1869.

BEATSON, LIEUTENANT-COLONEL ALEXANDER. *The War with Tippoo Sultaun*. London: Bulmer, 1800.

BELFOUR, F. C. *Macarius*. Paris: Oriental Translation Fund, 1829.

BELLEW, H. W. *The Races of Afghanistan*. Calcutta, 1880.

BELON, PIERRE. *Les Observations en Grece, Asie, Indee, Egypte, Arabie, &c*. Paris, 1554.

BERGMANN, DR. FREDERIC-GUILLAUME. *Histoire de la Castration et de la Circoncision*. Palermo, 1883.

BERMANN, RICHARD A. *The Mahdi of Allah*. New York: Macmillan, 1932.

BERNCASTLE, J. *Voyage to China*. 2 vols., London, 1850.

BERNIER, FRANCOIS. *Voyages*. 2 vols., Amsterdam, 1710.

BLOCH, DR. IWAN. *Anthropological Studies in the Strange Sexual Practices of all Races in all Ages, Ancient and Modern*. New York: Anthropological Press, 1933.

BLUNT, W. S. *Gordon at Khartoum*. London: Swift, 1911.

BOSE, S. C. *A Description of the Manners, Customs and Inner Life of Hindoo Society in Bengal*. Calcutta, 1881.

BRUGSCH BEY, DR. HENRY. *History of Egypt*. 2 vols., London, 1881.

BRUCE, JAMES. *Travels*. Edinburgh: Etheridge, 1798.

BUCHANAN, CLAUDIUS. *Christian Researches in Asia*. London, 1819.

BURCKHARDT, JOHN LEWIS. *Travels in Nubia*. London: Murray, 1822.

————. *Travels in Syria*. London: Murray, 1822.

————. *Travels in Arabia*. London: Murray, 1829.

————. *Arabic Proverbs*. London: Murray, 1830.

BRIGGS, JOHN. *Firishta*. 4 vols., London, 1829.

BURNES, LIEUT. ALEXANDER. *Travels into Bokhara*. 3 vols., London: Murray, 1834.

BURNES, J. *A Visit to the Court of Scinde*. London, 1831.

BURTON, ISABEL. *The Life of Captain Sir Richard F. Burton*. 2 vols., London: Chapman & Hall, 1893.

BURTON, SIR RICHARD F. *Pilgrimage to El-Medinah and Meccah*. 3 vols., London: Longman, 1856.

————. *The Book of the Thousand Nights and a Night*. 17 vols., London: Burton Club, 1885–88.

————. *Kama Sutra*. London: Burton Club, 1887.

BUSTEED, H. E. *Echoes of Old Calcutta*. Calcutta, 1882.

BUTCHER, REV. DEAN. *Armenosa of Egypt*. London: Blackwood, 1898.

CAMPBELL, CALDER. *The War-Life of a Soldier*. London: Skeffington, 1857.

CAMPBELL, MAJ.-GEN. JOHN *The Wild Tribes of Khordistan*. London, 1864.

CARRACCIOLI, CHARLES. *Life of Lord Clive*. 4 vols., London, *circa* 1785.

CARSTAIRS, R. *Human Nature in Rural India*. London: Blackwood, 1898.

CATROU, F. F. *A History of the Mogul Dynasty in India*, London, 1826.

CAUNTER, REV. HOBART. *Romance of India*. London: Warne, *circa* 1880.

CHAILLE-LONG, COLONEL M. *The Three Prophets*. New York: Appleton, 1884.

————. *My Life in Four Continents*. London: Hutchinson, 1912.

CHARDIN. *Voyages en Perse*. 10 vols., Paris: Langles, 1811.

CHENNELLIS, MISS E. *Recollections of an Egyptian Princess*. London: Blackwood, 1898.

CHICK, N. A. *Annals of the Indian Rebellion*. Calcutta, 1859.

CLARKE, CAPT. H. W. *The Sikandar Nama of Nizami*. London, 1881.

COLBORNE, COLONEL THE HON. J. *With Hicks Pasha in the Soudan*. London: Smith, 1884.

COLOMB, CAPT. R. N. *Slave-Catching in the Indian Ocean*. London, 1873.

COMPTON, HERBERT. *Indian Life in Town and Country.* London: Putnam, 1904.

CORYAT, T. *Crudities.* 3 vols., London, 1776.

CREAGH, CAPT. JAMES. *Armenians, Koords and Turks.* 2 vols., London: Tinsley, 1880.

CROIX, PETIS DE LA. *Histoire de Timur-Bec.* 4 vols., Paris, 1723.

CROMER, EARL OF. *Modern Egypt.* 2 vols., London: Macmillan, 1908.

CROOKE, W. *The Popular Religion and Folk-lore of Northern India.* 2 vols., London, 1896.

CUMMING, LT.-COL. GORDON. *Wild Men and Wild Beasts.* New York: Scribner, 1872.

———. *Arabia.* New York: Scribner, 1872.

CUNNINGHAM, CAPTAIN JOSEPH DAVY. *History of the Sikhs.* London, 1853.

DALRYMPLE, A. *The Oriental Repertory.* 2 vols., London, 1808.

DALTON, COL. E. T. *Descriptive Ethnology of Bengal.* Calcutta, 1872.

Dampier's Voyages. 4 vols., London, 1729.

DARMESTETER, JAMES. *Ormazd et Ahriman.* Paris, 1877.

DAVENPORT, JOHN. *Curiositates Eroticaè Physiologiae.* London, 1875.

DAY, REV. LAL BEHARI. *Govinda Samanta.* 2 vols., London, 1874.

DINGWALL, DR. ERIC JOHN. *Male Infibulation.* London, 1925.

DIROM, MAJOR A. *War with Tippoo Sultan.* London: Faden, 1793.

D'OHSSON, BARON C. *Histoire des Mongols.* 4 vols., Paris: La Haye, 1834.

DORN, BERNHARD. *History of the Afghans.* Paris: Oriental Translation Fund, 1829–36.

DOSABHAI FRAMJI. *History of the Parsis.* 2 vols., London, 1884.

DUBOIS, ABBÉ J. A. *Hindu Manners, Customs and Ceremonies.* 2 vols., Oxford, 1897.

DULAURE, JACQUES ANTOINE. *The Gods of Generation.* New York: Panurge Press, 1933.

DUNCAN, SARAH JEANNETTE. *Adventures of a Memsahib.* London: Nelson, *circa* 1900.

EASTWICK, E. B. *Lutfullah.* Madras, 1857.

ELPHINSTONE, THE HON. MOUNT-STEWART. *Account of the Kingdom of Caubool.* 2 vols., London, 1839.

ELTON, LORD GODFREY. *General Gordon.* London: Collins, 1954.

FALKLAND, VISCOUNTESS. *Chow-Chow,* 2 vols., London, 1857.

FERRIER, J. P. *Caravan Journeys in Persia, Afghanistan, Turkestan and Beloochistan.* London, 1856.

FITZGERALD, EDWARD. *Rubaiyat of Omar Khayyam.* (1st Version, 1859; 4th Version, 1879.)

FORBES, JAMES. *Oriental Memoirs.* 4 vols., London, 1813.

FORREST, SIR GEORGE. *The Life of Lord Roberts.* New York: Stokes, *circa* 1920.

FOSTER, SIR WILLIAM. *John Company.* London: Bodley Head, 1926.

FRANCE, HECTOR. *Sous le Burnous.* Paris: Charpentier, 1886.

FRASER, JAMES BAILLIE. *The Kuzzilbash.* 3 vols., London, 1828.

———. *The Persian Adventurer.* 3 vols., London, 1830.

———. *Historical and Descriptive Account of Persia.* London, 1836.

FRAZER, SIR JAMES GEORGE. *The Golden Bough.* 12 vols., London: Macmillan, 1935.

FRYER, DR. JOHN. *A New Account of East India and Persia.* London, 1698.

GALLAND, ANTOINE. *Journal Pendant son Séjour à Constantinople.* 2 vols., Paris, 1881.

GARNIER, FRANCOIS. *Voyage d'Exploration en Indo-Chine.* 2 vols., Paris, 1873.

GEDDIE, JOHN. *Beyond the Himalayas.* London: Nelson, 1884.

GESSI, ROMOLO. *Seven Years in the Sudan.* London: Sampson Low, 1892.

Gordon Memoirs. London, 1895.

GLADMIN. *Memoirs of Khozęh Abdulkurreem.* Calcutta, 1788.

GOODLAND, ROGER. *A Bibliography of Sex Rites and Customs.* London: Routledge, 1931.

GRAHAM, MARIA. *Journal of a Residence in India.* Edinburgh, 1812.

GRIER, SYDNEY C. *In Furthest Ind.* London: Blackwood, 1898.

GROSE. *A Voyage to the East Indies.* 2 vols., London, 1772.

HAAFNER, M. J. *Voyages dans l'Inde,* 2 vols., Paris, 1811. *Hajji Baba of Isfahan.* 2 vols., London, 1824.

HAKE, A. EGMONT. *The Journals of Major-Gen. C. G. Gordon, C.B., at Khartoum.* London: Kegan Paul, 1885.

HALHED, N. B. *Code of Gentoo Laws.* London, 1776.

HAMILTON, CAPTAIN ALEXANDER. *A New Account of the East Indies.* 2 vols., Edinburgh, 1727.

HANNA, COLONEL H. B. *The Second Afghan War.* 2 vols., London: Constable, 1899.

HARGREAVES, REGINALD. *The Enemy at the Gate.* London: MacDonald, 1945.

HARRIS, WALTER B. *From Batum to Baghdad.* London: Blackwood, 1898.

———. *Tafilet.* London: Blackwood, 1898.

———. *A Journey Through the Yemen.* London: Blackwood, 1898.

HERBERT, LORD GEORGE. *A Night in a Moorish Harem.* London: Erotica Biblion Society.

HERBERT, SIR THOMAS. *Some Yeares Travels into Divers Parts of Asia and Afrique.* London, 1638.

HERKLOTS, G. B. *Qanoon-e-Islam.* Madras, 1863.

Herodotus. 4 vols., London, 1880.

HILL, DR. BIRKBECK. *Colonel Gordon in Central Africa.* London: De La Rue, 1881–83.

HODSON, REV. GEORGE H. *Twelve Years of a Soldier's Life in India.* Boston: Ticknor and Fields, 1860.

HUC AND GABET. *Souvenirs d'Un Voyage dans la Tartarie, le Thibet, et la Chine.* 2 vols., Paris, 1850.

HUGEL, BARON CHARLES. *Travels in Kashmir and the Punjab.* London, 1845.

HUGHES, THOMAS PATRICK. *A Dictionary of Islam.* London: Allen, 1885.

HUNTER, SIR WILLIAM W. *History of British India.* 2 vols., London, 1899–1900.

JACKSON, A. V. WILLIAMS. *History of India.* 9 vols., London: Grolier Society, 1906.

JACQUEMONT, VICTOR. *Correspondance.* 2 vols., Paris, 1832.

JENNINGS, HARGRAVE. *Nature Worship.* New York, 1929.

KAEMPFER, ENGLEBERT. *Histoire Naturelle, Civile et Ecclesiastique du Japon.* Paris: La Haye, 1729.

KAPUDAN, SIDI ALI. *The Mohit.* London.

KAYE, SIR JOHN, AND MALLESON, COLONEL. *History of the Indian Mutiny of 1857–8.* 6 vols., London: Longmans, 1899–1909.

KAYE, JOHN WILLIAM. *Lives of Indian Officers.* 3 vols., London: Strahan, 1869.

KHAN, GHOLAM HUSSIAN. *Seir Mutaqherin.* 2 vols., Calcutta, 1789.

KINCAID, DENNIS. *British Social Life in India.* London: Routledge, 1938.

KIRKPATRICK, COLONEL W. *Select Letters of Tippoo Sultan.* London, 1811.

KIRMANI, MEER HUSSEIN ALI KHAN. *History of Hydur Naik.* Paris: Oriental Translation Fund, 1842.

———. *History of Tipu Sultan.* Paris: Oriental Translation Fund, 1864.

KLAPROTH, JULES. *Magasin Asiatique.* 2 vols., Paris, 1825.

LACROIX, PAUL. *History of Prostitution.* 2 vols., Chicago: Covici, 1926.

LA CROZE, M. V. *Histoire du Christianisme des Indes.* Paris: La Haye, 1724.

LANE, EDWARD WILLIAM. *Manners and Customs of Modern Egyptians.* 2 vols., London: Murray, 1871.

———. *The Arabian Nights' Entertainments.* 3 vols., London: Murray, 1841.

LA ROQUE. *Voyage to Arabia the Happy.* London, 1726.

LEARED, DR. ARTHUR. *Morocco and the Moors.* London, 1876.

LEON, E. DE. *The Khedive's Egypt.* London: Sampson Low, 1877.

LEON, ROUSSET. *A Travers la Chine.* Paris, 1878.

Lettres Edifiantes et Curieuses. 26 vols., Paris, 1780–83.

LEWIN, LT.-COL. T. *The Wild Races of South-Eastern India.* London, 1870.

———. *A Fly on the Wheel.* London, 1885.

LEYDEN, JOHN, AND ERSKINE, WILLIAM. *Memoirs of Zehir-ed-din Muhammed Baber.* London, 1826.

Life in the Mofussil. 2 vols., London, 1878.

LORD. *Display of Two Forraigne Sects in the East Indies.* London, 1630.

Lustful Turk, The. London, 1828.

MACGREGOR, COLONEL CHARLES. *A Journey Through Khorassan.* 2 vols., Edinburgh, 1875.

MACKINTOSH, CAPT. A. *An Account of the Origin and Present Condition of the Tribe of Ramoosies*. Bombay, 1833.

MACLENNAN, J. F. *An Inquiry into the Origin of the Form of Capture in Marriage Ceremonies*. Edinburgh, 1865.

Macoudi. 9 vols., Paris, 1861–77.

MAJOR, R. H. *India in the XVth Century*. London: Hakluyt Society, 1857.

MAKRIZI. *Historie des Sultans et Mamlouks de l'Egypte*. 2 vols., Paris: Oriental Translation Fund, 1837–42.

MANTEGAZZA, PAOLO. *L'Amour dans L'Humanité*. Paris, 1886.

MALCOLM, SIR JOHN. *History of Persia*. 2 vols., London, 1815.

————. *History of Central India*. 2 vols., London, 1823.

MASPERO, G. *The Dawn of Civilisation*. London, 1894.

Maundeville, Sir John. London, 1866.

MAYNE, J. D. *A Treatise on Hindu Law and Custom*. Madras, 1880.

MCCRINDLE, J. W. *Ancient India*. 5 vols., London, 1877–96.

Merveilles de l'Inde. Leide, 1883.

MEYER, JOHANN JAKOB. *Sexual Life in Ancient India*. 2 vols., New York: Dutton, 1930.

MEYNARD, BARBIER DE. *Histoire et Littérature de la Perse*. Paris: Large, 1861.

MILLINGEN. *Wild Life Among the Koords*. London, 1870.

MINNEY, R. J. *Clive*. New York: Appleton, 1931.

MIRABEAU, HONORE. *Errotika Biblion*. Bruxelles, 1866.

MOCQUET, JEAN. *Voyages en Afrique, Asie, Indes Orientales et Occidentales*. Paris, 1617.

MORIER, J. *A Journey Through Persia, Armenia and Asia Minor*. London, 1812.

MONTAIGNE, MICHEL DE. *Essays*. (In numerous editions.)

MUIR, SIR WILLIAM, AND COLDSTREAM, WILLIAM. *Records of the Intelligence Department of the Government of India*. 2 vols., Edinburgh, 1902.

MUIR, SIR WILLIAM. *Annals of the Early Caliphate*. Edinburgh, 1883.

MUNSON, ARLEY. *Kipling's India*. New York: Doubleday, 1915.

NEUFELD, CHARLES. *A Prisoner of the Khalifa*. London: Chapman & Hall, 1899.

NEWMAN, HENRY STANLEY. *What I saw in India*. London: Partridge, *circa* 1880.

NIEBUHR, CARSTEN. *Voyage en Arabie*. 2 vols., Amsterdam, 1774.

————. *Description de l'Arabie*. Amsterdam, 1774.

OHRWALDER, FATHER JOSEPH. *Ten Years' Captivity in the Mahdi's Camp*. London: Sampson Low, 1892.

OLIPHANT, LAURENCE. *Haifa*. London: Blackwood, 1887.

OLIPHANT, MRS. *Zaidee*. 3 vols., London: Blackwood, 1857.

OLIVER, F. S. *The Endless Adventure*. 3 vols., London: Macmillan, 1935.

OSBORNE, HON. W. G. *Court and Camp of Runjeet Singh*. London, 1840.

OUSELY, SIR WILLIAM. *Travels in Various Countries of the East*. 3 vols., London, 1819–23.

OVINGTON, REV. F. *A Voyage to Surratt*. London, 1696.

OWEN, CAPT. W. F. W. *Narrative of Voyages to Explore the Shores of Africa, Arabia and Madagascar*. 2 vols., London, 1833.

PALGRAVE, W. GIFFORD. *Narrative of a Year's Journey Through Central and Western Arabia*. 2 vols., London, 1865.

PANDURANG HARI. *Memoirs of a Hindoo*. 3 vols., London: Whitaker, 1826.

PEARCE, N. *Life and Adventures in Abyssinia*. 2 vols., London, 1831.

PEARSE, MAJOR HUGH. *Soldier and Traveller*. London: Blackwood, 1898.

Perfumed Garden of the Cheikh Nefzaoui. London: Kama Shastra Society, 1886.

PLAYFAIR, G. *Taleef-i-Shereef*. Calcutta, 1883.

POWER, FRANK. *Letters from Khartoum*. London: Sampson Low, 1885.

PRICE, MAJOR D. *Memoirs of the Emperor Jahanguier*. Paris: Oriental Translation Fund, 1829.

PRINSEP, AUGUSTUS. *Baboo*. London: Smith & Elder, 1834.

PURCHAS. *Pilgrims*. 4 vols., London, 1625–26.

RASHIDUDDIN. *Histoire des Mongols de la Perse*. Paris: Quatremere, 1836.

Rati Shastra. Calcutta, 1908.

REINAUD, M. *Relation des Voyages Faites par les Arabes et les Persans*. 2 vols., Paris, 1845.

REMONDINO. *History of Circumcision*. Philadelphia: Davis, 1891.

REYNOLDS, REGINALD. *The White Sahibs in India*. London: Secker & Warburg, 1937.

ROBERTS, LORD FREDERICK. *Forty-One Years in India*. 2 vols., London: Bentley, 1897.

ROE, SIR THOMAS. *Embassy to the Court of the Great Mogul*. 2 vols., London: Hakluyt Society, 1620.

ROWLANDSON, LIEUT. M. J. *Tohfut-ul-Mujahideen*. Paris: Oriental Translation Fund, 1833.

ROYLE, CHARLES. *The Egyptian Campaigns*. London: Hurst and Blackett, 1900.

RUSSELL, WILLIAM HOWARD. *My Diary in India*. 2 vols., London: Routledge, 1860.

Sacred Books of the East. 10 vols., London, 1880.

SACY, SILVESTRE DE. *Chrestomathie Arabe*. 3 vols., Paris, 1826–27.

SALE, GEORGE. *The Koran*. London, 1735.

SALE, LADY. *A Journal of the Disasters in Afghanistan*. London: Murray, 1843.

SANGUINETTI, DR. B. R. *Voyages d'Ibn Batoutah*. 4 vols., Paris: Société Asiatique, 1853–58.

SCHUYLER, EUGENE. *Turkistan*. 2 vols., London, 1876.

SHAW, ROBERT. *Visits to High Tartary, Yarkand and Kashghar*. London, 1871.

SHAW, DR. T. *Travels or Observations Relating to Several Parts of Barbary and the Levant*. London, 1738.

SHEA, DAVID, AND TROYER, ANTHONY. *The Dabistan*. 3 vols., Paris: Oriental Translation Fund, 1843.

SHERRING, REVEREND M. A. *Hindu Tribes and Castes*. 3 vols., Calcutta, 1872–81.

SKEEN, GENERAL SIR ANDREW. *Passing It On*. Aldershot: Gale & Polden, 1932.

SLANE, BARON MCGUCKIN DE. *Ibn Khallikan's Biographical Dictionary*. 4 vols., Paris, 1842–71.

SLATIN PASHA, COLONEL SIR R. *Fire and Sword in the Sudan*. London: Arnold, 1906.

SLEEMAN, LIEUTENANT-COLONEL SIR WILLIAM H. *Rama-seeana*. Calcutta, 1836.

———. *Rambles and Recollections*. 2 vols., London, 1844.

———. *A Journey Through the Kingdom of Oudh*. 2 vols., London, 1858.

SMITH, R. BOSWORTH. *Life of Lord Lawrence.* 2 vols., New York: Scribner, 1883.

Society in India. 2 vols., London, 1841.

Society, Manners, Tales and Fictions of India. 3 vols., London, 1844.

SOLVYNS, F. B. *Les Hindous.* 4 vols., Paris, 1808.

SONNERAT. *Voyages.* 3 vols., Paris, 1782.

SONNINI, BARON C. S. *Voyages.* Paris, 1800.

STANLEY, SIR HENRY M. *Autobiography.* London: Sampson Low, 1909.

STAVORINUS. *Voyage to the East Indies.* 3 vols., London, 1798.

STEEVENS, G. W. *With Kitchener to Khartum.* London: Blackwood, 1898.

————. *Egypt in 1898.* London: Blackwood, 1899.

————. *With the Conquering Turk.* London: Blackwood, 1898.

STEWART, MAJOR C. *Private Memoirs of the Emperor Humayun.* Paris: Oriental Translation Fund, 1832.

STONE, LEE ALEXANDER. *The Story of Phallicism.* 2 vols., Chicago: Covici, 1927.

STRACHEY, LYTTON. *Eminent Victorians.* London: Chatto & Windus, 1918.

SURRIDGE, VICTOR. *India.* London: Jack, *circa* 1920.

TASSY, GARCIN DE. *Particularites de la Religion Musulmane dans l'Inde.* Paris, 1851.

TAVERNIER, J. B. *Les Six Voyages en Turquie, en Perse, et aux Indes.* 2 vols., Paris 1676.

TAYLOR, CAPTAIN MEADOWS. *Confessions of a Thug.* 3 vols., London: Bentley, 1839.

TAYLOR, COLONEL MEADOWS. *The Story of My Life.* London: Blackwood, 1898.

TELFER, CAPT. J. BUCHAN. *The Bondage and Travels of Johann Schiltberger.* London: Hakluyt Society, 1879.

TERRY, EDWARD. *A Voyage to East India.* London, 1655.

THEVENOT, J. DE. *Voyages en Europe, Asie et Afrique.* 5 vols., Paris, 1727.

THOMAS, P. *Kama Kalpa.* Bombay: Taraporevala, *circa* 1950.

THOMPSON, EDWARD J. *The Other Side of the Medal.* London: Woolf, 1925.

THUNGBERG, C. P. *Travels in Europe, Africa and Asia.* 4 vols., London, 1799.

TREVELYN, SIR GEORGE. *Cawnpore*. London: Macmillan, 1907.

TWEEDIE, MAJOR-GENERAL W. *The Arabian Horse: His Country and People*. London: Blackwood, 1898.

VAMBERY, A. *Sketches of Central Asia*. London, 1868.

WALLACE, LEW. *The Prince of India*. 2 vols., New York: Harper & Brothers, 1893.

WARBURTON, SIR ROBERT. *Eighteen Years in the Khyber*. London: Murray, 1900.

WARD, W. *A View of the History, Literature and Religion of the Hindoos*. 4 vols., London, 1817–20.

WESTERMARCK, EDWARD. *The Origin and Development of Moral Ideas*. London: Macmillan, 1906.

————. *Marriage Ceremonies in Morocco*. London: Macmillan, 1914.

————. *Ritual and Belief in Morocco*. London: Macmillan, 1920.

WESTROPP, HODDER M., AND WAKE, C. STANILAND. *Ancient Symbol Worship*. New York: Bouton, 1874.

WILKINS, W. H. *The Romance of Isabel, Lady Burton*. 2 vols., London: Hutchinson, 1897.

WILLS, C. J. *Behind an Eastern Veil*. London: Blackwood, 1898.

WILSON, ARNOLD. *The Abode of Snow*. Edinburgh, 1875.

WINGATE, SIR F. R. *Mahdiism and the Egyptian Sudan*. London: Macmillan, 1891.

————. *The Sudan, Past and Present*. London: Macmillan, 1892.

YULE, COL. HENRY, AND BURNELL, A. C. *Hobson-Jobson*. London: Murray, 1903.

ABOUT THE AUTHOR

ALLEN EDWARDES is one of the most famous scholars exploring the sexual customs of Africa, the Middle East and the Orient. *The Jewel in the Lotus* has been internationally hailed as a masterpiece of modern anthropology and sex research. Mr. Edwardes is also the author of the long-awaited sequel, *The Cradle of Erotica*, which scrutinizes the erotic practices of peoples whose behavior is unknown to all but a few western scholars.

Bantam
On Psychology

☐	PSYCHOANALYSIS AND RELIGION, Erich Fromm	2188 ●	$1.25
☐	FRITZ, Martin Shepard	2202 ●	$1.95
☐	WHEN I SAY NO, I FEEL GUILTY, Manuel Smith	2268 ●	$1.95
☐	SIMULATIONS OF GOD: THE SCIENCE OF BELIEF, John C. Lilly, M.D.	2442 ●	$2.25
☐	TRANSCENDENTAL MEDITATION, Jack Forem	2675 ●	$1.95
☐	IN AND OUT THE GARBAGE PAIL, Fritz Perls	6369 ●	$1.95
☐	THE GESTALT APPROACH & EYE WITNESS TO THERAPY, Fritz Perls	6414 ●	$1.95
☐	THE DISOWNED SELF, Nathaniel Branden	7502 ●	$1.50
☐	BREAKING FREE, Nathaniel Branden	8031 ●	$1.50
☐	AWARENESS: exploring, experimenting, experiencing, John O. Stevens	8053 ●	$1.95
☐	PSYCHOSOURCES, A Psychology Resource Catalog, Evelyn Shapiro, ed.	8501 ●	$5.00
☐	THE PSYCHOLOGY OF SELF-ESTEEM: A New Concept of Man's Psychological Nature, Nathaniel Branden	10189 ●	$1.95
☐	WHAT DO YOU SAY AFTER YOU SAY HELLO? Eric Berne, M.D.	10251 ●	$2.25
☐	GESTALT THERAPY VERBATIM, Fritz Perls	10470 ●	$2.25
☐	PSYCHO-CYBERNETICS AND SELF-FULFILLMENT, Maxwell Maltz, M.D.	10535 ●	$1.95
☐	THE FIFTY-MINUTE HOUR, Robert Lindner	10537 ●	$1.95

Buy them at your local bookstore or use this handy coupon for ordering: